IMAGES
of America

MAYWOOD

IMAGES of America

MAYWOOD

City of Maywood
and Edward W. Ahrens

Edited by Patricia Urbina

ISBN 0-7385-3000-X

Published by Arcadia Publishing
Charleston SC, Chicago IL, Portsmouth NH, San Francisco CA

Printed in Great Britain

Library of Congress Catalog Card Number: 2005929113

For all general information contact Arcadia Publishing at:
Telephone 843-853-2070
Fax 843-853-0044
E-mail sales@arcadiapublishing.com
For customer service and orders:
Toll-Free 1-888-313-2665

Visit us on the Internet at www.arcadiapublishing.com

Contents

ACKNOWLEDGMENTS

The list of contributors who provided photographs and information for this history of the City of Maywood is long indeed. Hopefully no one was forgotten or missed.

Thanks go to the current Maywood City Council, including Mayor George Martinez, mayor pro tem Samuel Peña, and council members Luis Lara, Jose Zuniga, and Thomas Martin. We also thank chief of police Bruce Leflar; ACAO Michael Williams; David Mango, director of Building and Planning; city attorney Cary Reisman; Pete Parra, assistant director of Community Services ; recreation supervisor Fernando Martinez; former mayors Rose Busciglio, Thomas Engle, and Ben Lang; former CAO Ron Lindsey; Vic Heintzman, former assistant director of Community Services, former chief of police Ted Heidke; Linda Dovalis, former director of Building and Planning, deputy city clerk Hector Duarte Jr., and senior planner Julia Gonzalez. The Maywood Lions deserve special mention, including Art Sherman, Bob Smith, photographer Hal Link, Bob Thew, and W. R. Barnett. Publications that helped guide research include the newspapers *Maywood Herald, Daily Signal, Maywood Journal, Industrial Post* Silver Jubilee Edition, and various City of Maywood–area and chamber of commerce publications: Maywood Lions Club 50th anniversary book, Maywood's Annual report 1956–1957, Maywood 60th anniversary program, and Maywood newsletters. The entire City of Maywood staff helped make this book possible.

Special thanks are extended to photographer Bill Japport for his dedication, time, and effort.

A Residential Isle in a Sea of Industry

The land on which the city of Maywood is situated was deeded in 1781 to Spanish War veteran Manuel Nieto, a favorite of his nation's crown. The land was recorded with the establishment of the Pueblo De Nuestra Señora de Los Angeles. There was no marked change in this vast wilderness, which had been inhabited by Native American groups in previous centuries, for scores of years thereafter.

Although Los Angeles grew from a dusty pueblo into a raucous frontier town, Maywood, located only 10 miles away, remained a cow pasture. In the 20th century, the area that became Maywood changed from ranchlands to almost entirely vegetable farms. With transportation developments, truck gardening flourished, with products being sold in the City of Los Angeles. Cauliflower became the principal crop.

Plans for a community, which developed into the city of Maywood, were first generated in 1912, when the Laguna Maywood Land and Water Company incorporated for $2 million. The corporation was formed to acquire and develop the 2,800-acre De Baker Rancho, comprised of land now occupied by the city. Work began in 1913 to mold the prospective community. But plans were interrupted by the events of World War I.

In 1915, Thomas Ross was credited with building the first dwelling in the region. It was a frame shack on Cudahy Road. Cudahy Road was later named Atlantic Boulevard.

Other men of vision, sensing opportunity in the Laguna-Bell region, filtered in to build homes, stores, and industries. By 1919, there were enough inhabitants to warrant a name for the town. The land company sent out cards to the people living in the area, asking them to vote on a name. The selection of Maywood has a history all its own. According to historical records, a young lady working for the land corporation was so popular that her name, May Wood, was chosen by those who voted. Christening of the town took place on May 4, 1919, and some 300 persons attended the event.

Built in 1920, the first school in Maywood was Washington School, now called Loma Vista. The next schools to be built were Lincoln, now called Fishburn Avenue, and then Jefferson, which became Heliotrope. Some of the early known Washington teachers were Sarah Bradley, Laura Waddell Malberry, and Maud Phifer Primasing. Edna Wilson, mother of Mrs. Primasing, one of the city's pioneer women realtors, was also one of the first organizers of a realty board in Maywood.

In 1926, the three schools came under the jurisdiction of the Los Angeles City Public School System, which changed the school names to the streets on which they were located.

"When I arrived in Maywood in September of 1922," remembered Anna M. Clarke, an early Maywood resident, who became active in real estate, "the early sub-dividers had already decided on the name of Maywood for approximately 1,000 acres of sandy land at the bend of the Los

Angeles River. This was a rural settlement of people who built their homes on acre plots and raised their own fruit, vegetables, and chickens. The northern strip of Maywood," Clarke recalled, "was a big potato patch."

In September 1924, Maywood was incorporated. The first council meeting was held on the night of September 8, 1924, at Glen L. Saxton's real estate office at 4438 East Slauson Avenue. Frank H. Pepper emerged as president of the Maywood Board of Trustees, or mayor. The other members of the council were Frank Sabin, J. P. Packard, Herman Bejack, and Aaron Hoover.

One of the first official acts of the city council was to write Uncle Sam, asking that a branch of the Los Angeles Post Office be placed in Maywood. Within the first month, the council wrote and adopted 20 ordinances regulating fire, health, gambling, and other issues. The initial officials, appointed in September 1924, were city treasurer John W. Garrett, acting city clerk Loren J. Walter, city attorney O. A. Gerth, city engineer Vaughn Wood, police chief Vere H. S. Meadows, police officers George D. Dunphy (later replaced by E. C. Lansing) and Edward B. Elliott, and policewoman Marie W. Horton.

On March 19, 1925, the old Egyptian Theatre opened. Constance Talmadge was featured in a thriller entitled *Learning to Love*.

Only one short year passed from the city's incorporation before a bitter battle to de-incorporate the city was launched by citizens who called themselves the Maywood Taxpayers League. Rafael Chacon and Mary Fowler were the leaders of the league's concerted effort to topple the city. Along with fellow citizens, they amassed 614 signatures from the city's approximately 800 registered voters on "dis-incorporate" petitions.

This majority was sufficient to place the issue on the ballot for the November 1925 election. The final vote was 822 to discontinue the city government and 534 in support of it. Maywood lived only because the law required a two-thirds majority to dissolve.

Despite the outcome, Mrs. Fowler continued in her cause to wage an all-out fight against the city in 1927. She, along with F. E. Goodway, circulated petitions for the City of Huntington Park to annex the Maywood "Strip," a portion of the city in which her home was located on Gifford Avenue. An election followed and the proposal won by an overwhelming vote of 365 to 65. However, this election was declared invalid because of a legal technicality.

Never one to "say die," Mrs. Fowler wasn't finished yet. She led the drive again for annexation and circulated more petitions, gaining enough signatures for a second election. The "Strip" was then annexed by Huntington Park. Ironically the vote count in the second election was the same as the first—365 to 65 in favor of annexation.

Maywood's first library was established in February 1921, in the Lincoln School (now Fishburn Avenue School). In 1921, the library had 141 borrowers and 407 books. In 1924, the library moved to 5820 Pine Avenue. It remained at that location until 1938, growing each year, when it moved to 4318 East Slauson Avenue, adjacent to Maywood City Hall.

Early in 1948, the library was unable to renew its lease, and it seemed that it might have to go into storage. It was saved due to the interest of citizens and the Maywood Chamber of Commerce, which arranged for it to be moved into a vacant building at 5822 Pine Avenue. More than a decade later, a modern structure was built to accommodate the library, next to the city hall, and was dedicated on October 20, 1961.

Back in 1924, when the signs read "Welcome to Greater Maywood," mail was received from Los Angeles, dispatched and delivered by bicycle from a small store located at 828 East Slauson Avenue (now 4428 East Slauson). That year, postcards were a penny, first-class mail was 2¢ an ounce, and airmail (weather permitting) was 8¢ an ounce.

In 1925, the Maywood Post Office became a branch of Huntington Park's postal system, and later in the 1920s, moved into a building at 5816 Pine Avenue. In 1934, the Maywood branch was converted into an individual post office. And in March 1935 Charles Hollar, the Maywood city clerk, was appointed the first postmaster. With the continued growth of Maywood quite evident, city officials set their sights on the acquisition of a new and independent post office building.

Thanks to the efforts of Herman Bejack, one of the original council members, the site of the northwest corner of Pine and Slauson was selected, and a new building erected and officially dedicated in 1938.

With the death of Charles Hollar, George Archer was appointed postmaster on June 9, 1938. In 1946, Archer officially retired, and on October 1, 1946, Jack Freemen became acting postmaster until July 31, 1950, when he resigned to enter private enterprise.

In September 1973, in keeping with the United States Postal Services economy move, Maywood then became a branch of the Bell Postal area (Bell, Bell Gardens, Cudahy, and Maywood).

Infrastructure issues practically began with the cityhood. By mid-1925, 70 percent of the property owners along East Slauson Avenue were demanding a paved road, and bids were accepted for the project. The council's decision to use concrete for paving on Slauson instead of asphalt brought about member Aaron Hoover's resignation on June 26. Member Bejack also quit, saying he needed time to "make a living."

In 1926, a loan from the bank was authorized to complete the paving—"not to exceed $3,000." Things began looking brighter in February of that year when the Los Angeles County Board of Supervisors wrote that $29,000 was on the way for the Slauson improvement project, and they offered a like amount to improve Atlantic Avenue.

The election on April 12, 1926, retired the pioneer politicians from office. William Schleppy became the new mayor, and the new council consisted of members Walt E. Staring, R. Plaisted, Oscar Johnson, and James H. Champion. Less than two weeks later, on April 24, one of the biggest celebrations and parades staged in the city took place to celebrate the opening of the New Slauson Avenue. The "main street" had been closed for months of paving. The occasion heralded the beginning of a settled political period, and was regarded by all as a sign of a more optimistic future for Maywood.

Among other things, the Slauson improvement had been held up to allow other streets to be refurbished, as, naturally, nearly every resident wanted "his street" to be improved first. But Slauson was a main thoroughfare and vitally necessary to the impatient civic boosters. The mammoth parade was held at 3:00 p.m., and local organizations all turned out in grand style, including the chamber of commerce, Moose, American Legion, Women's Club, and other groups. All stores in Maywood ran "special prices."

An evening program at Slauson and Atlantic featured talks by F. M. White, president of the Laguna-Maywood Land Corporation; supervisor Cogswell of the county administration; Wynn Sanborn, East Side representative of the Los Angeles City Council, and Fred Beatty, president of the East Side Organization. The *Industrial Post* newspaper came out with a big edition in which the editor provided this banner headline, "Maywood's New Day Is Dawning."

By 1928, Maywood was the center of a thriving community of over 4,000 residents. Frank M. Gardner was mayor, supported by councilmen Earl G. Horton, Fred H. Brewer, Thomas F. Driscoll, and William E. Heath.

"It is easy to explain why the city has grown so rapidly," said F. W. White, president of the Laguna-Maywood Land and Water Company in 1928. "Here the climate is marvelous. The scenery, made up of rugged mountains, rolling hills, fertile and flowering fields, enthralls and entrances one. Clear-visioned men of business and of industry have located in and around Maywood because they have found a climate ideal for all—[for] year labor and factory efficiency. They found inexpensive fuel, oil, gas, and hydro-electric power. Such nationally known firms as Willy-Overland, Firestone Tire Company, Goodyear, and Goodrich have recognized the advantages our community offers them, and they are only forerunners of other great industrial giants which will build huge plants in our midst.

"Maywood is the hub of this great industrial development and her future is bright with cooperation on the part of her people; with coordination of the forces that build up a community, there is no reason why Maywood should not continue to grow and become one of the most important factors in the up-building of Southern California," White said.

The first official census figures, taken in 1930, indicated there were 6,794 residents in the city. Efforts were made for the elimination of open gambling, bookies, slot machines, and the separation of dance and liquor establishments.

Maywood was saluted by other Southeast Cities (in relation to Los Angeles) in 1938 when it "bought and paid for" a city hall building at 4319 East Slauson Avenue for an approximate cost of $21,500. At first, the city council members thought they wanted a Spanish Mission type of building. But they later rejected the plans in favor of what was then "the modern style." The council met as often as three times a week to arrange the property's purchase. Joseph Schlapp was the building contractor and Dr. Edwards the architect and engineer.

Construction, which was expected to take 120 days, started in February and was completed 90 days later. On June 11, 1938, the hall was dedicated with a big celebration. The city council members were composed of Mayor V. F. Quinzy, Y. L. Creed, Frank Dowell, Ben Lang, and Harold Hammond. These five men were credited with being the most forward-looking council during Maywood's formative years.

By 1928, the Maywood Police Department had published its first "annual," showing a personnel strength of a police chief, four uniformed officers, and four detectives. One of the biggest police-involved incidents of the early years occurred in April 1935. Maywood, Bell, and Huntington Park officers arrested 18 persons on charges of disturbing the peace, refusing to disperse, and intoxication at the Rose Beer Garden in Maywood. Members of the Maywood Fire Department turned their hoses on the brawlers, and the water's force knocked many individuals to the floor.

By 1964, the police department had grown to a 23-man force with five sergeants, four marked patrol cars, two unmarked vehicles, two motorcycles, and a three-wheeled cycle. By 1984, the department continued to have 23 sworn officers as well as non-sworn personnel, including a parking control officer, four police clerk-dispatchers, one senior records clerk, two records clerks, five school crossing guards, and two reserve police officers.

The city also added a contract to police the City of Cudahy in late 2003. The number of department assignments in 2005 has increased to 41 sworn officers, 6 dispatchers, 9 reserve officers, 6 community service officers, 5 record bureau employees, and 5 technical reserves—a grand total of 72. Three officers have died in the line of duty since 1924—Clarence Bower (1944), John Hoglund (1992), and Daniel Kelley (1999). They made the ultimate sacrifice.

Maywood Park, located at Fifty-eighth Street and Heliotrope Avenue, had its beginning in the 1930s when the present-day baseball outfield was a large meadow used as a play area. The postwar years found a veterans housing center at Maywood Park, where the landscape was dotted with many apartment buildings, one of which was renovated and used as a recreation room and office. The Maywood Parks and Recreation Department came into being in 1955, when the leisure time of residents heightened. In 1957, a major change came over the park when additional property adjacent to the park was purchased, increasing the park area twofold.

In the 1960s, the Parks and Recreation department saw the need for participatory recreation programs, which allowing equal time for everyone regardless of ability or experience. It was an idea that has been emulated by many other recreational departments in the Southeast area.

In November 1975, a new $120,000 recreational facility was completed. It was financed by funds provided by the State Park Bond Act of 1974, matched by federal revenue sharing funds.

The 1980s saw major changes for the city as a swimming pool and tennis court were constructed. The demolition of two city-owned houses on Heliotrope to add additional open space was a welcomed development along with new field lighting and new security lighting.

In 1997, construction began on a new $5.1 million multipurpose building that was funded through federal monies from the Department of Housing and Urban Development. The two-story complex has been utilized for basketball, volleyball, aerobics, weight training, professional boxing, and various classes and other sports and activities.

Today, 81 years from its official creation, Maywood has retained its small-town, suburban atmosphere, even though it's surrounded by a massive group of industrial complexes.

Maywood still offers an ideal residential community for the men and women who work in those surrounding industries.

Anyone who looks around Maywood today can see 14 miles of residential streets that were repaved, as well as a new median on Slauson Avenue, erection of two new schools, completion of 7.3 acres of new parklands, and a revived redevelopment effort.

The city council, comprised of Mayor Samuel Peña, mayor pro tem Luis Lara, and council members George Martinez, Thomas Martin, and Jose Zuniga, has directed Maywood's progress in recent years, and the residents look forward to a vibrant city for years to come.

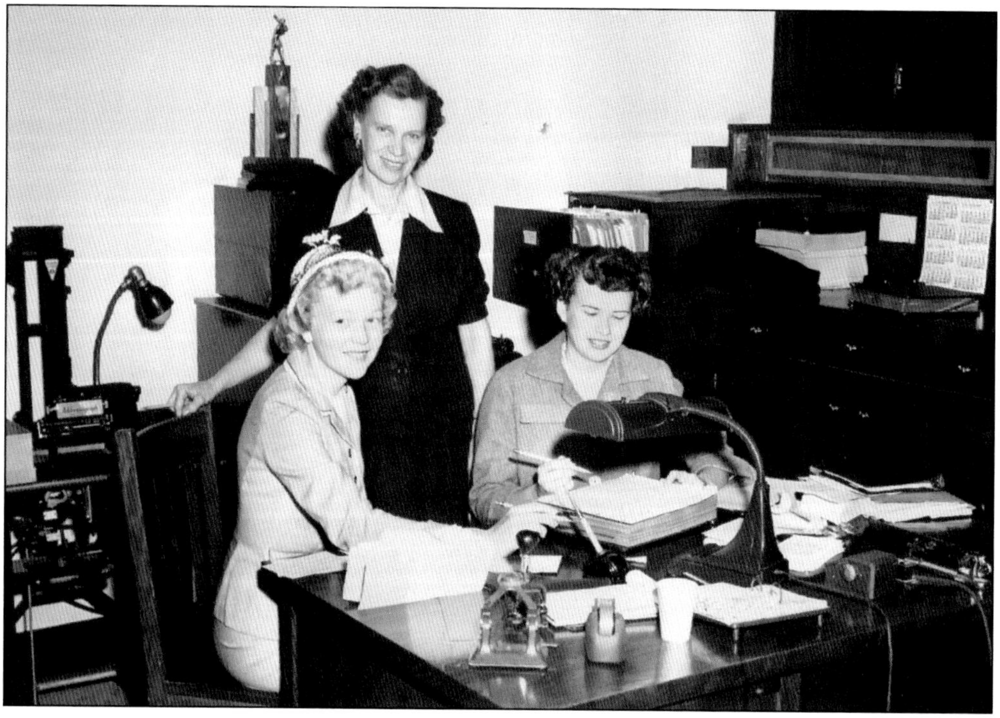

This book is dedicated to Maywood historian Isabel Dedmore, who served as city clerk from 1953 to 1971.

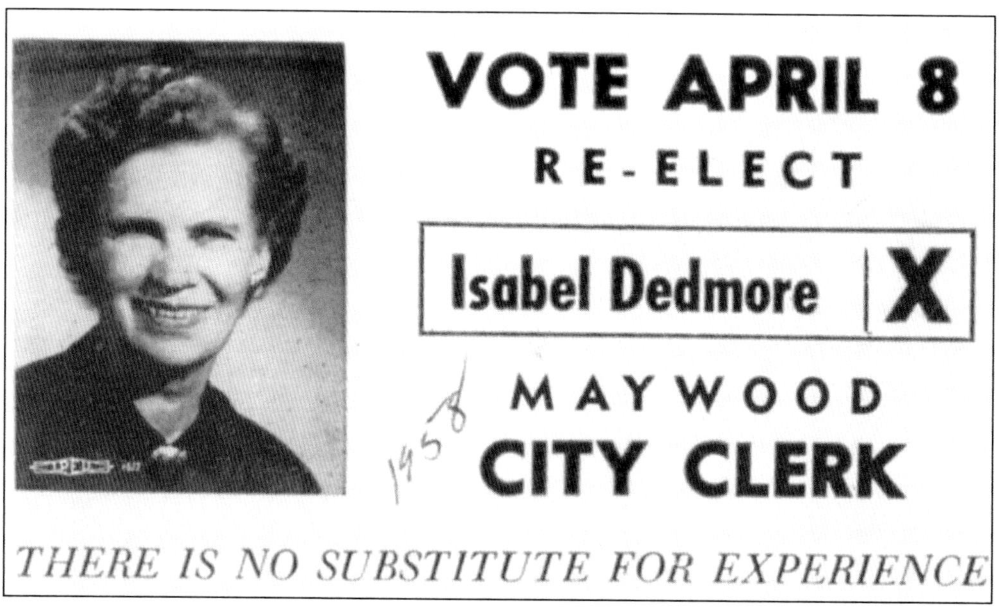

One

The 1920s

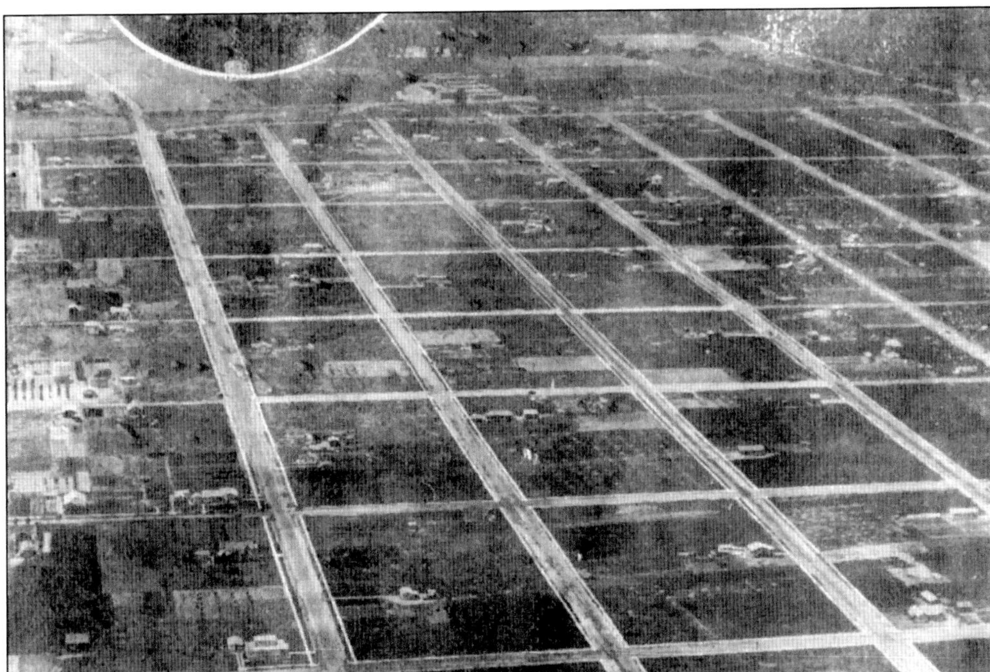

This is a 1920 aerial view of Maywood. The building at the bottom was a hotel located at Slauson and Atlantic Avenues. Atlantic Avenue was then called Cudahy Road.

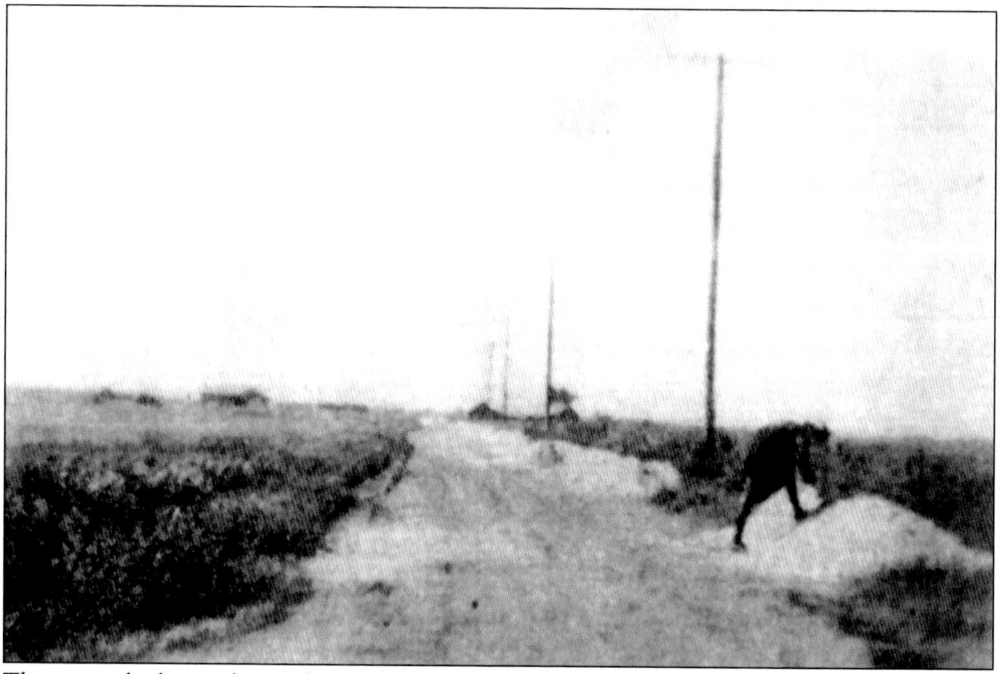

This image looks north at Atlantic Avenue, then called Cudahy Road, from Sixtieth Street.

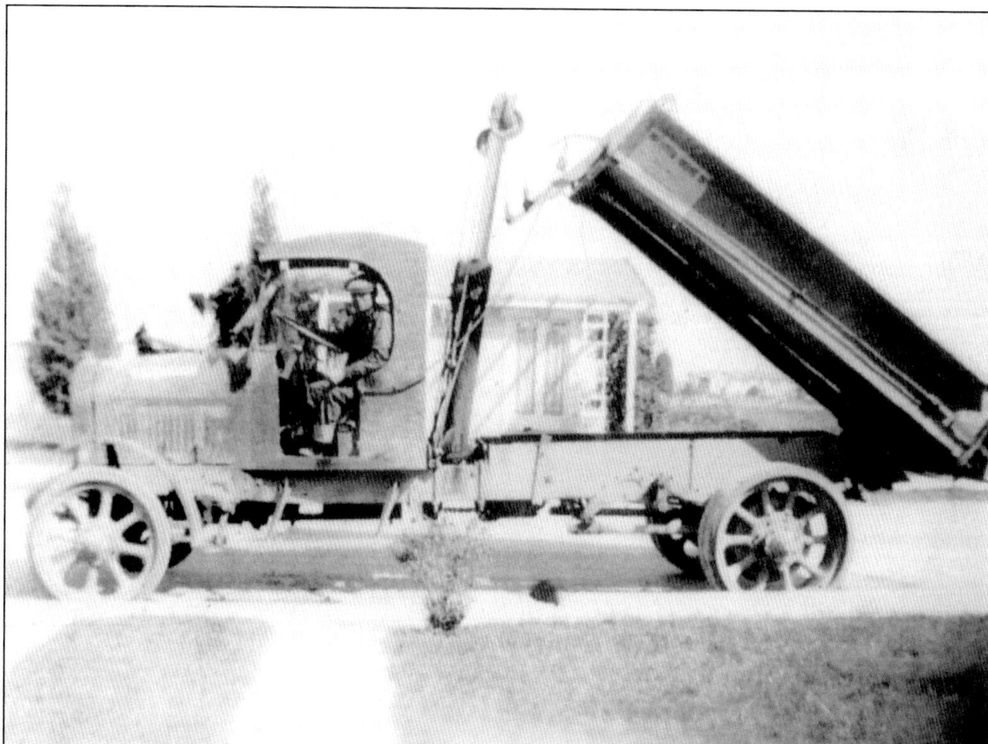

A cement company, located at Alamo Avenue and Sixtieth Place, was one of Maywood's early industrial locations.

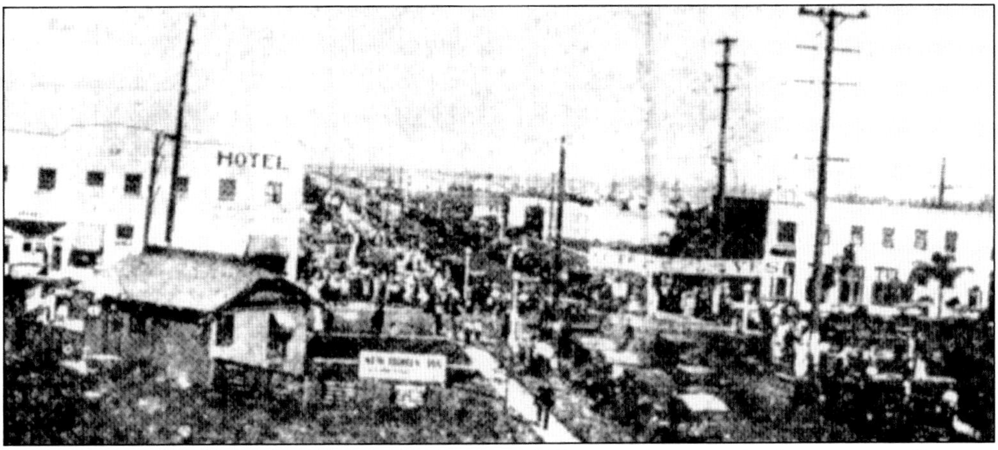

This 1924 picture shows the corner of Atlantic and Slauson Avenues, looking east on Slauson, on incorporation election day. Notice the narrow streets, short lampposts, automobiles, and the banners across the street bearing the words "Vote Yes."

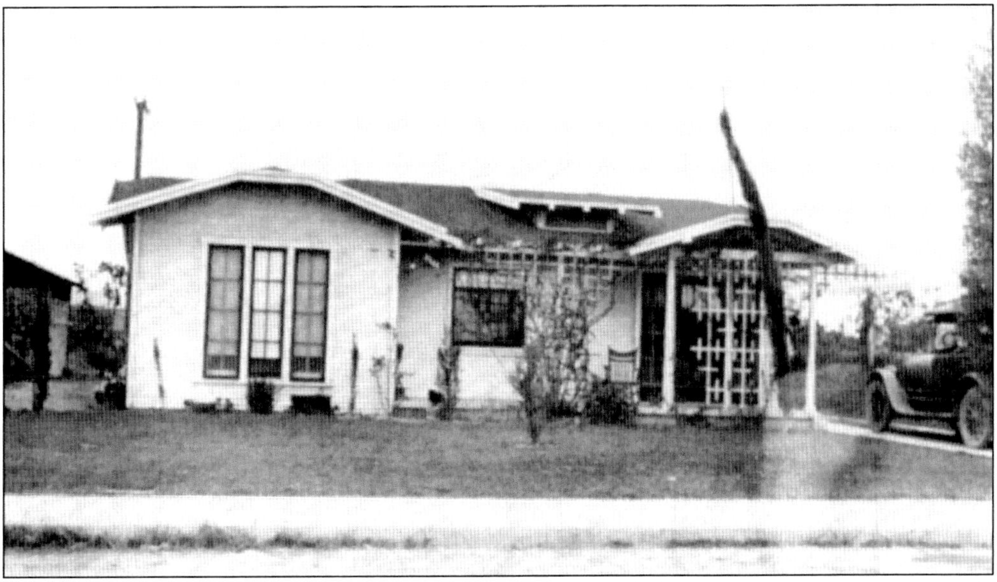

A typical new house in the city of Maywood is depicted in 1924, the year the city incorporated.

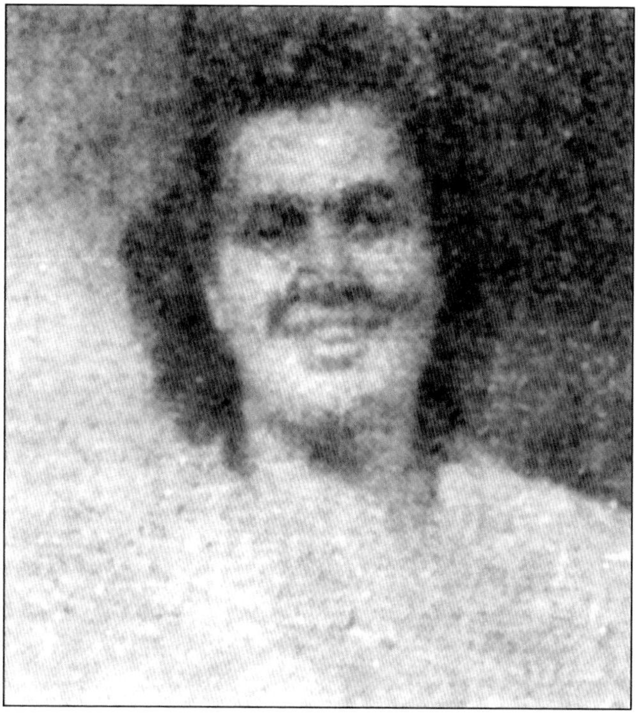

Billie Cooper was the first baby born in the city. Billie's parents, Otto and Faye Cooper, resided in the 4200 block of Fifty-fourth Street.

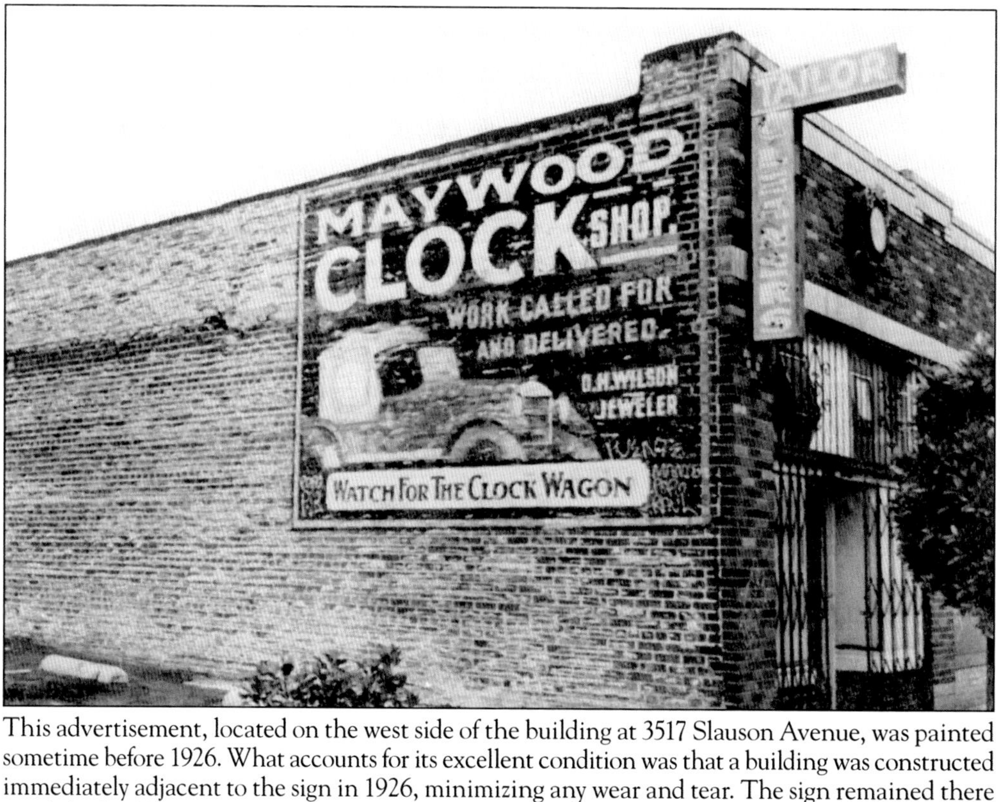

This advertisement, located on the west side of the building at 3517 Slauson Avenue, was painted sometime before 1926. What accounts for its excellent condition was that a building was constructed immediately adjacent to the sign in 1926, minimizing any wear and tear. The sign remained there until the building was razed in 1976 to make room for new construction.

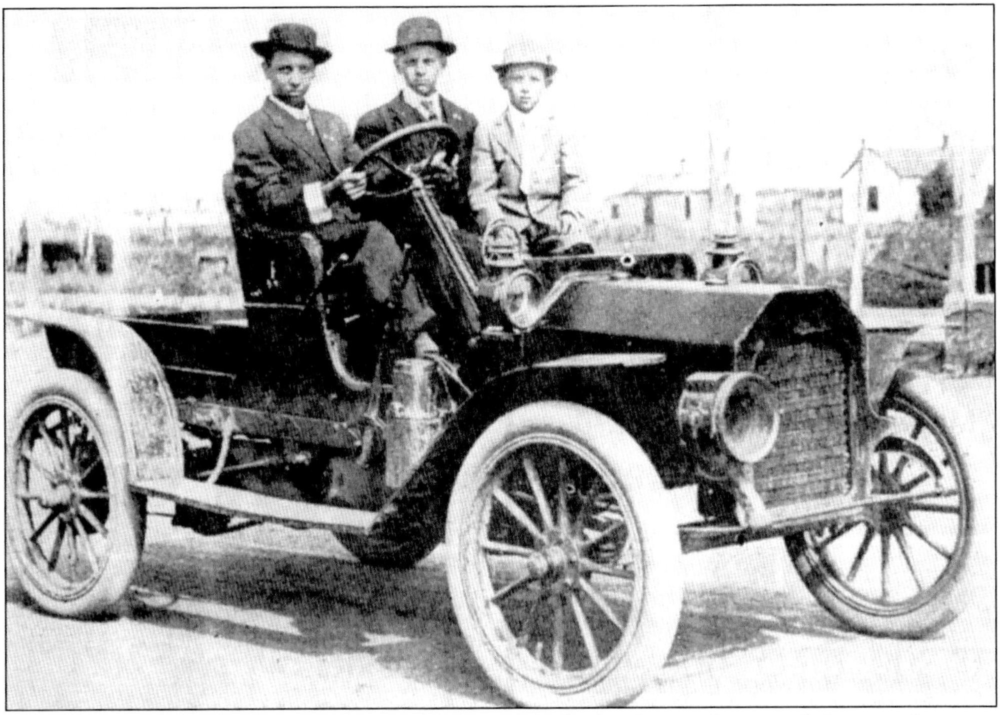

Driving a 1908 Reo in 1925, J. E. Dugan later owned a brake shop and automobile repair business on Atlantic Boulevard.

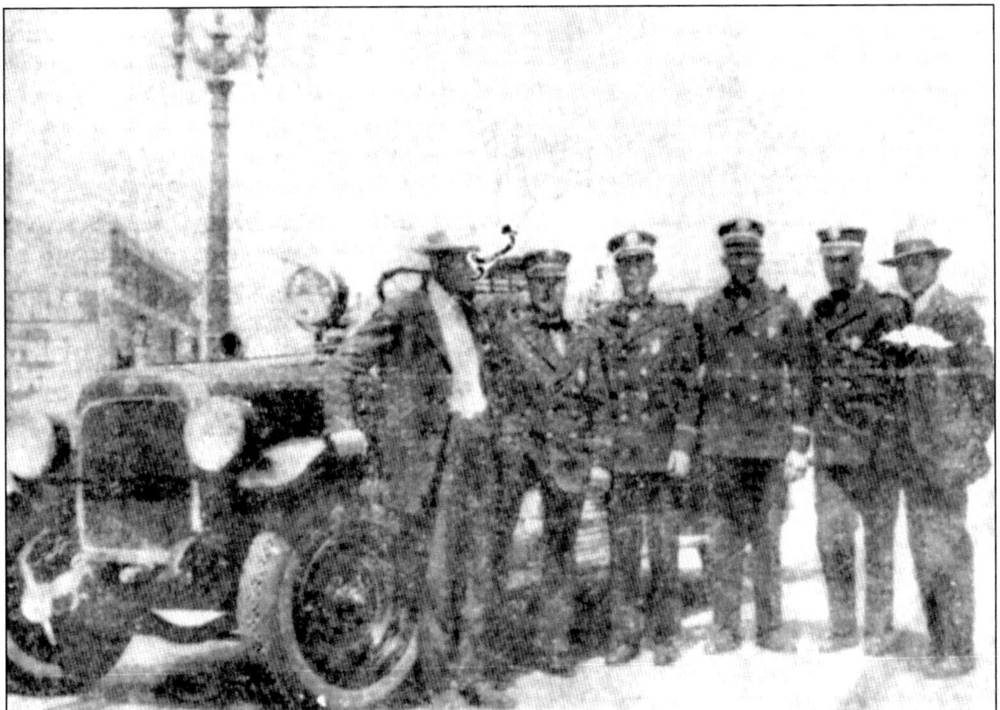

This was the first City of Maywood Fire Department. Fires never had a chance in those days.

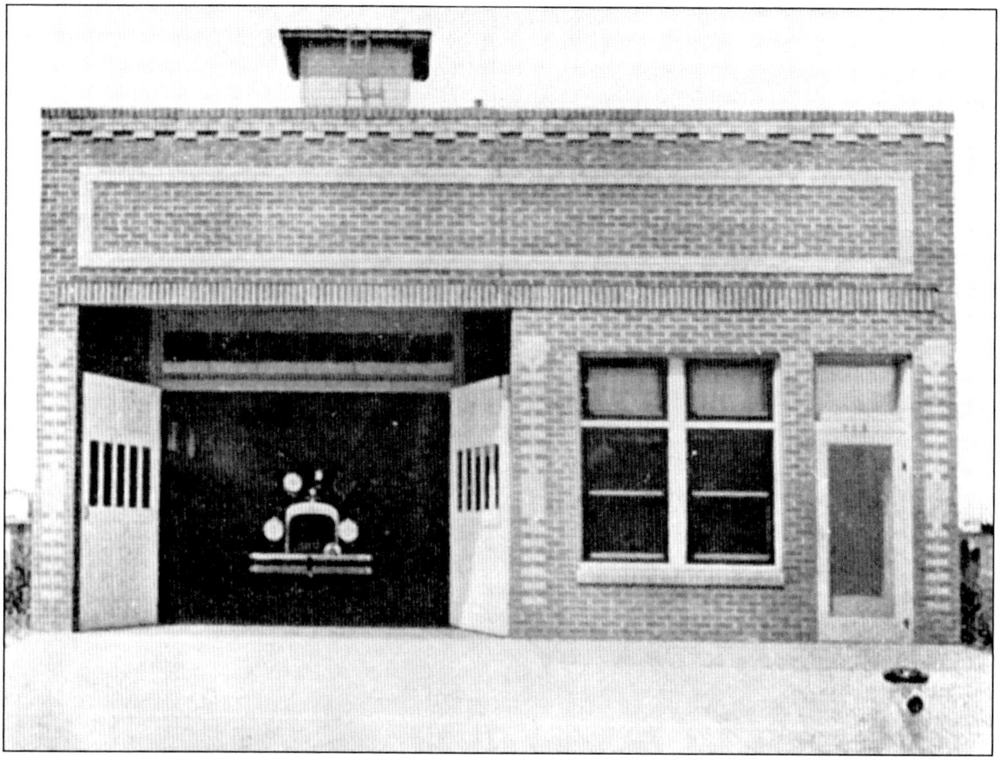

This photograph depicts the Maywood Fire Department.

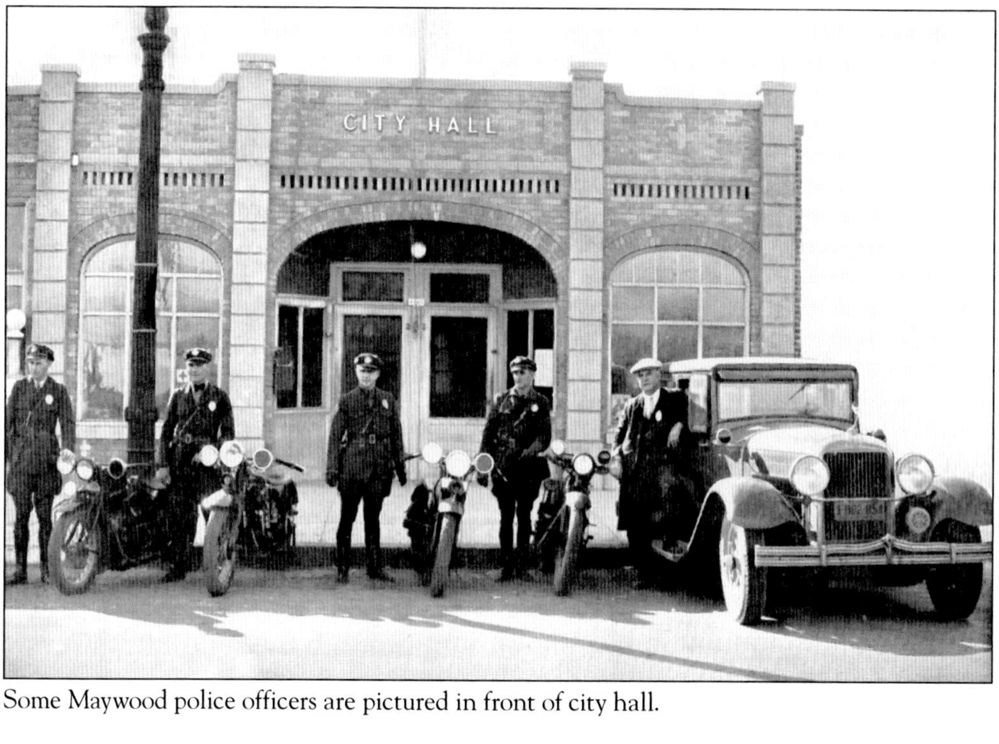

Some Maywood police officers are pictured in front of city hall.

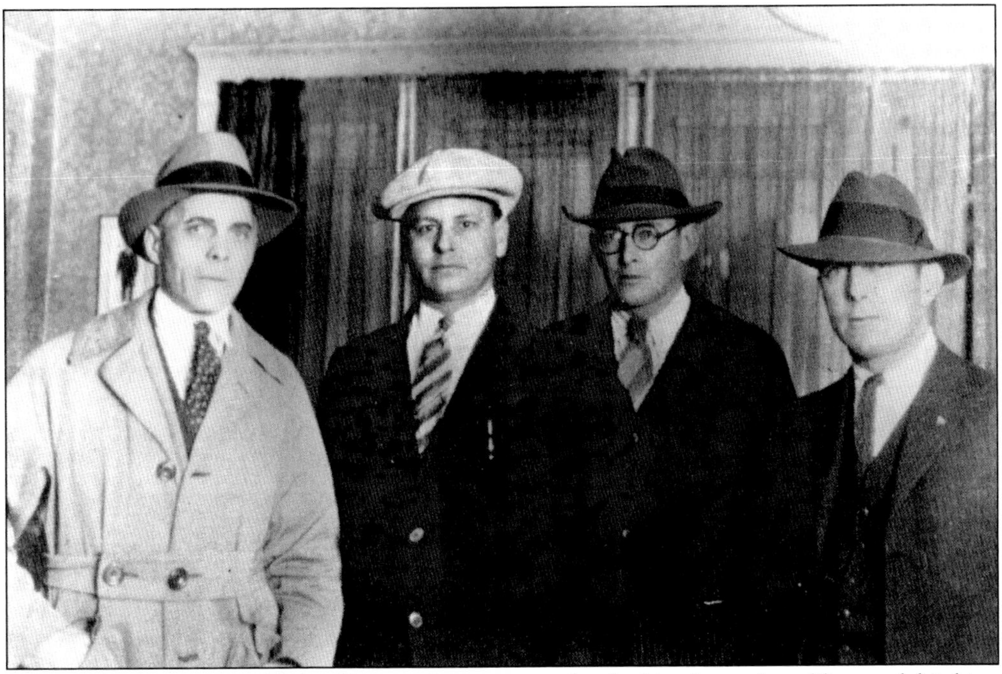

Maywood's shotgun squad helped keep order in a town that had its share of gambling and drinking establishments in the late 1920s.

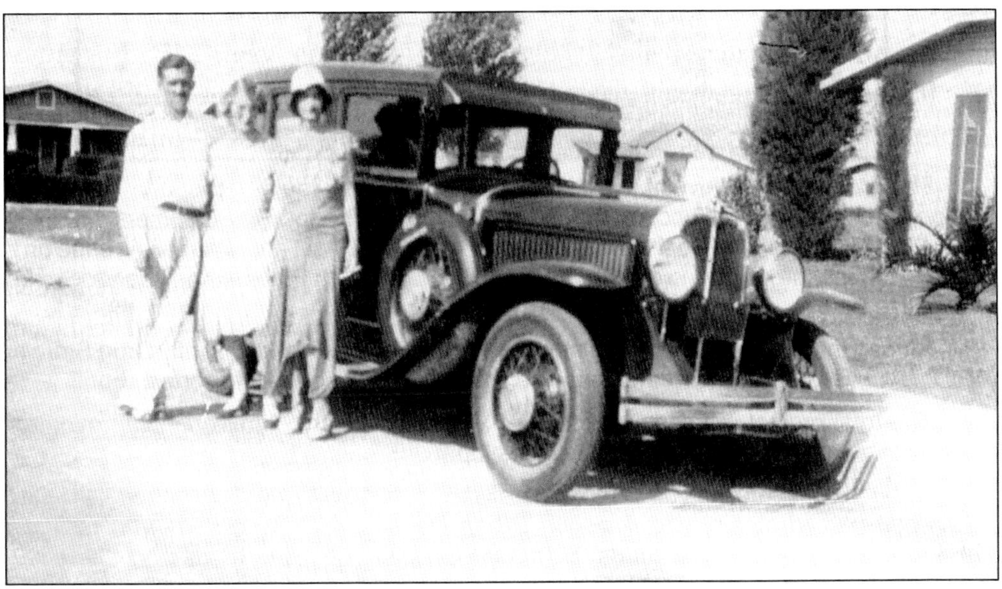

Early Maywood residents pose here.

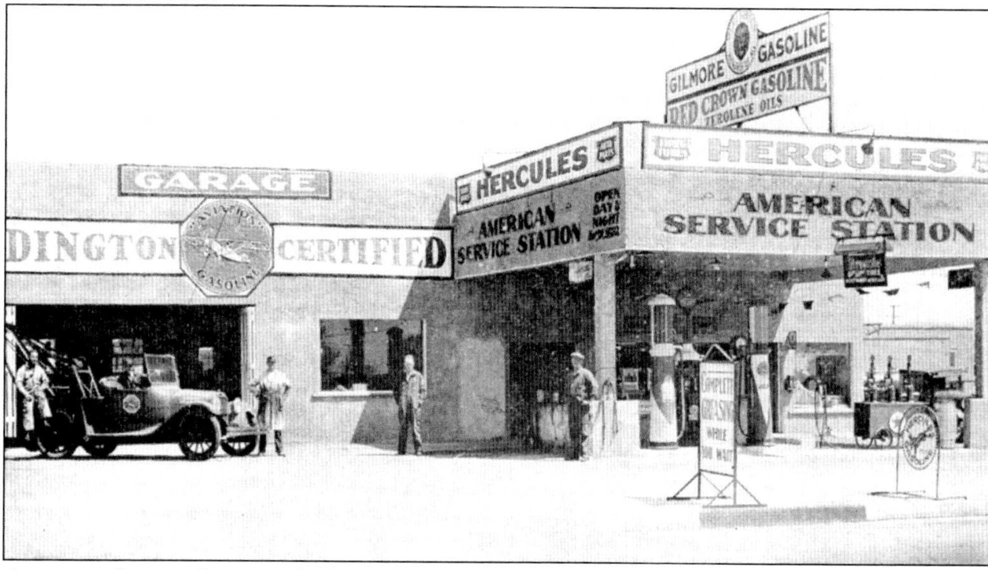

American Service Station, which was located on Slauson Avenue and King Street, offered all the amenities of the day, including towing, batteries, tire repair, new tires, inner-tubes, and parts.

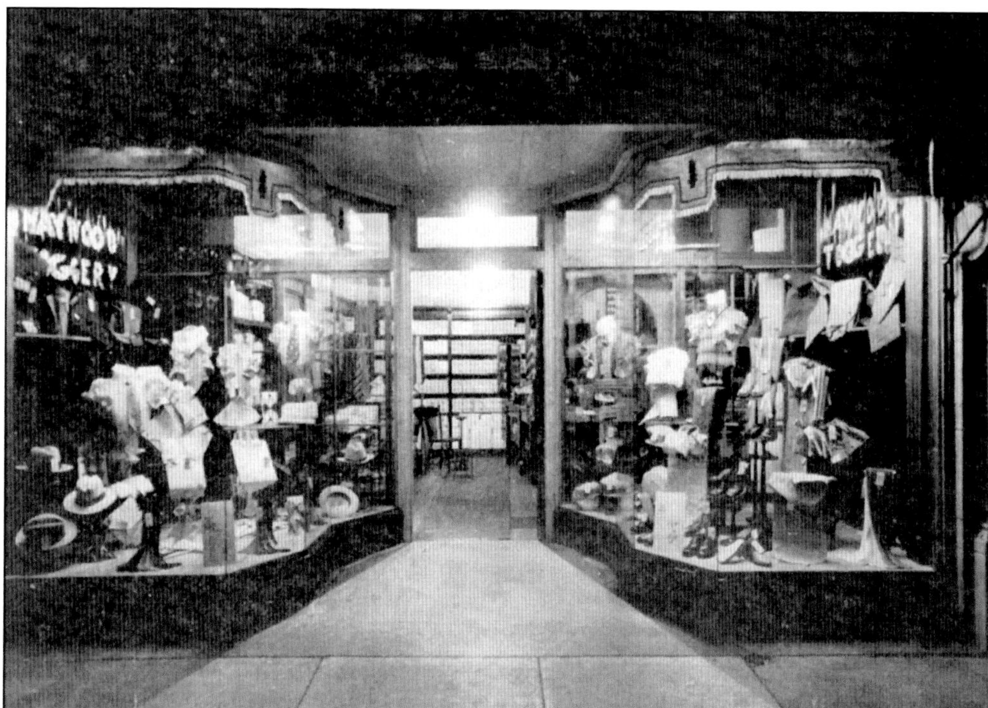

This front view shows the display windows of the Maywood Toggery on Slauson Avenue. While the word toggery has practically left the language, it is still defined in Webster's Dictionary as "clothing store."

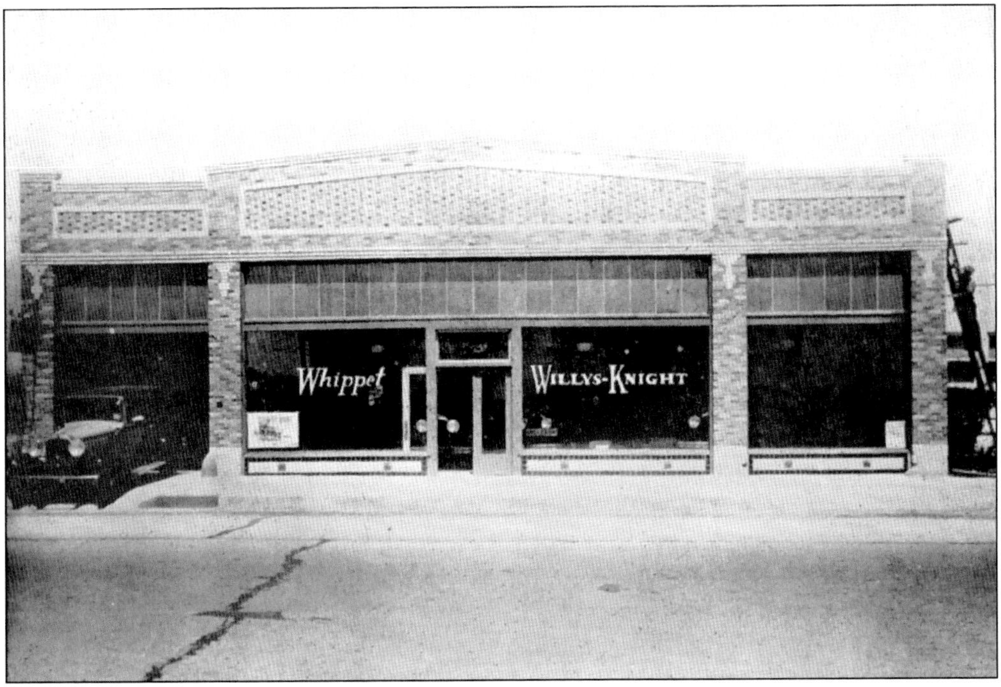

Willys-Knight Garage offered general repairs, sales, and service. The originally Toledo, Ohio–based Willys later became famous for producing the all-around World War II military vehicle of choice—the Jeep.

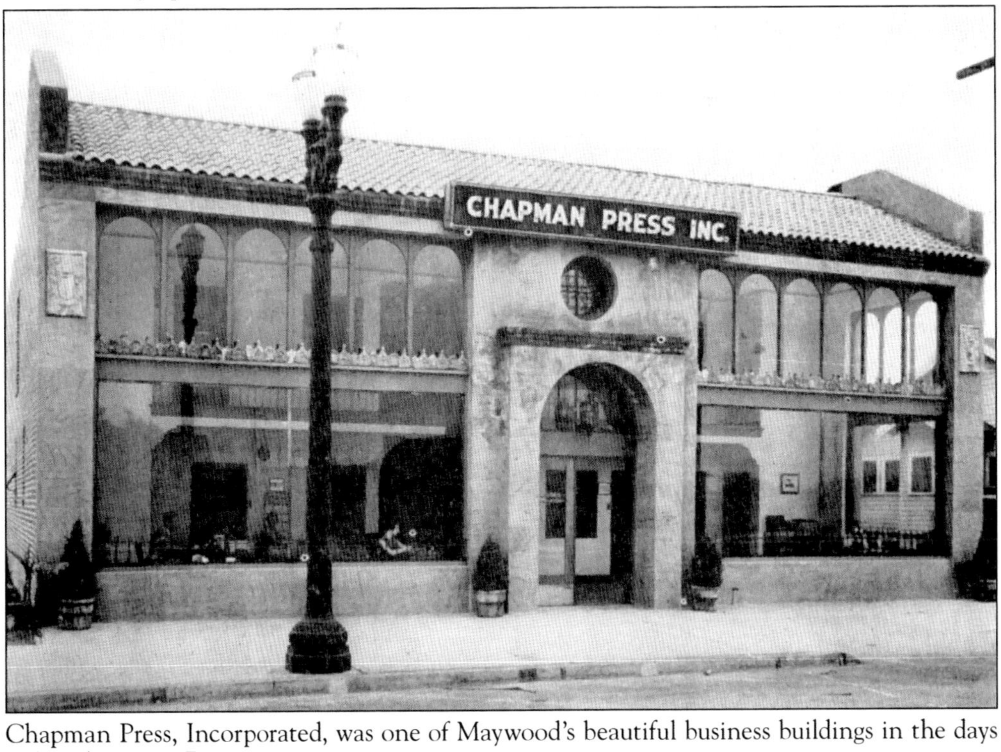

Chapman Press, Incorporated, was one of Maywood's beautiful business buildings in the days before the Great Depression era.

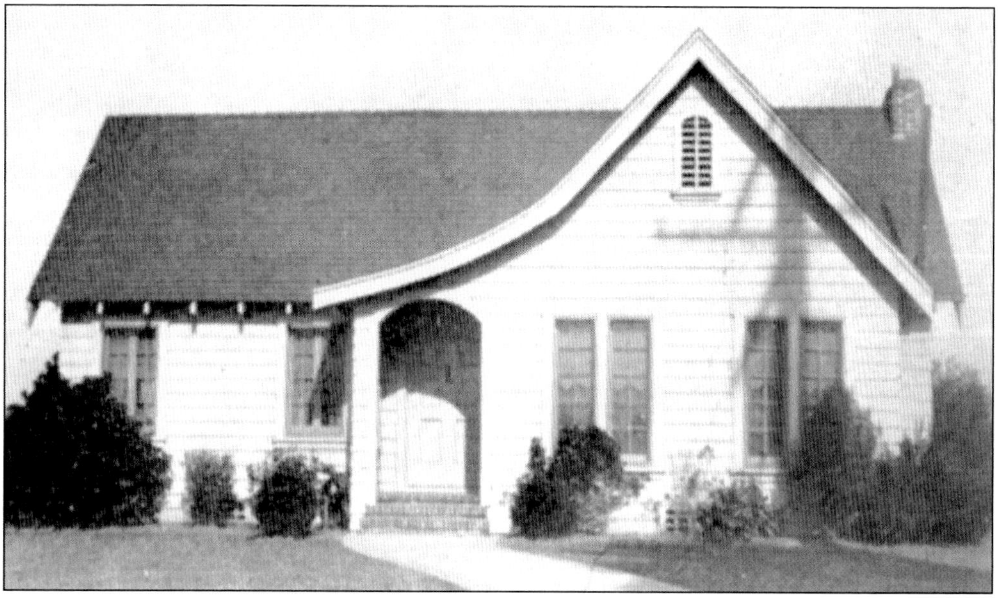

A typical home in Maywood, where careful plans were laid to insure the continued growth of the city, had special emphasis placed on attractiveness and functional construction.

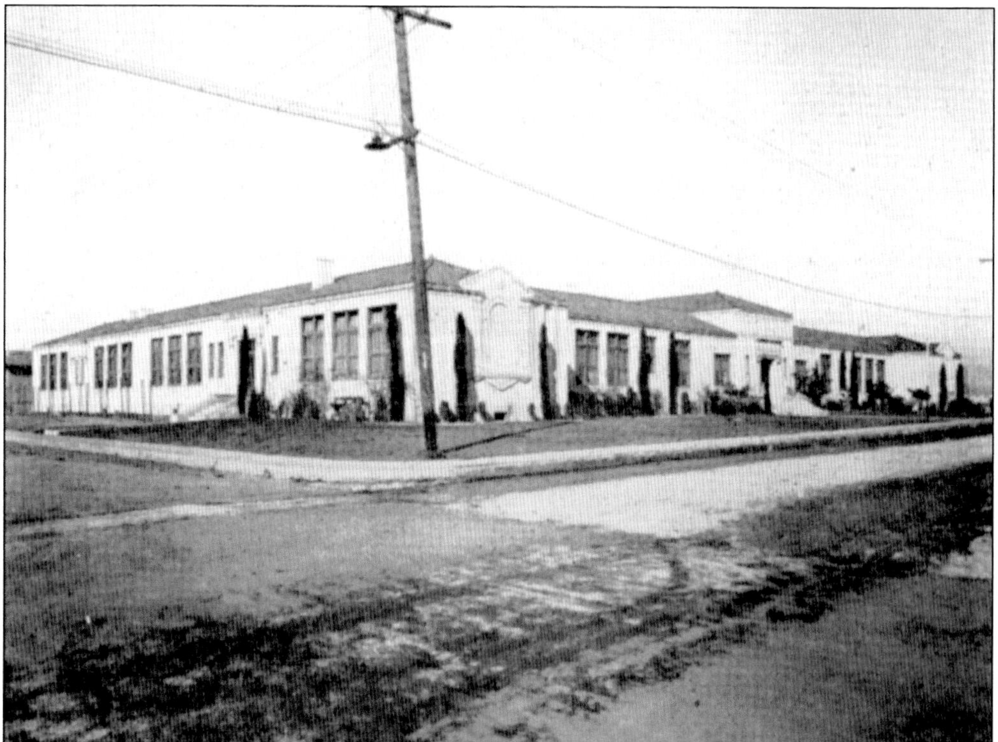

Heliotrope Avenue Elementary School, kindergarten through fifth grade, was originally named Jefferson School.

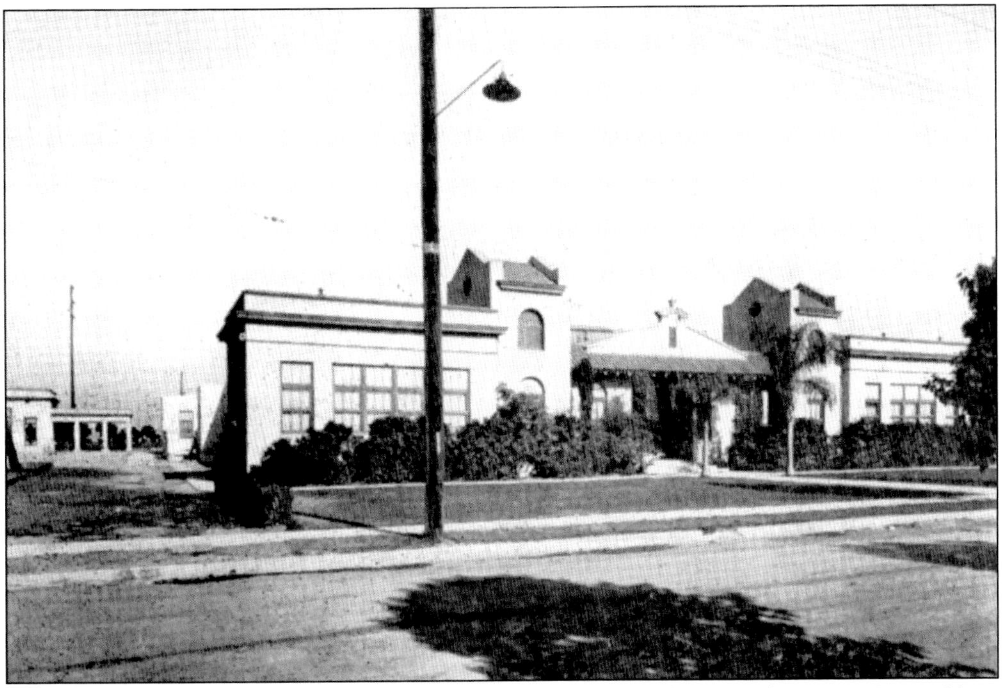

Washington School, the first school constructed in Maywood, is now known as Loma Vista Elementary School.

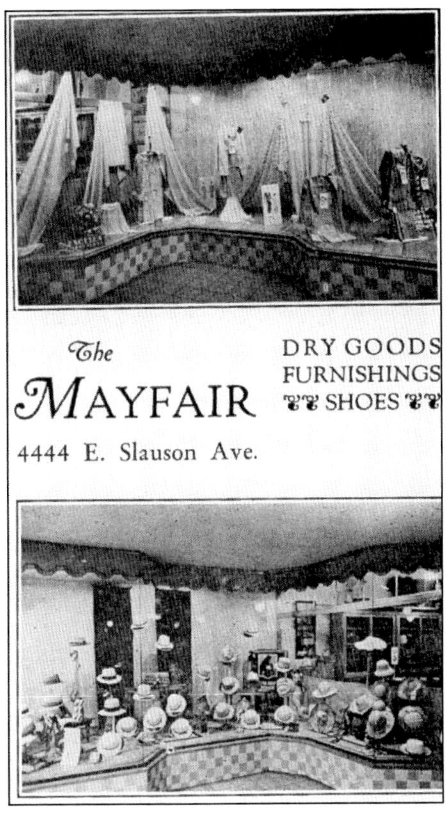

The Mayfair Dry Goods Furnishings, which supplied many area families with textiles and other clothing materials, was located on East Slauson Avenue in Maywood.

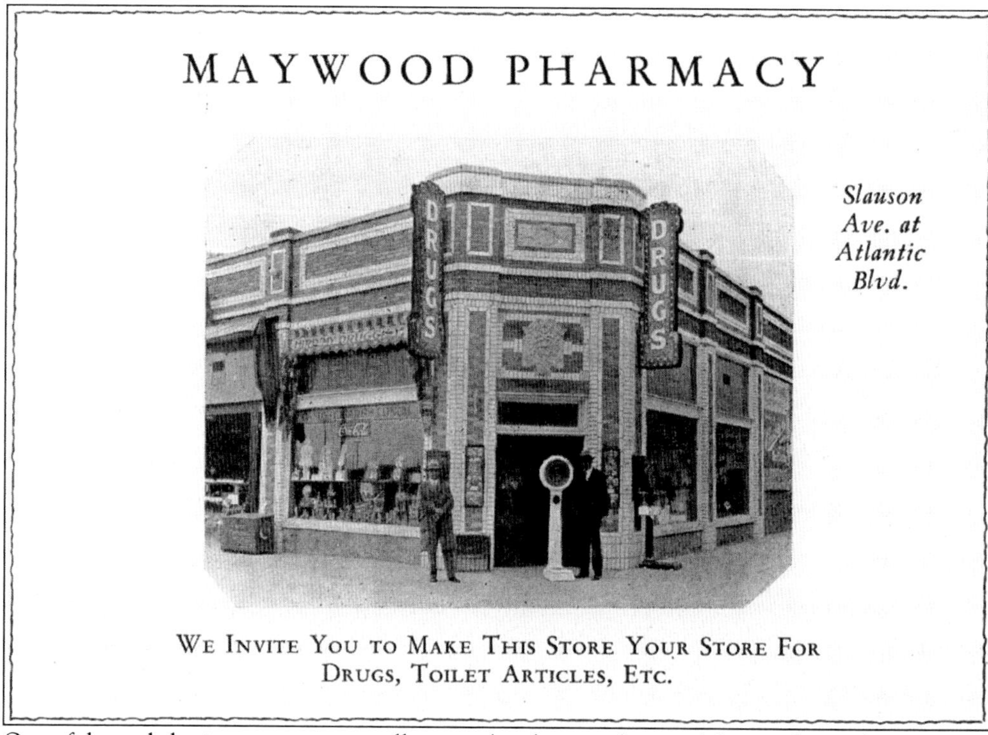

One of the early business centers, as well as social gathering places in Maywood, was the Maywood Pharmacy, located at Slauson Avenue and Atlantic Boulevard.

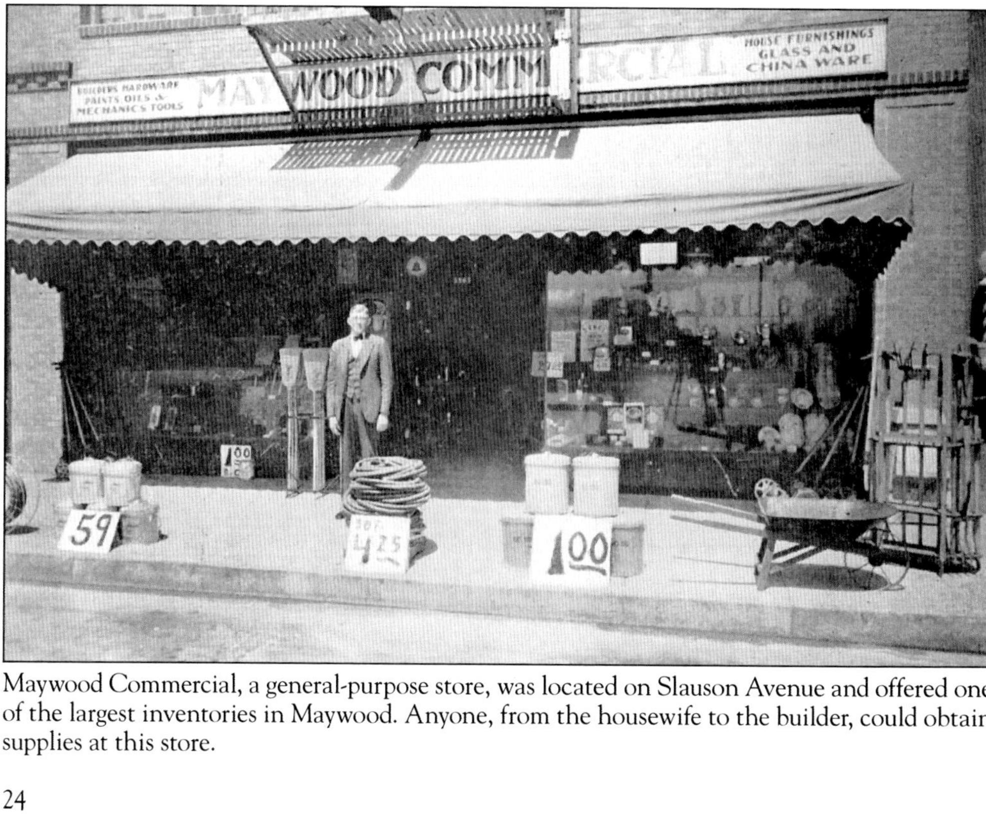

Maywood Commercial, a general-purpose store, was located on Slauson Avenue and offered one of the largest inventories in Maywood. Anyone, from the housewife to the builder, could obtain supplies at this store.

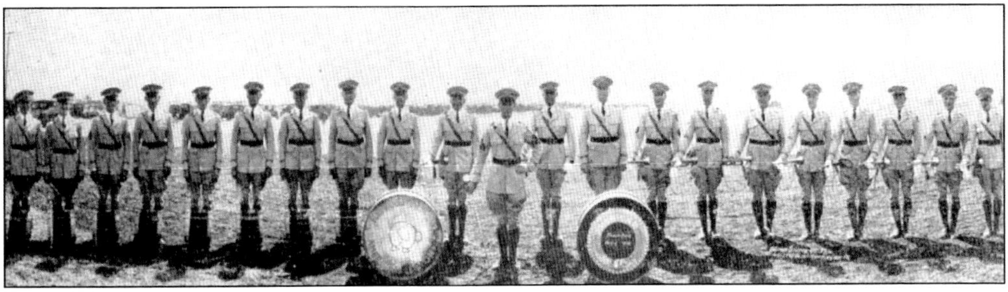

Maywood Post No. 223 of the American Legion was originally started in the fall of 1921 as a community ex-servicemen's club. Many Civil War–era veterans were at retirement age or older, and dozens of Army, Navy, and Marine veterans had returned a scant three years earlier from the European battlefields of the First World War.

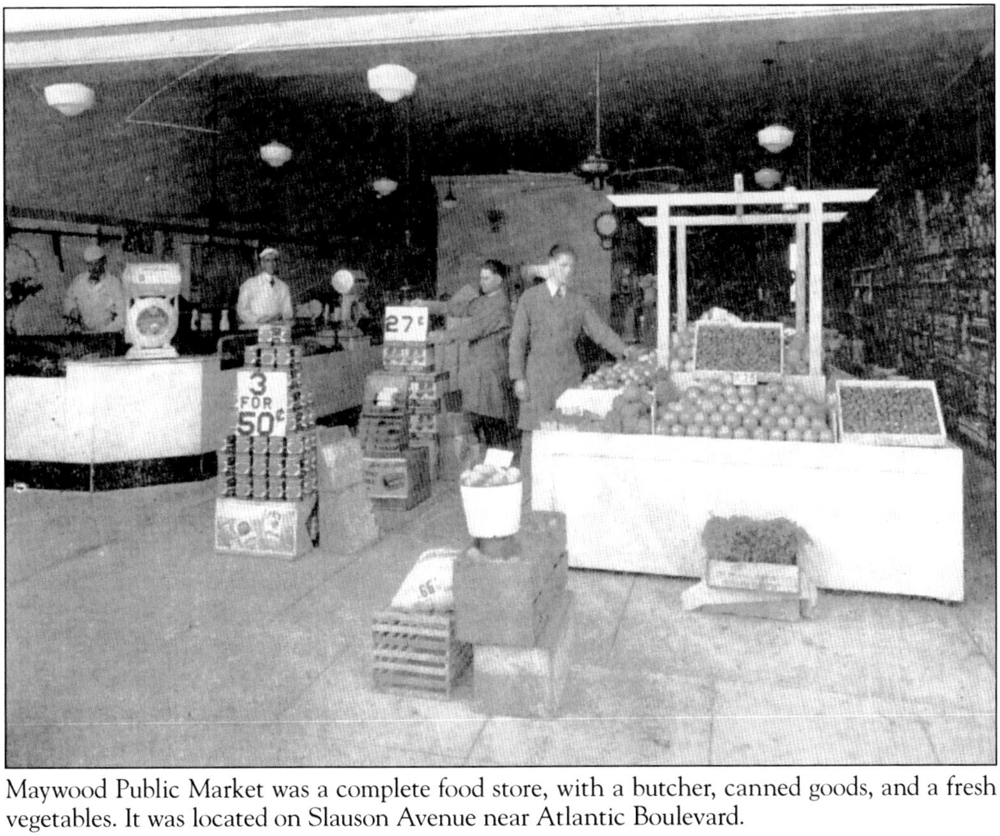

Maywood Public Market was a complete food store, with a butcher, canned goods, and a fresh vegetables. It was located on Slauson Avenue near Atlantic Boulevard.

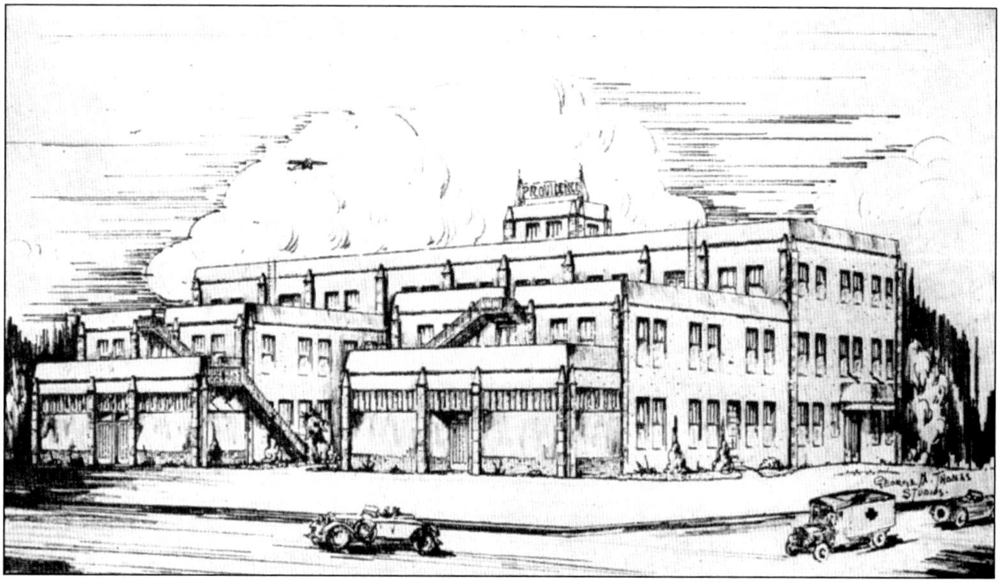

The rapid growth and development of Maywood created a need for a larger, more modern hospital. As a result, New Providence Hospital was built and equipped at a cost of over $200,000, a whopping sum in 1920s dollars.

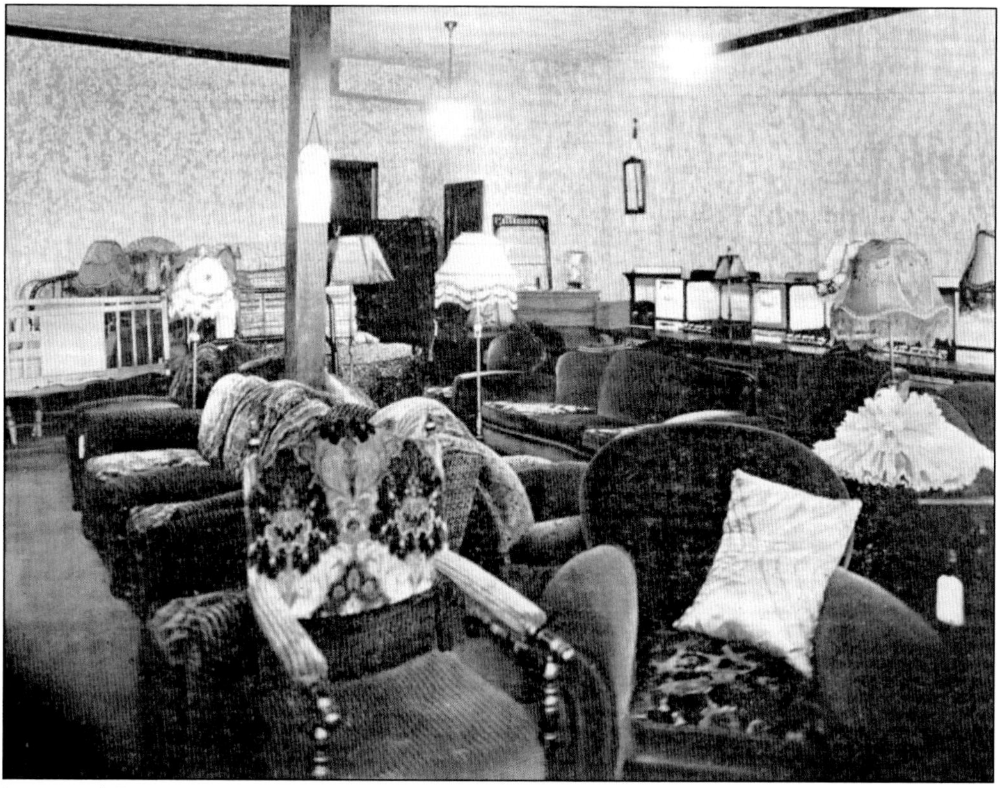

Maywood Furniture Company, located at 3511 East Slauson Avenue (at Maywood Avenue), carried furniture and radios. For convenience, the company accepted old furniture as a trade-in for new pieces. Radio broadcasting was still in its infancy in the 1920s.

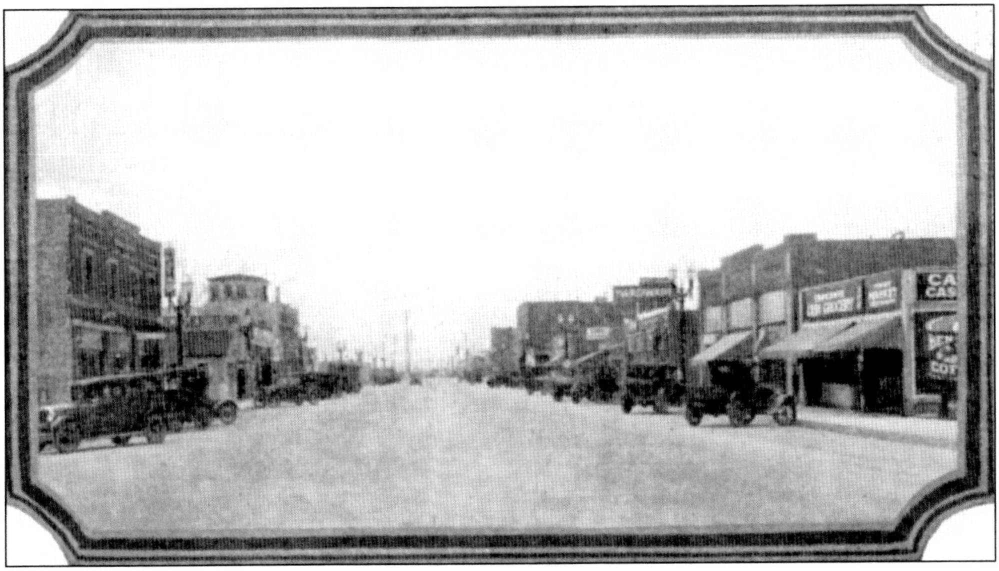

This view shows Slauson Avenue, looking west toward Maywood Avenue.

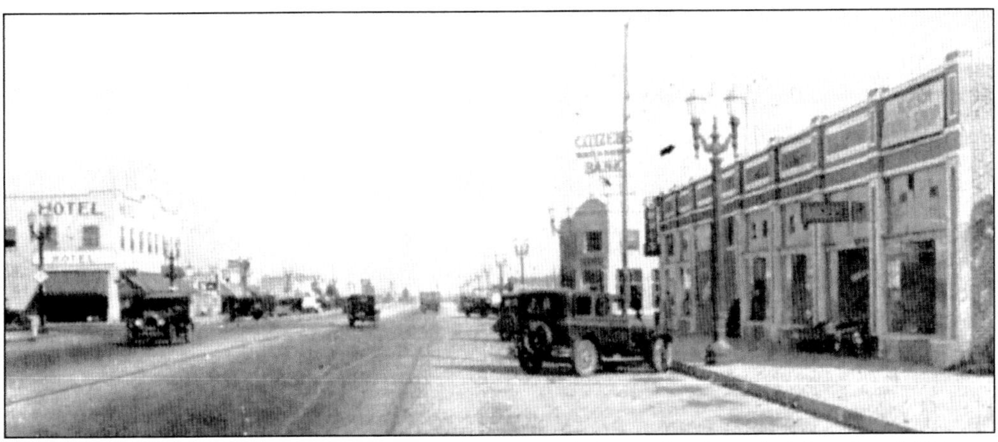

Looking east, this is the corner of Slauson Avenue at Atlantic Boulevard. A hotel and Citizens National Bank stand on opposite corners.

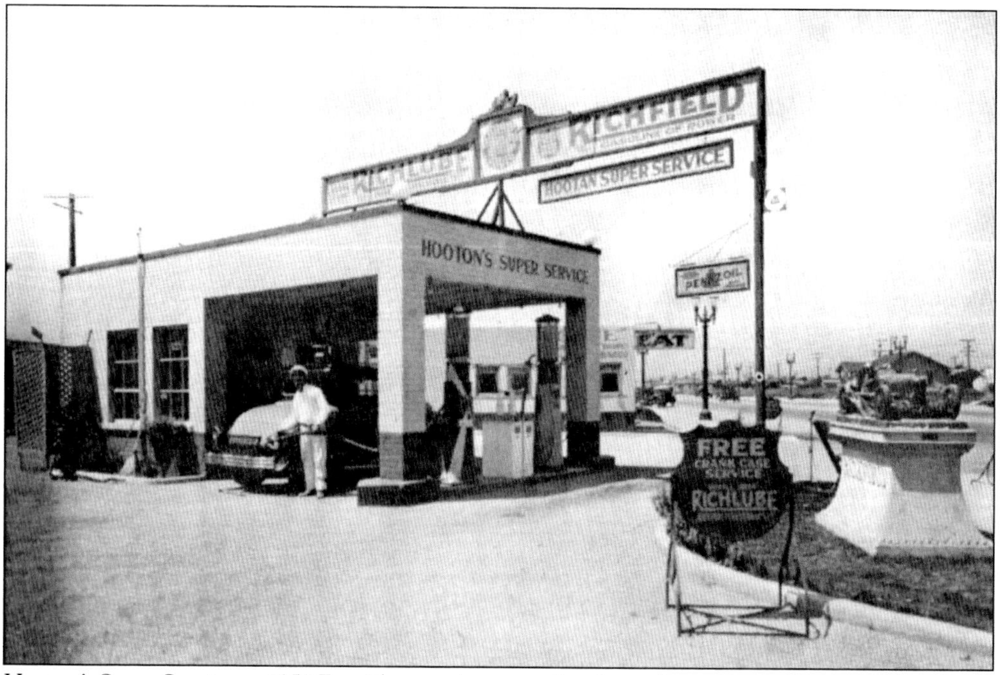

Hooton's Super Service at 4058 East Slauson Avenue offered speedy service for Maywood motorists.

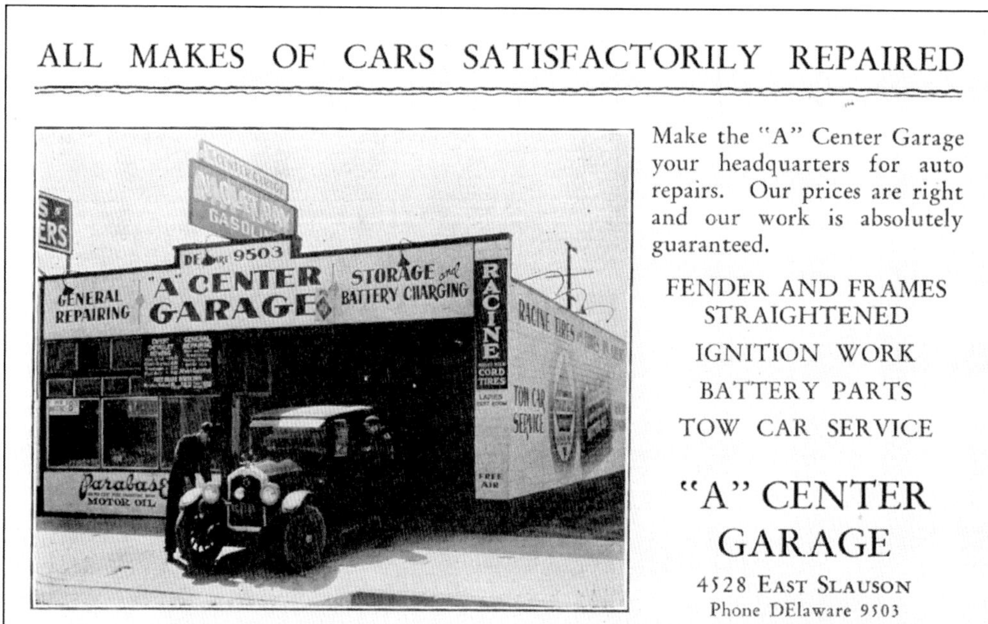

"A" Center Garage offered itself as the headquarters for auto repairs. The garage specialized in straightening fenders and frames, ignition work, battery parts, and towing service.

Two

The 1930s

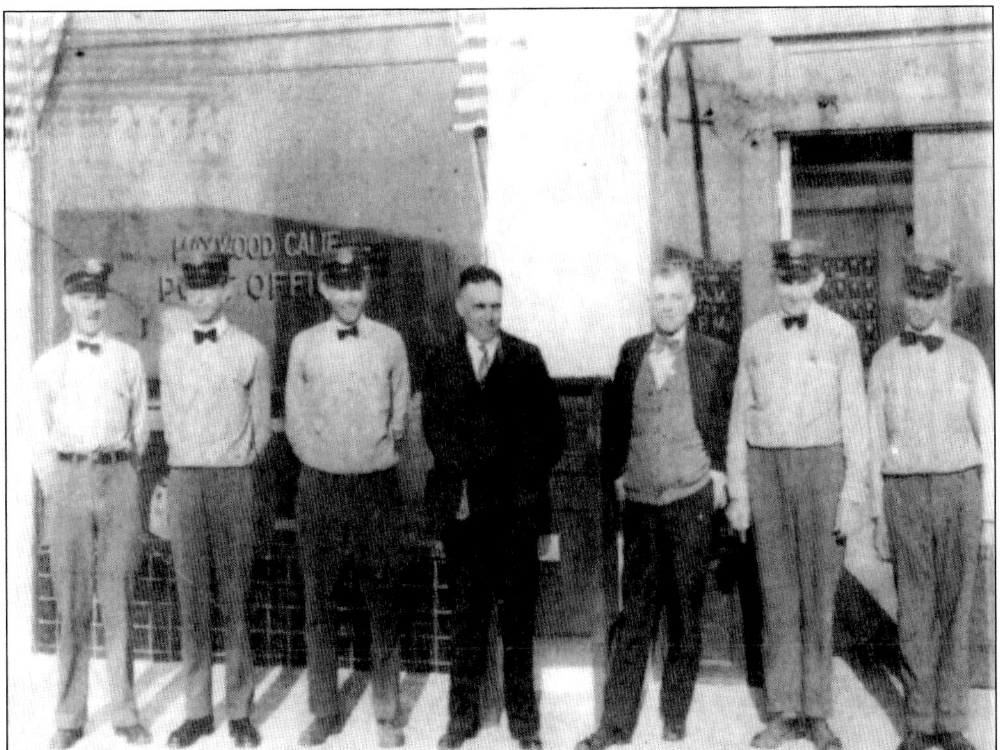

This picture, reportedly taken in 1930, shows the full complement of the Maywood Post Office, with two supervisors and five carriers. The post office was located at 5816 Pine Avenue. Mail was received from Los Angeles through the Huntington Park Post Office.

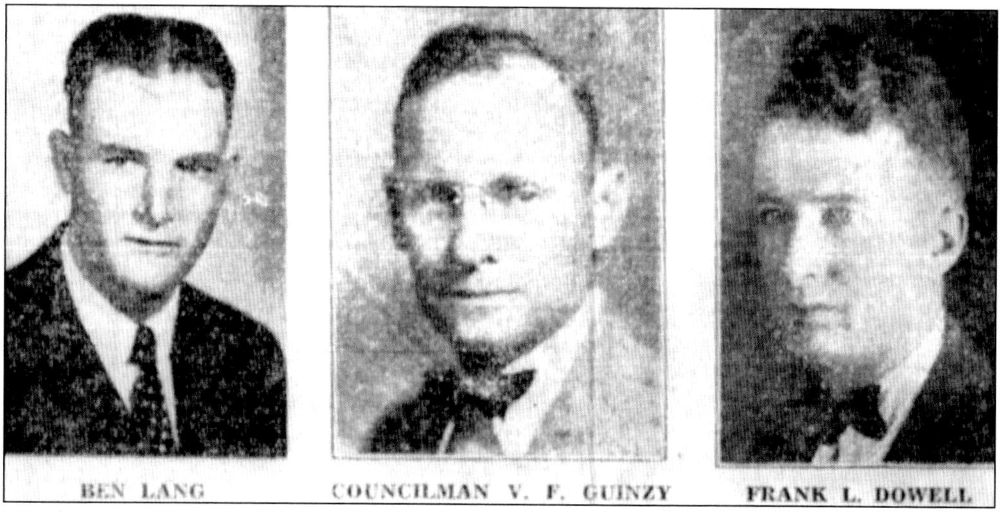

Members running on the Citizens' Ticket for the Maywood city council at the regular municipal election are depicted on a photograph dated Tuesday, April 14, 1936. Pictured, from left to right, they are Ben Lang, councilman Vennard F. Guinzy, and Frank L. Dowell.

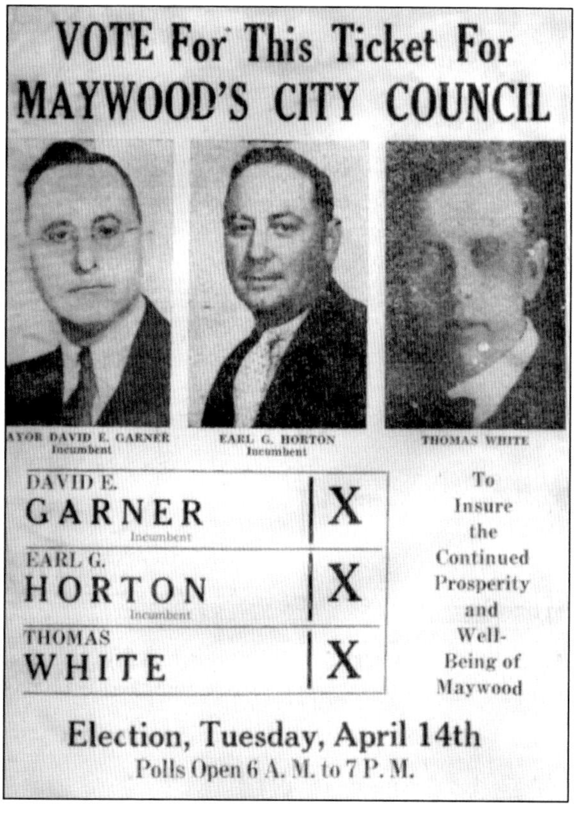

This is a political ticket for Maywood City Council from the *Industrial Post* dated Friday, April 23, 1936.

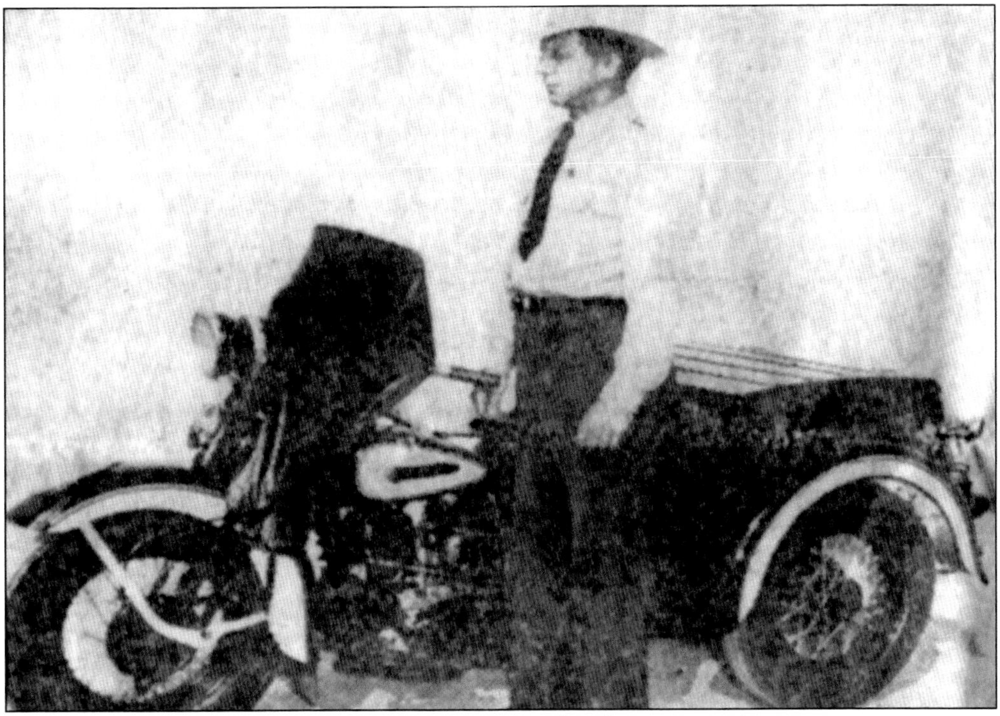

Former chief of police Kenneth Blackburn is depicted with a motorcycle.

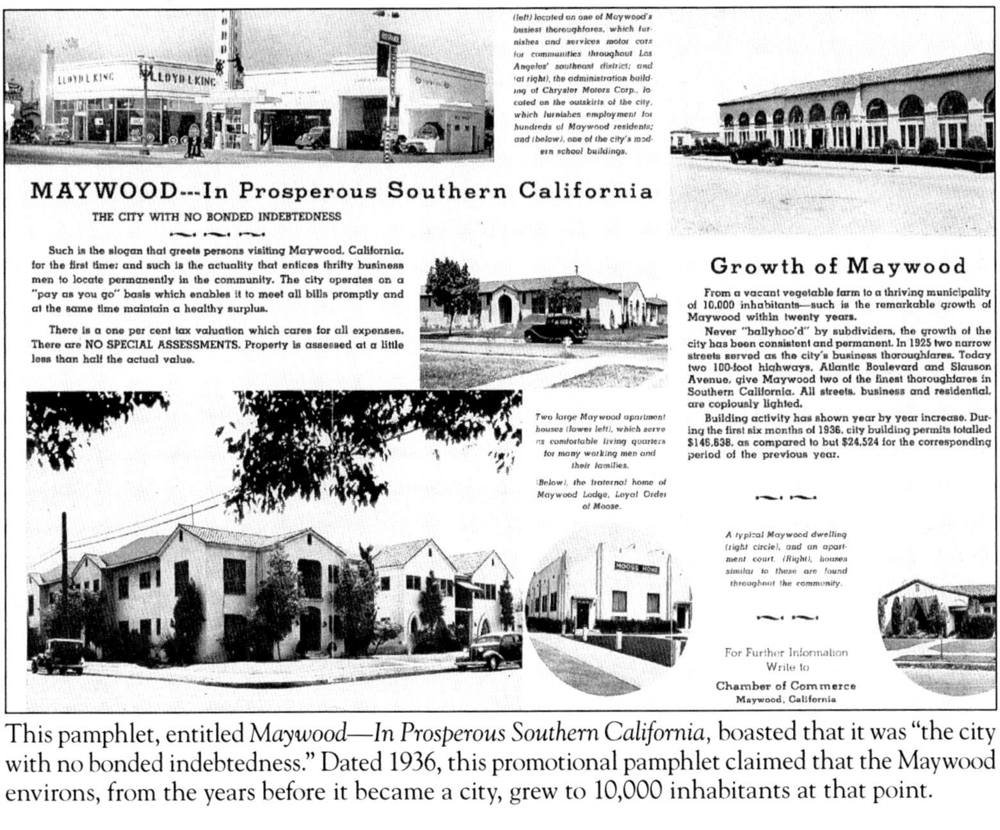

(left) located on one of Maywood's busiest thoroughfares, which furnishes and services motor cars for communities throughout Los Angeles' southeast district; and (at right), the administration building of Chrysler Motors Corp., located on the outskirts of the city, which furnishes employment for hundreds of Maywood residents; and (below), one of the city's modern school buildings.

MAYWOOD---In Prosperous Southern California

THE CITY WITH NO BONDED INDEBTEDNESS

Such is the slogan that greets persons visiting Maywood, California, for the first time; and such is the actuality that entices thrifty business men to locate permanently in the community. The city operates on a "pay as you go" basis which enables it to meet all bills promptly and at the same time maintain a healthy surplus.

There is a one per cent tax valuation which cares for all expenses. There are NO SPECIAL ASSESSMENTS. Property is assessed at a little less than half the actual value.

Growth of Maywood

From a vacant vegetable farm to a thriving municipality of 10,000 inhabitants—such is the remarkable growth of Maywood within twenty years.

Never "ballyhoo'd" by subdividers, the growth of the city has been consistent and permanent. In 1925 two narrow streets served as the city's business thoroughfares. Today two 100-foot highways, Atlantic Boulevard and Slauson Avenue, give Maywood two of the finest thoroughfares in Southern California. All streets, business and residential, are copiously lighted.

Building activity has shown year by year increase. During the first six months of 1936, city building permits totalled $146,638, as compared to but $24,524 for the corresponding period of the previous year.

Two large Maywood apartment houses (lower left), which serve as comfortable living quarters for many working men and their families.

(Below), the fraternal home of Maywood Lodge, Loyal Order of Moose.

A typical Maywood dwelling (right circle), and an apartment court. (Right), houses similar to these are found throughout the community.

For Further Information
Write to
Chamber of Commerce
Maywood, California

This pamphlet, entitled *Maywood—In Prosperous Southern California,* boasted that it was "the city with no bonded indebtedness." Dated 1936, this promotional pamphlet claimed that the Maywood environs, from the years before it became a city, grew to 10,000 inhabitants at that point.

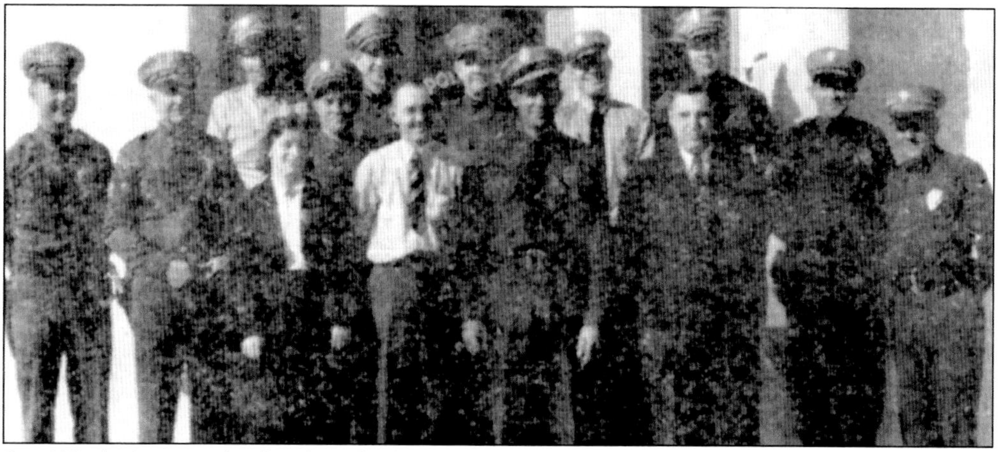

By 1937, the Maywood police force had grown to top-level efficiency. It had come a long way from the incorporation days of 13 years before.

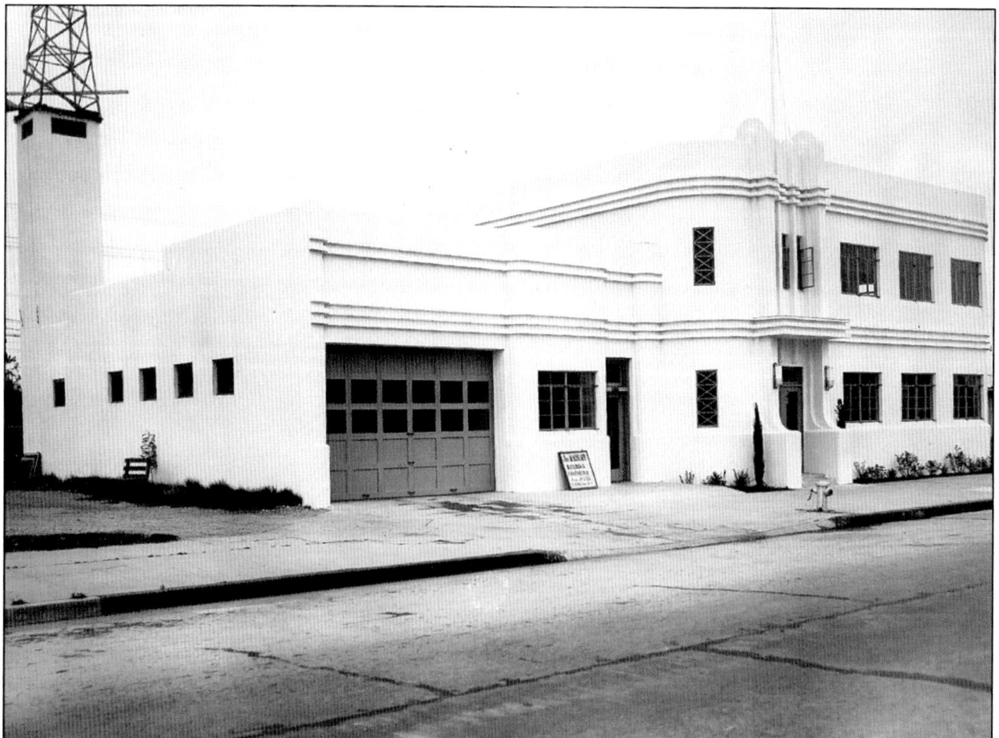

The new Maywood City Hall is shown in 1938 at 3419 East Slauson Avenue. The Maywood Fire Department kept their truck in the left side and the police department was located at the rear of the building.

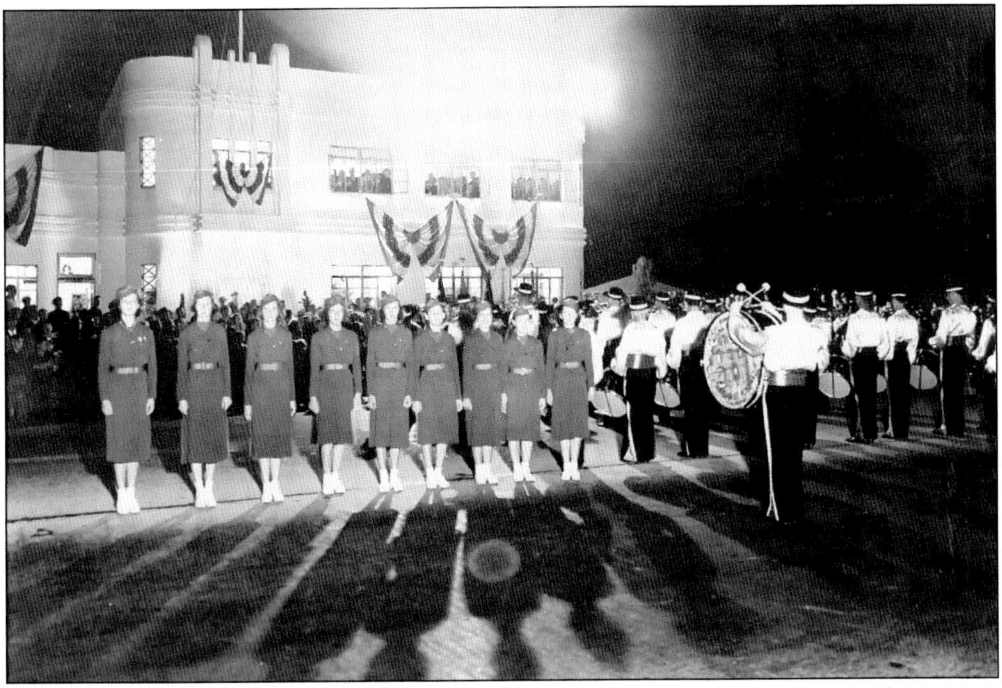

On June 11, 1938, the new city hall building was dedicated. Pictured are the San Gabriel American Legion Drum and Bugle Corps, who were the reigning national champion group. Their director was Bill Osborne.

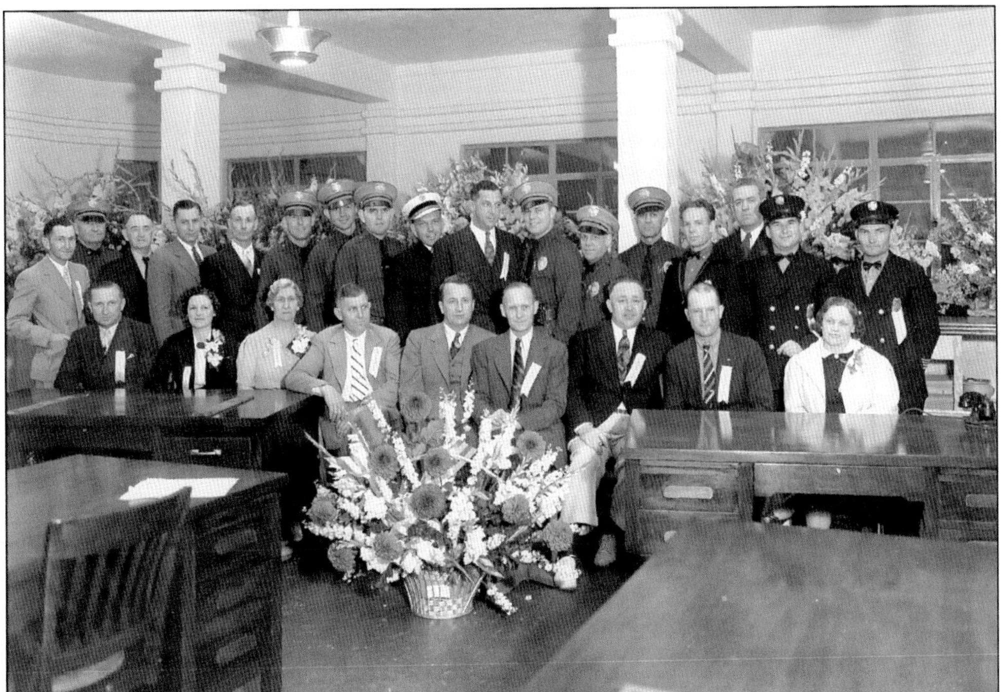

The interior of the new city hall building is shown here with employees, policemen, and firemen celebrating the opening.

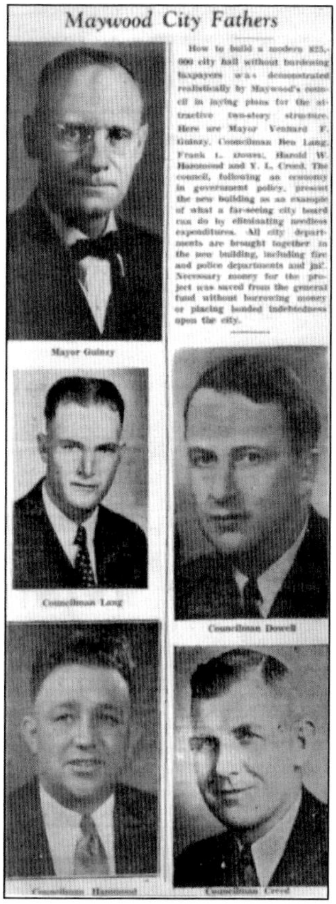

Maywood City Fathers

How to build a modern $25,000 city hall without burdening taxpayers was demonstrated realistically by Maywood's council in laying plans for the attractive two-story structure. Here are Mayor Vennard F. Guinzy, Councilman Ben Lang, Frank L. Dowell, Harold W. Hammond and Y. L. Creed. The council, following an economy in government policy, present the new building as an example of what a far-seeing city board can do by eliminating needless expenditures. All city departments are brought together in the new building, including fire and police departments and jail. Necessary money for the project was saved from the general fund without borrowing money or placing bonded indebtedness upon the city.

Mayor Guinzy

Councilman Lang

Councilman Dowell

Councilman Hammond

Councilman Creed

This is the council whose wisdom paved the way for the new city hall to be built without general funds. The members, from left to right, are Mayor Vennard F. Guinzy and fellow councilmen Ben Lang, Frank L. Dowell, Harold W. Hammond, and Y. L. Creed.

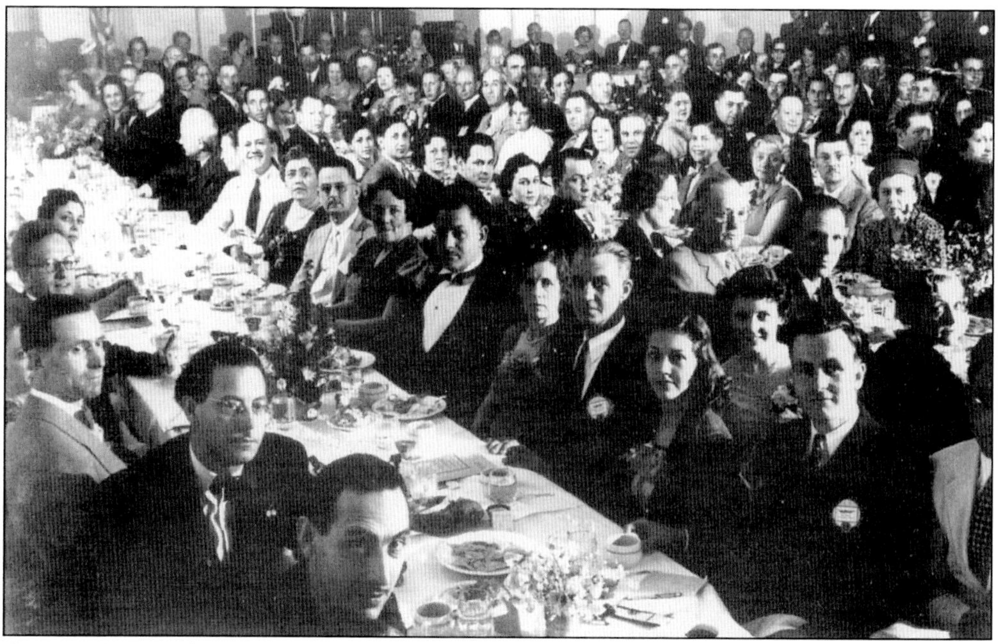

On May 27, 1939, charter night for the Lions Club was held at the Maywood City Hall Auditorium. The Maywood Lions have been a vital member of the community for more than 60 years.

Three

The 1940s

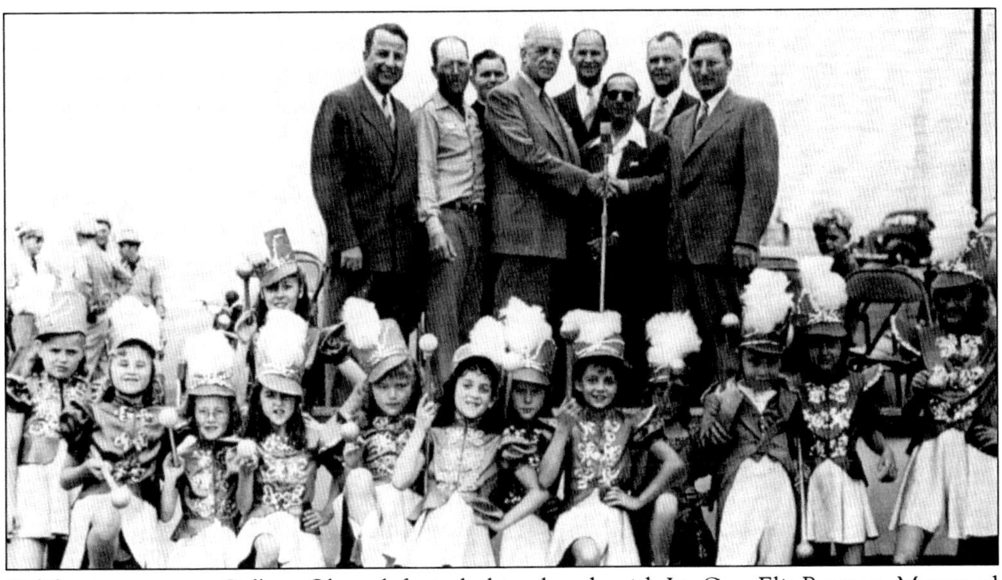

California governor Colbert Olsen, left, is shaking hands with Lt. Gov. Elis Rattson. Maywood mayor Ben Lang is next to the governor. Governor Olsen was in Maywood in 1940 for the opening of the Slauson Bridge. The councilman at the far left is Frank Dowell, and in the middle is Herman Bejack, a prominent Maywood civil leader.

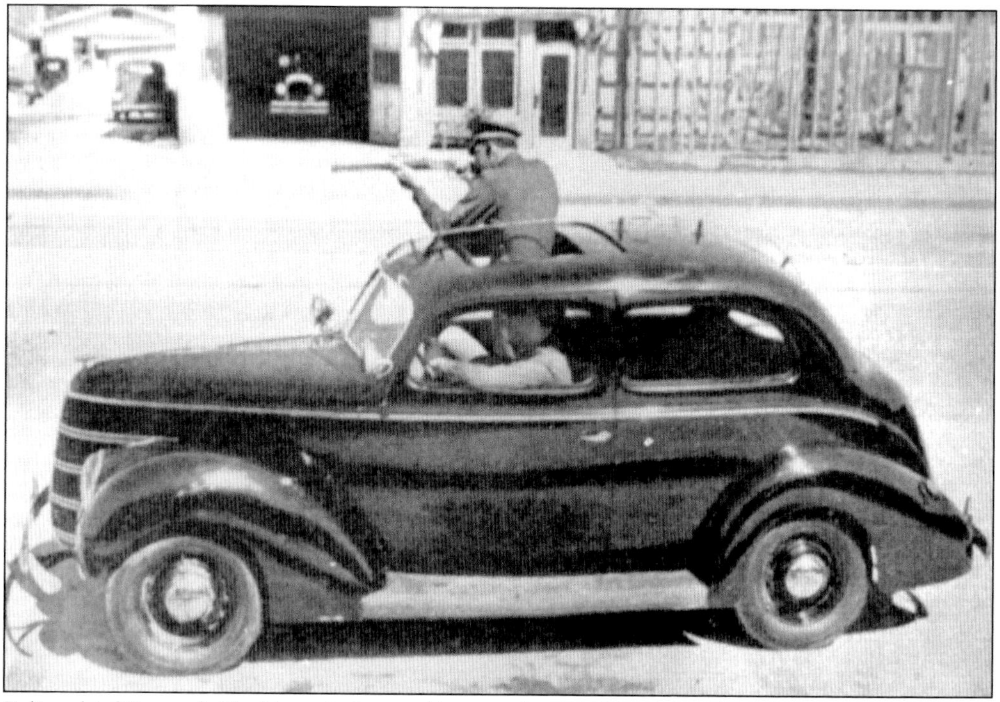

Police chief Kenneth Blackburn is depicted here with a 1938 Ford V-8, the standard 85-horsepower, two-door sedan. Chief Blackburn shows how this new aid can help crime prevention.

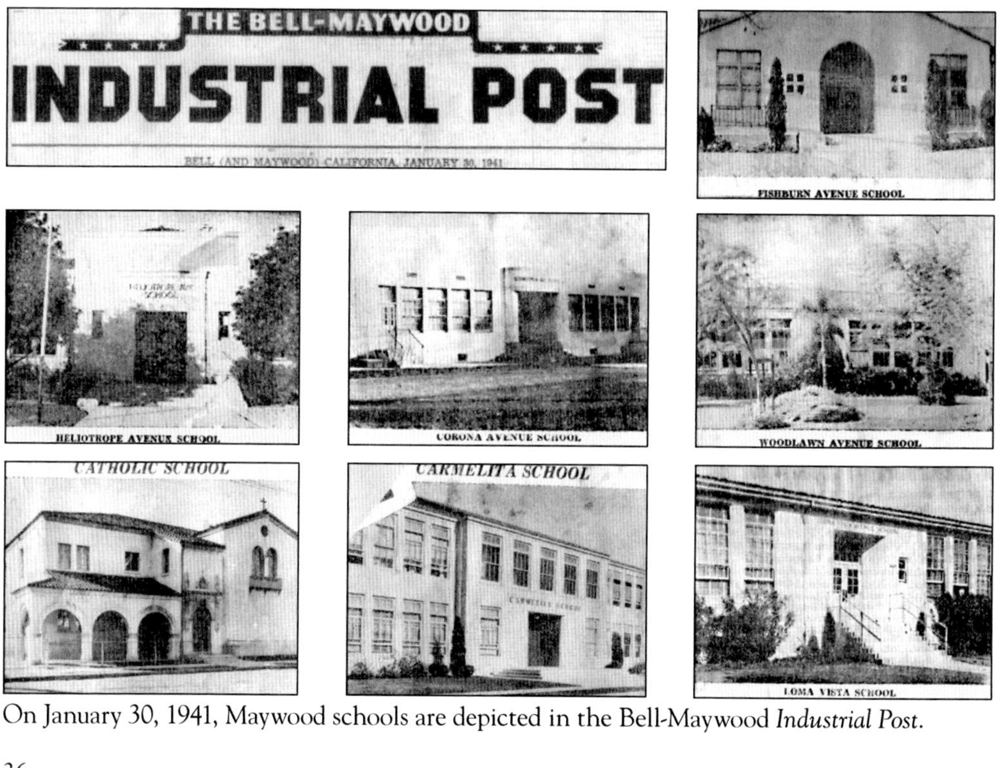

On January 30, 1941, Maywood schools are depicted in the Bell-Maywood *Industrial Post*.

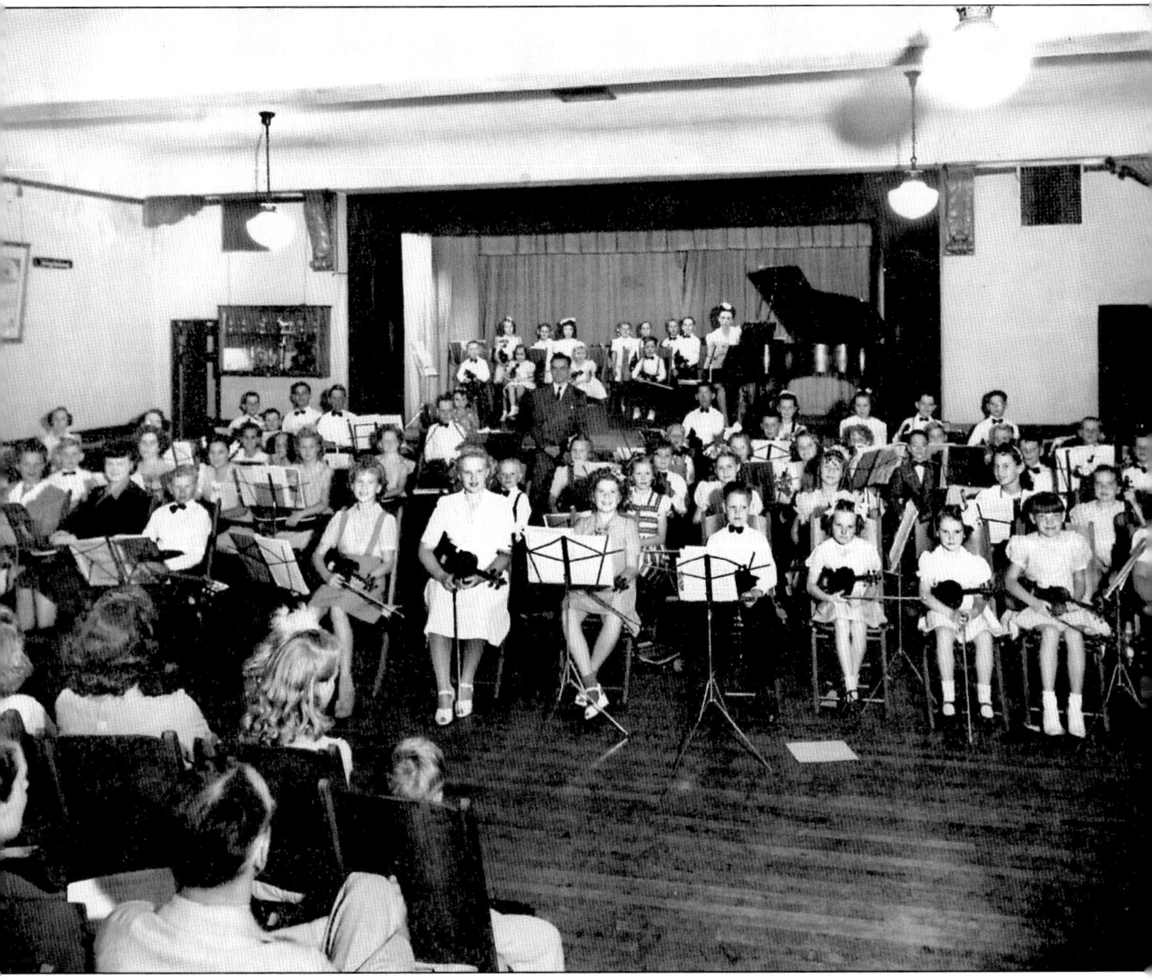

This youth concert was presented by a 50-piece band, including a grand piano.

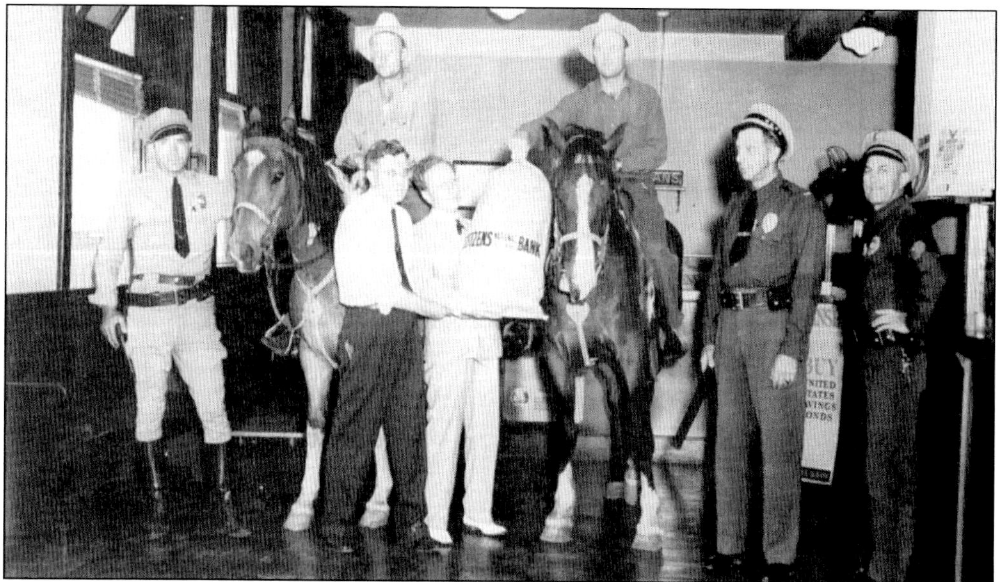

In this publicity shot at Citizens National Bank, Alma Lang (left) and Ben Lang are on horses to promote a rodeo at Maywood Park in the mid-1940s. Ernest Flanagan (far left), Chief Kenneth Blackburn (right), and Al Mauch (far right) are the other policemen in photograph.

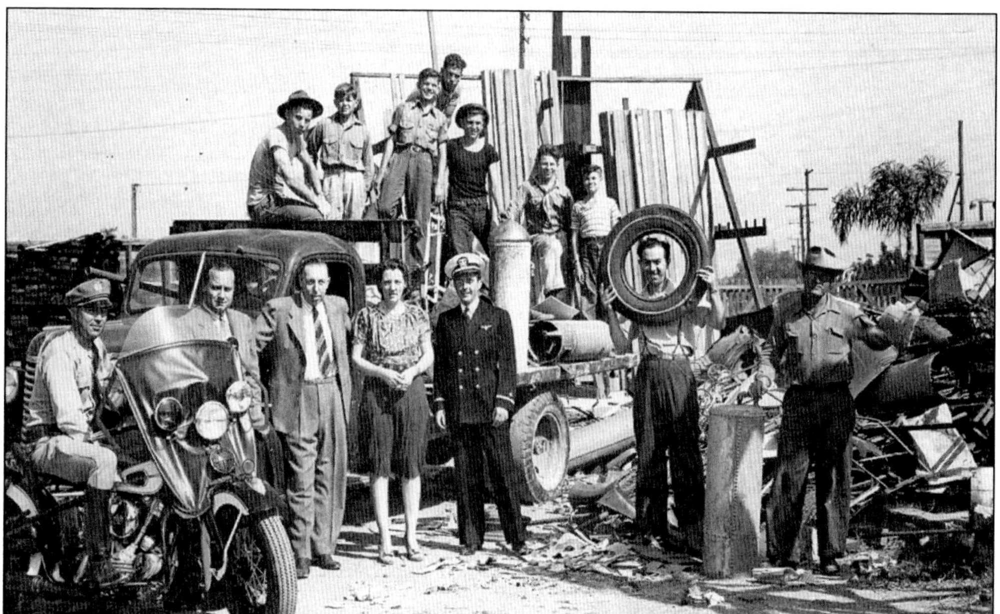

On September 1, 1942, the Maywood Salvage Crew, from left to right, is (first row) Officer White, Lion Dick Smith, Mr. Huey, Ann Aksom, Ensign Murphy, Jack Freeman, and Lion Ben Lang; (second row) Boy Scouts Bill Rath, Joe Gerdes, John Zaro, Phil Lang, Wally Gerdes, Bob Linkey, and Bob Horne.

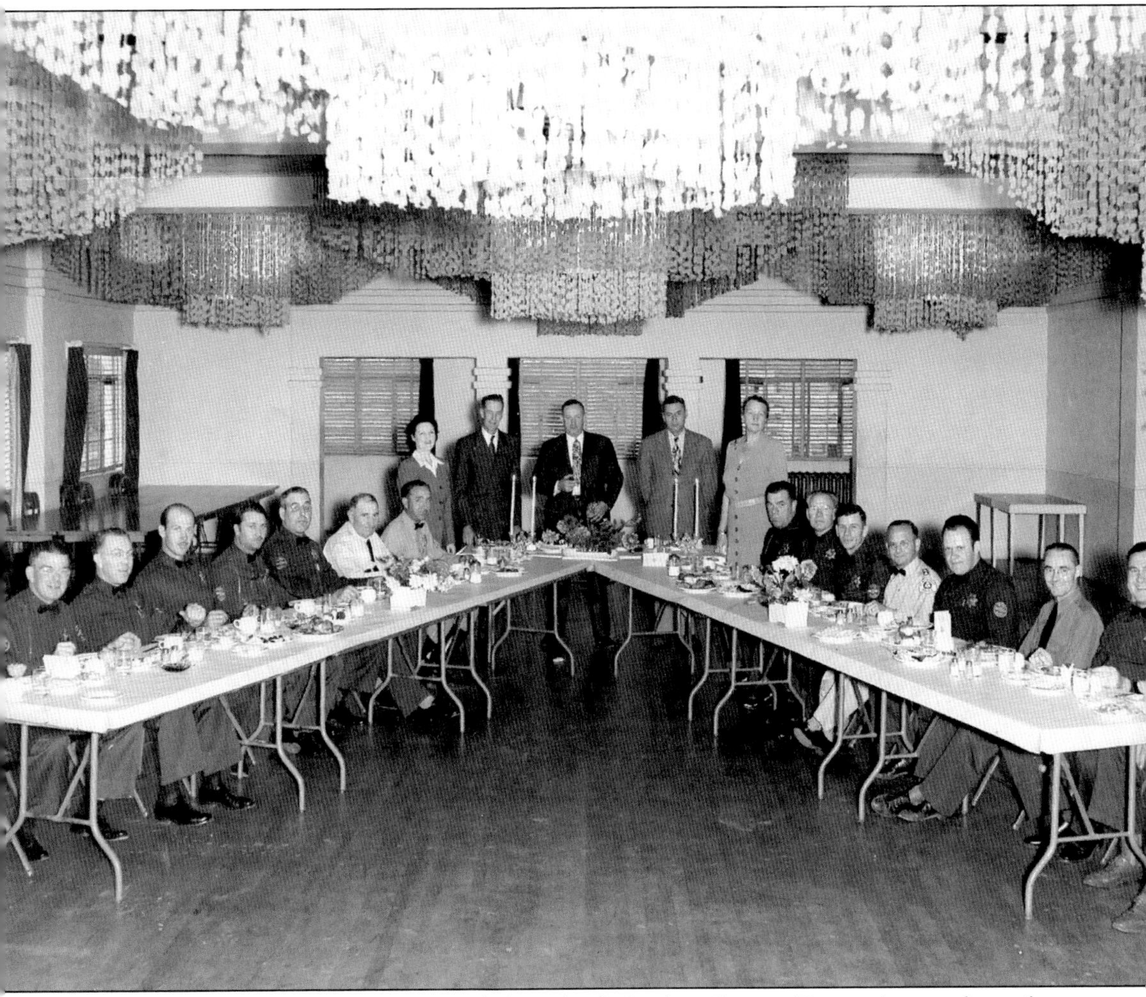

In November 1944, city employees, including chief of police George Tice and council member Harry Caldwell, enjoy a luncheon together.

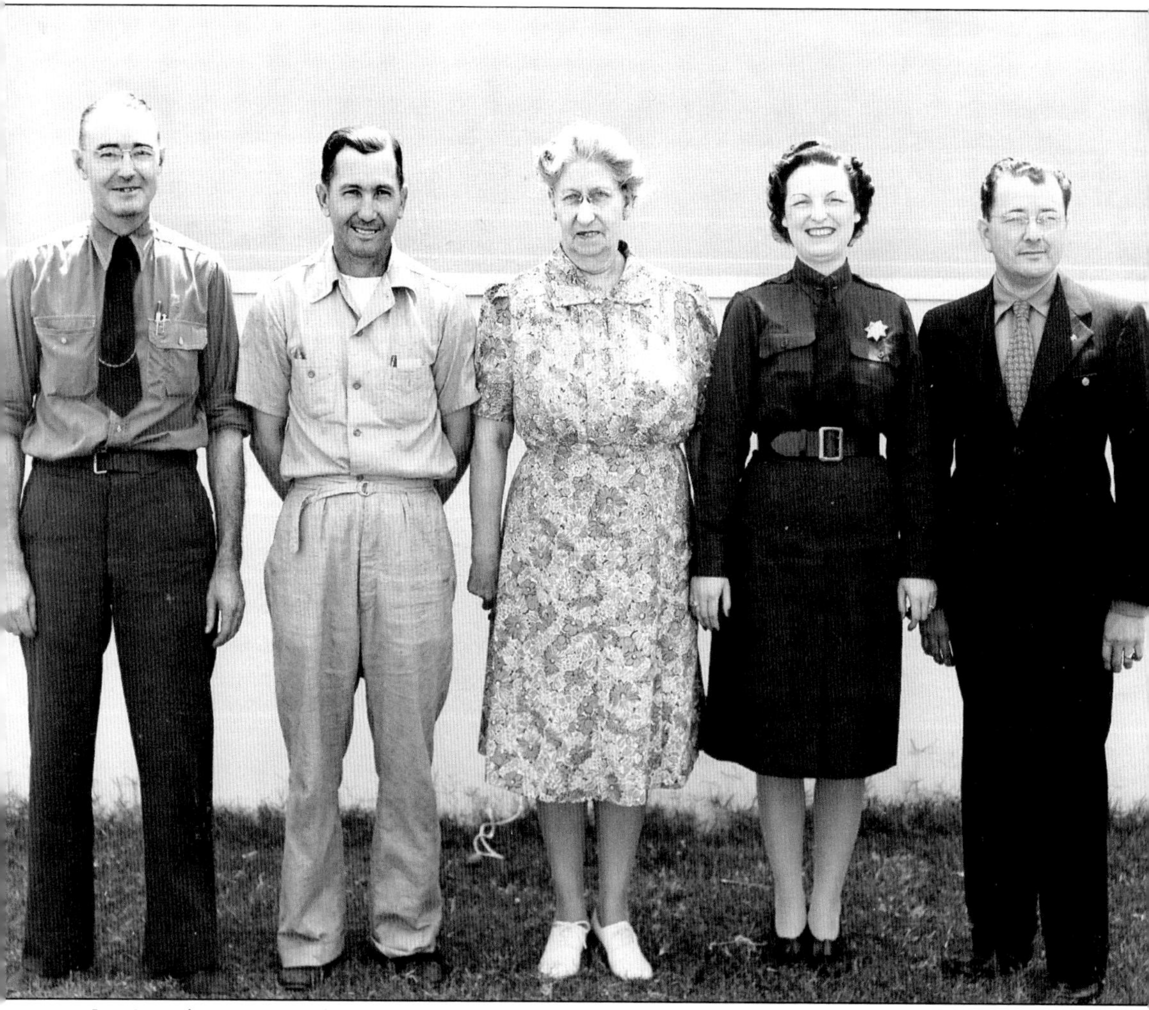

In 1944, these city employees, from left to right, are custodian Ralph Williss, street superintendent Henry Overholtzer, city clerk Isobel Hollar, police matron Reva Fairbanks, and city treasurer Milton Strauss.

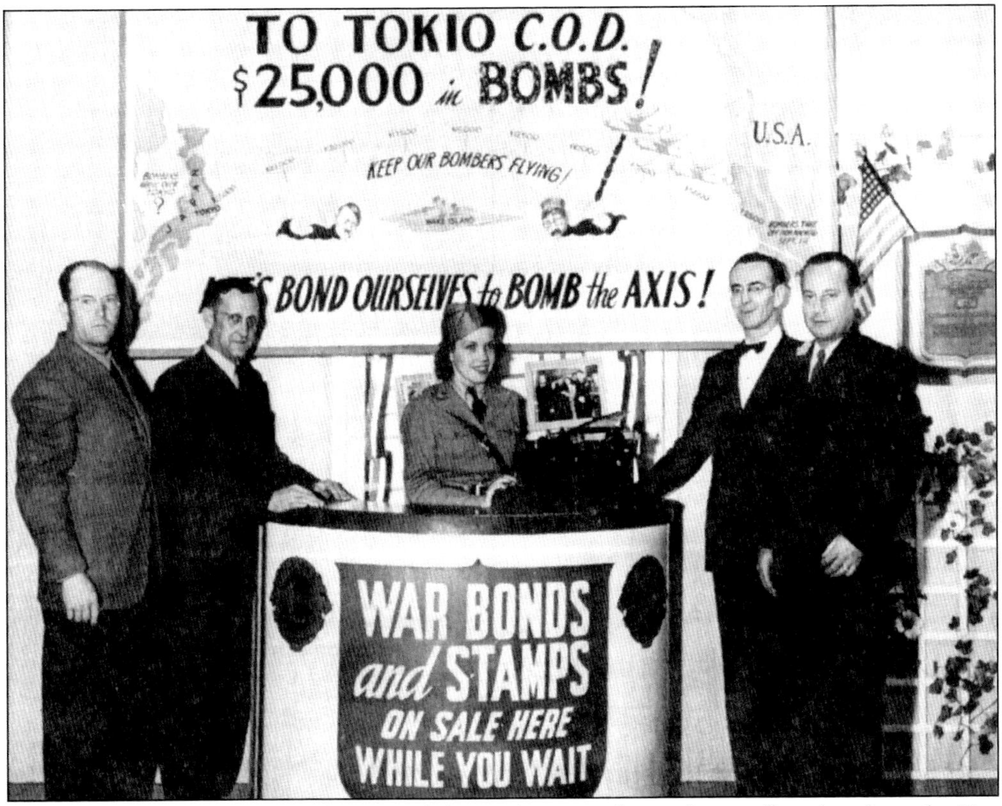

In September 1942, Maywood Lions Club members are shown here selling bonds at the Fox Maywood Theatre during the Salute to our Heroes Week. Maywood Lions Ben Lang, George Archer, and Dick Smith are shown in the photograph.

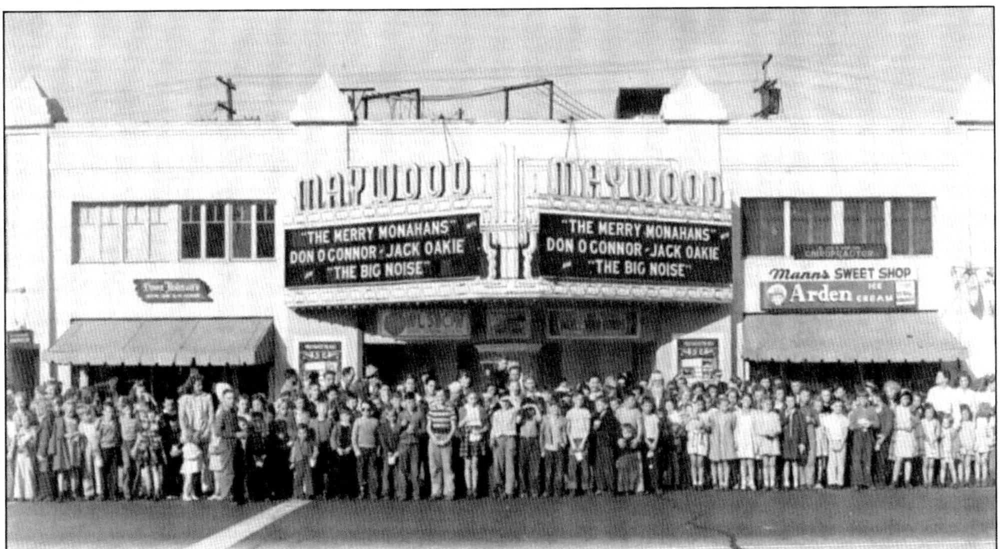

Every Christmas season during the World War II years of 1942 to 1945, the Maywood Lions Club sponsored a free show with complimentary candy at the Maywood Theater for all area youngsters.

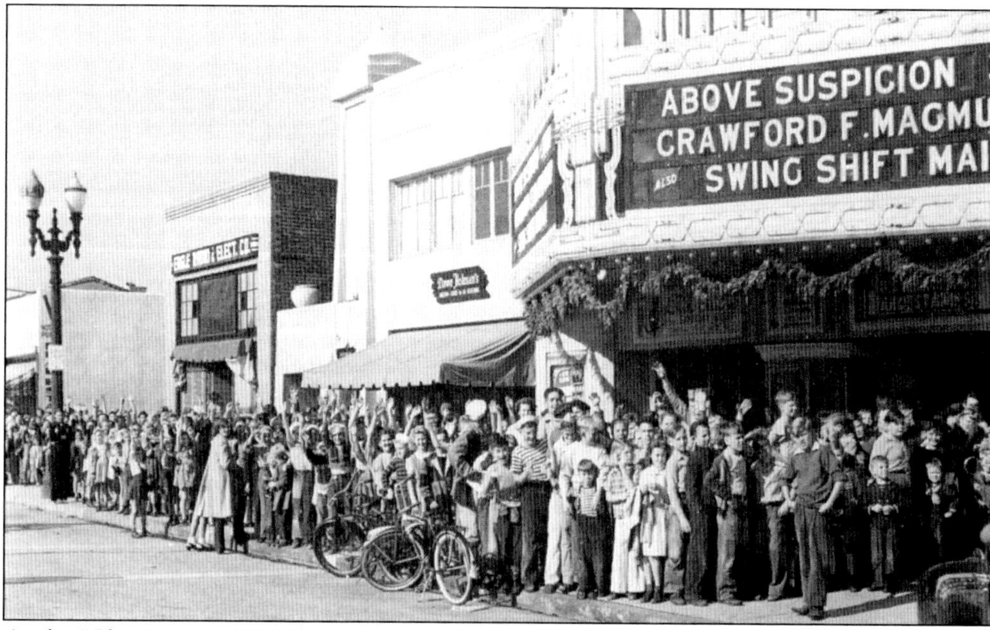

At the "Christmas Party at the Movies" in 1943, Lions Club members and their families line up at the Maywood Theater for the double feature of *Above Suspicion* with Joan Crawford and Fred MacMurray and *Swing Shift Maisie* starring Ann Sothern.

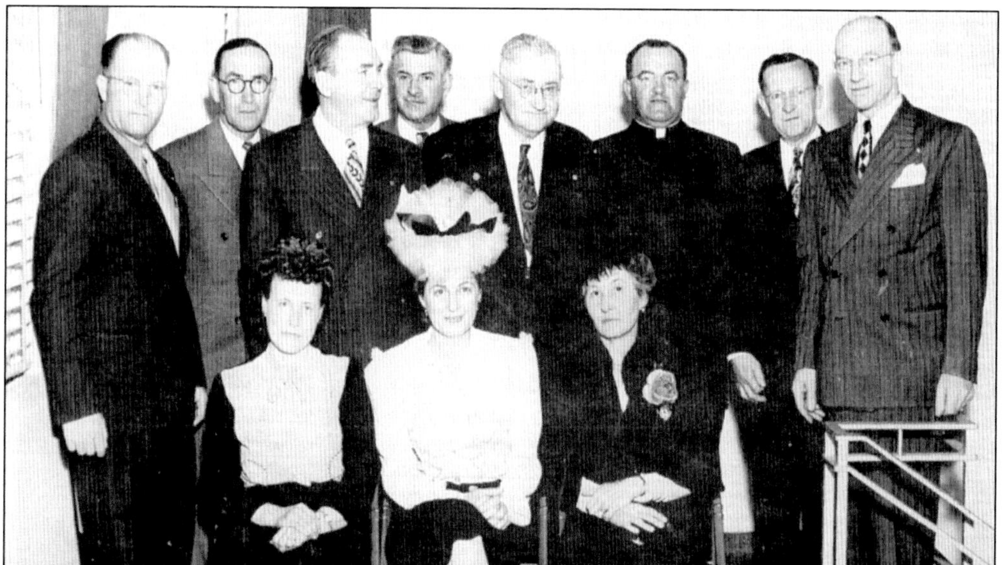

At a bonds party for the war effort on May 23, 1945, actor Pat O'Brien, third from left, and his wife, wearing the hat, are shown at the Maywood Lions Club. Ben Lang, George Archer, and Addis Kelley also are in photograph.

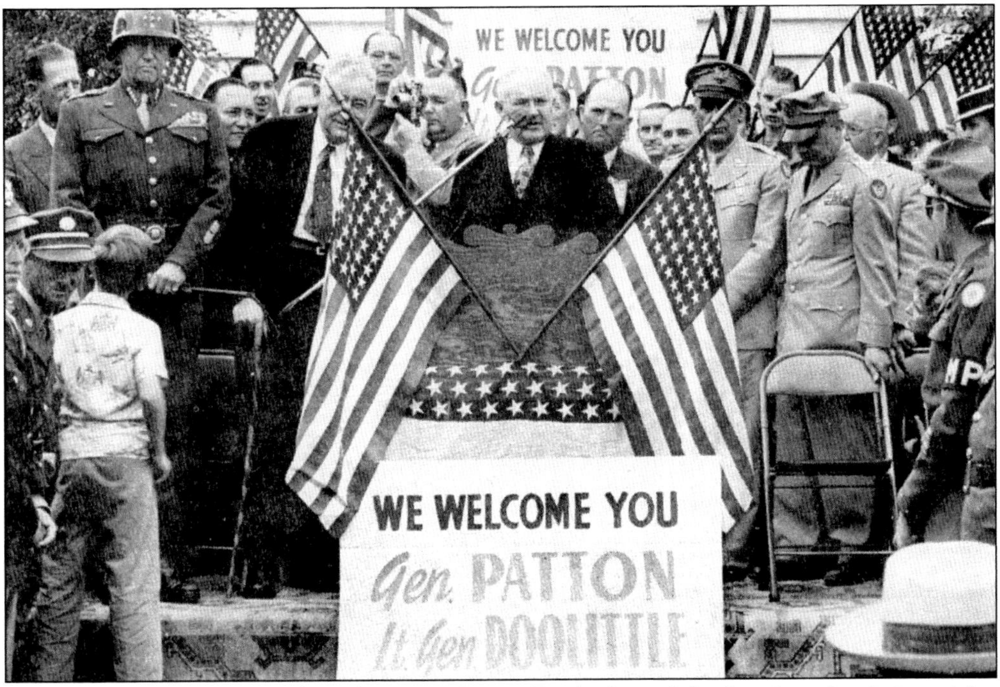

Gen. George S. Patton Jr., left, and Lt. Gen. Jimmy Doolittle, with his hand on the chair at right, are shown during their visit to Maywood in June 1945. Addis Kelley, Ben Lang, and mayor of Los Angeles Fletcher Bowron (dark suit, center) were also on hand for the festive occasion.

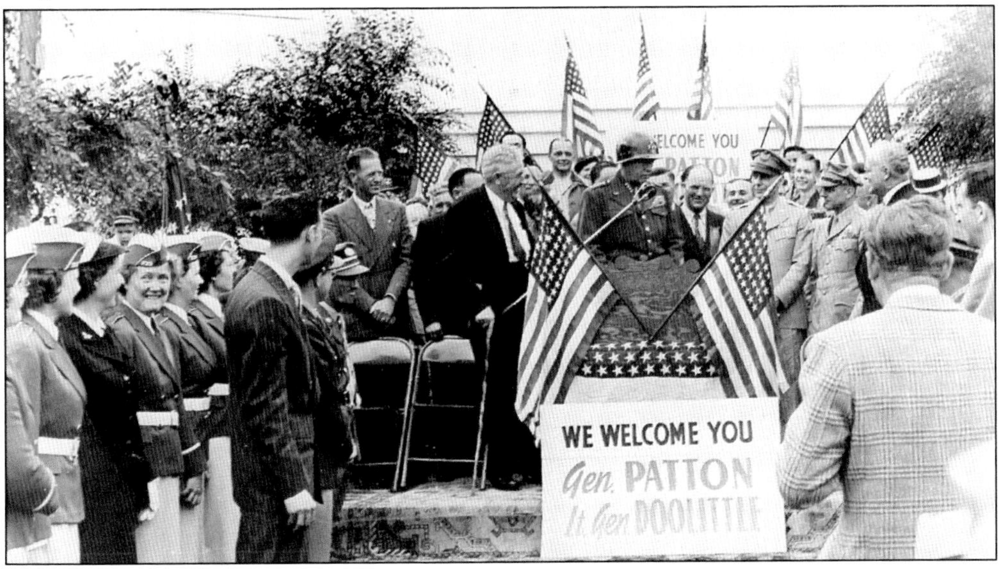

In June 1945, General Patton assumes command of the podium at the ceremony honoring both Patton and Lieutenant General Doolittle in Maywood. Patton commanded the U.S. Tank Corps in North Africa, the Seventh Army in Sicily, and the Third Army in France. His command decisions with the Third Army after D–Day helped the Allies to victory in the European Theater. "Doolittle's Raid," one of the great "impossible" missions of 1940s aviation warfare, was a bombing run by B-25s on Japanese munitions installations in Tokyo and other cities in April 1942. It was one of the great heroic events of World War II.

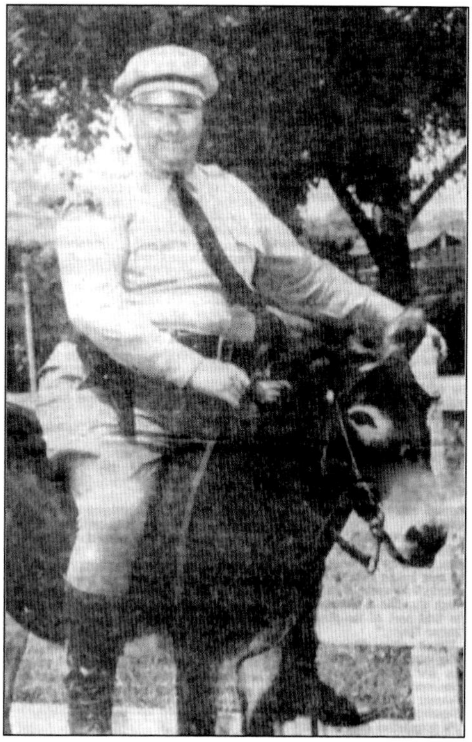

In the late 1940s, motorcycle officer C. O. Willis advertises a charity donkey softball game. Officer Willis was a 10-year veteran of the Maywood force from 1947 to 1957.

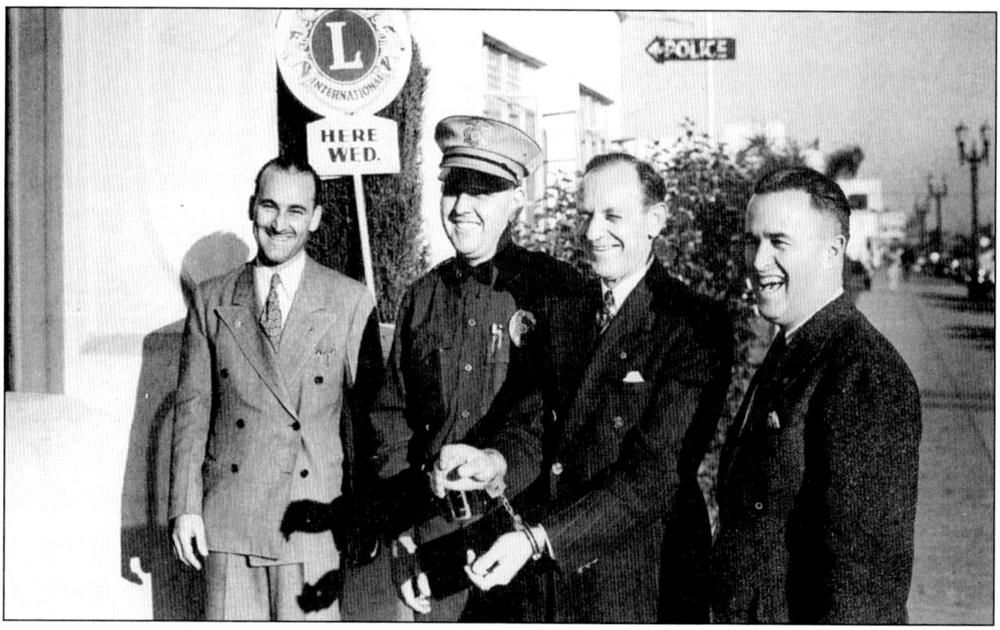

During the 1948 World Series, in which the Cleveland Indians eventually defeated the Boston Braves four games to two, Lions Club member George Strong won a $90 raffle, but was late for the weekly meeting. Maywood's finest went into action in the name of progress. Maywood police officer Robert Freeland was dispatched to George's office, along with secretary Oliver Mater, right, and they soon returned with a handcuffed Strong. Lions Club member Eddie Salitore, editor of the *Maywood Journal*, is on the left.

In 1924, Addis Kelley, a longtime community supporter and Maywood City Council member, moved to the city. He passed away in 1948.

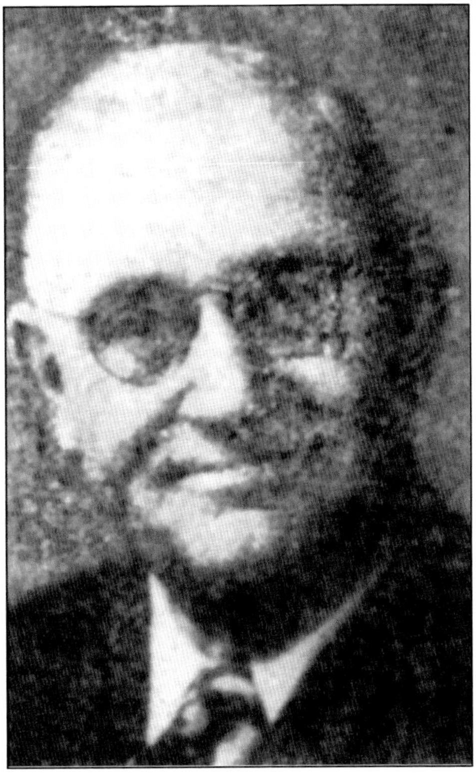

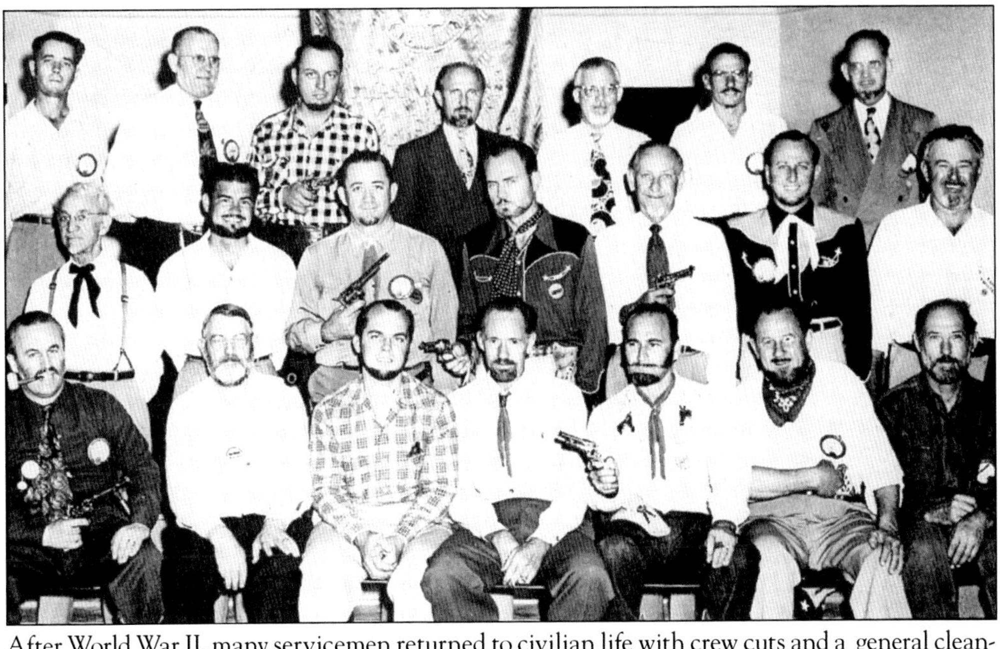

After World War II, many servicemen returned to civilian life with crew cuts and a general clean-cut, clean-shaven look, which became fashionable for men everywhere. The City of Maywood's 25th anniversary celebration in 1949, however, made some of Maywood's most distinguished citizens appear to be part of society's fringe rabble at the beard-growing contest. Luckily it was all in fun!

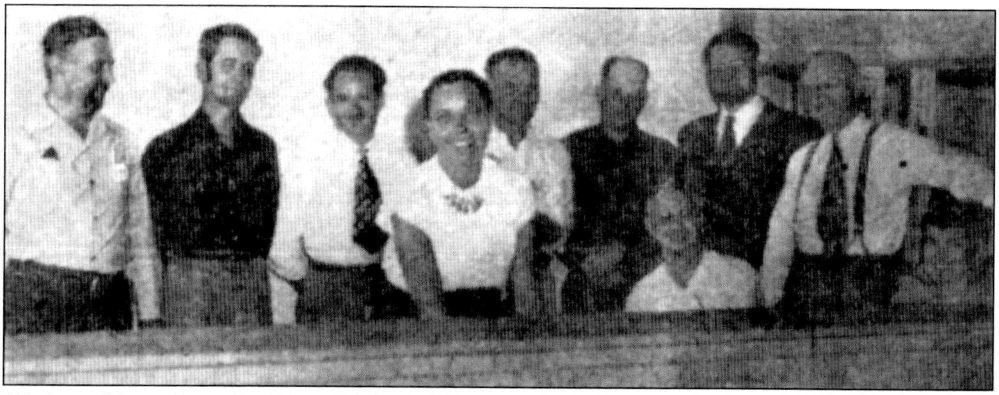

Working diligently on the Silver Jubilee celebration and other projects are the Maywood Chamber of Commerce officers and directors. Pictured, from left to right, are (first row, seated) chamber president John Clauser and secretary Shirley Wayne; (second row) James Vaughn, Bill Hill, Dr. Phil Glasser, treasurer Dorothy Zwiesler, Mark Law, Ben Lang, John Pomeroy, and L. R. Rice.

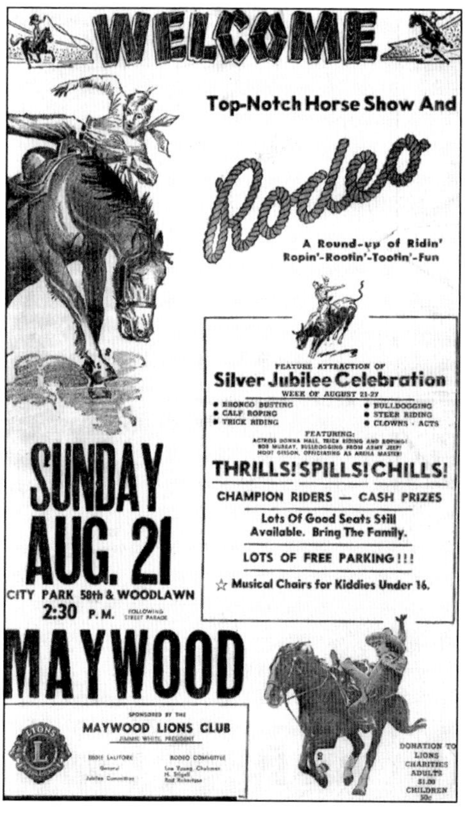

Maywood occasionally put on a rollicking good outdoors show. This poster advertises a rodeo at City Park, Fifty-eighth Street and Woodlawn Avenue, sponsored by the Lions Club. Lou Young was the chairman of the event, which promised "Thrills! Spills! Chills!"

The Silver Jubilee edition of the tri-city *Industrial Post* on August 22, 1949, carries this caption: "A historic photograph. Mayor Ben Lang receives gavel at the beginning of colorful term from the late Isobel Hollar, beloved city clerk and clubwoman." Both Lang and Hollar served long tenures in city service.

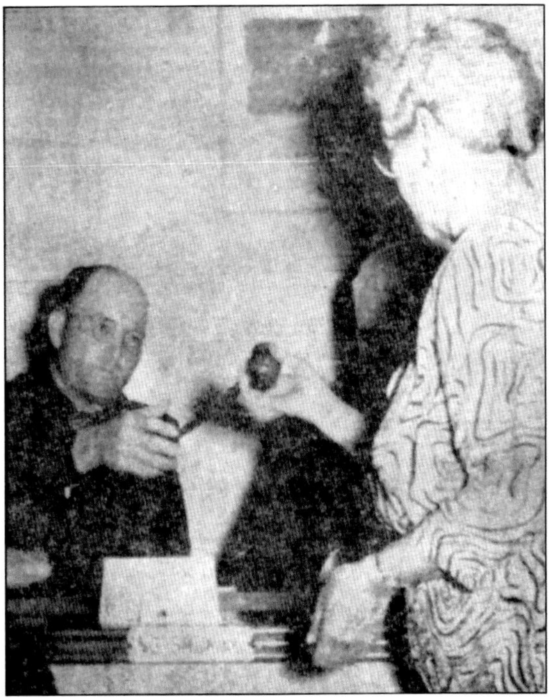

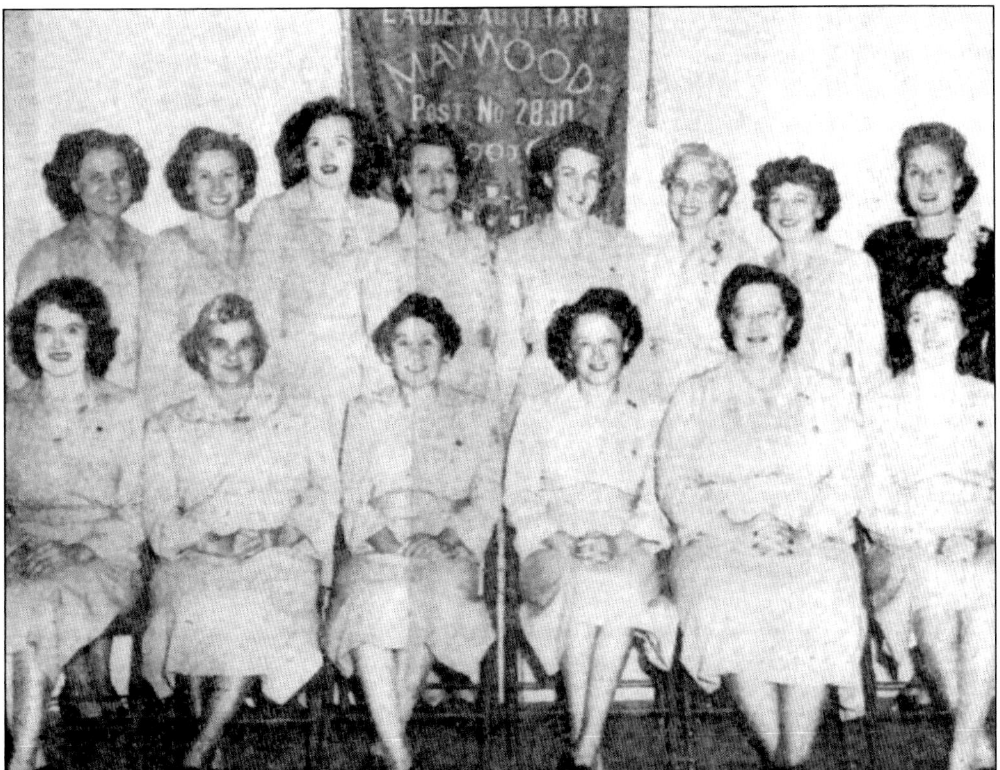

The tri-city *Industrial Post* carried this photograph of the 1949 officers of the Veterans of Foreign Wars Auxiliary No. 2830. Marian Newtols was the auxiliary's president.

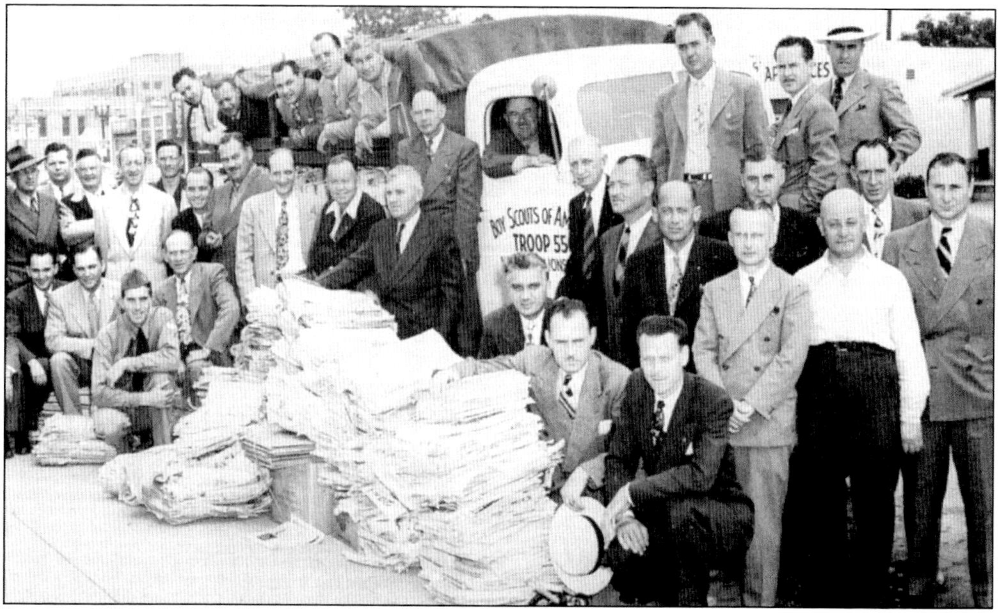

Shown in this late 1940s photograph are Lions Club members during a paper drive.

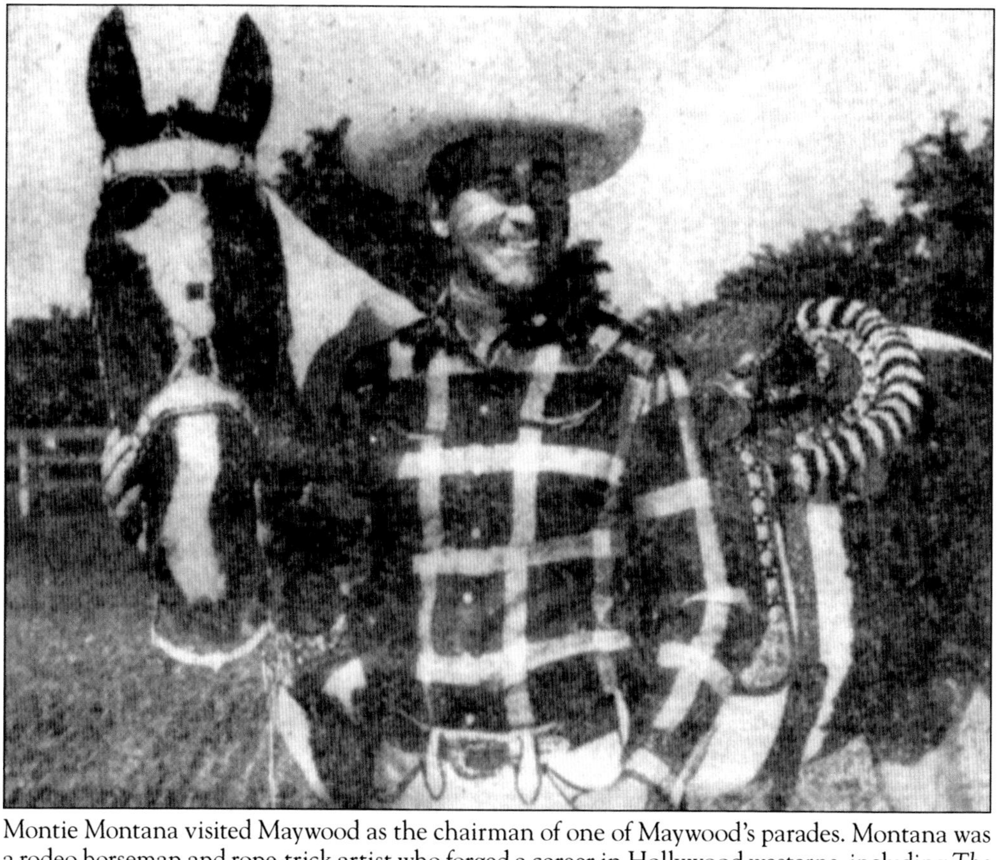
Montie Montana visited Maywood as the chairman of one of Maywood's parades. Montana was a rodeo horseman and rope-trick artist who forged a career in Hollywood westerns, including *The Kid from Texas* (1939), *Riders of the Deadline* (1943), and *Down Dakota Way* (1949).

Four

THE 1950S

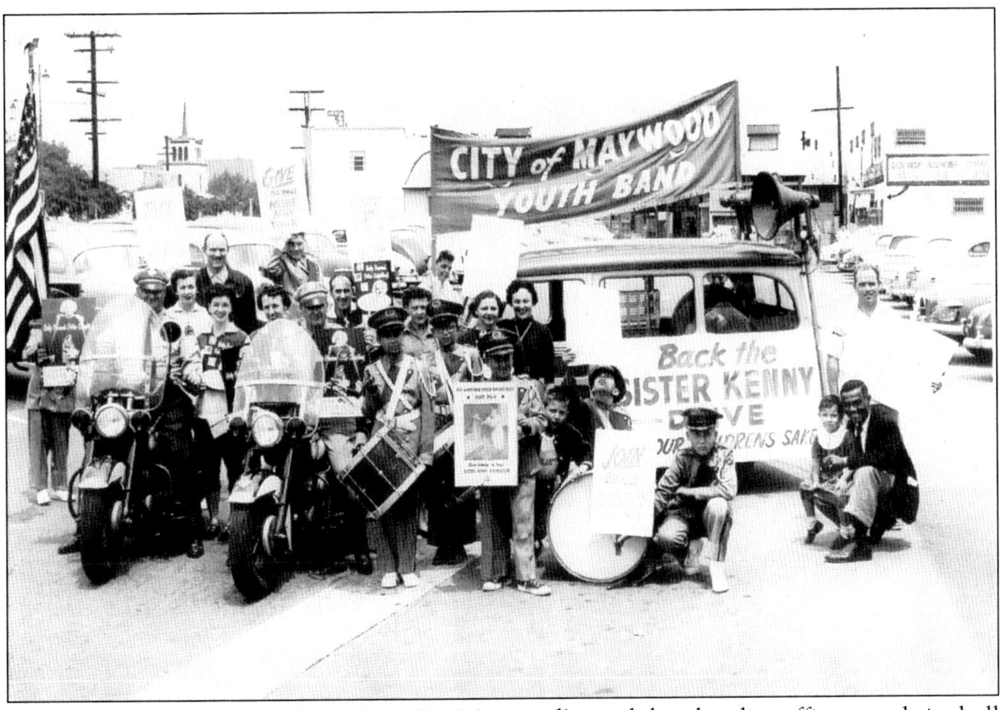

At a Sister Kenny Drive in the early 1950s, Maywood's youth band, police officers, and city hall staff raise funds to fight the advance of polio. Mary Kenny was an Australian nurse whose book, *And They Shall Walk*, chronicled her efforts to find a polio cure.

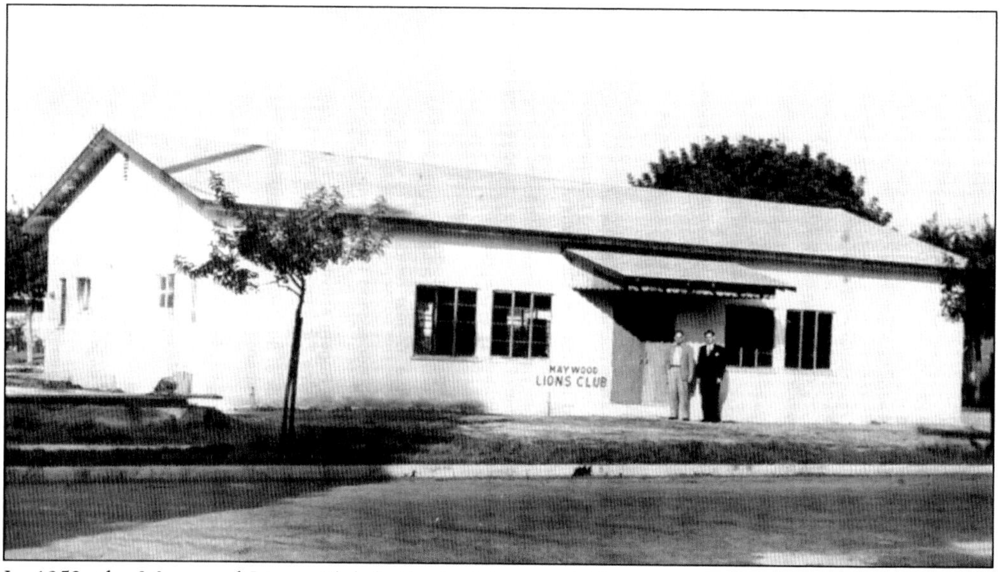

In 1952, the Maywood Lions Club built the Maywood Community Center and later donated it to the city. Located at 4747 East Fifty-sixth Street, it was used by the Block Watchers, Boy Scouts, senior citizens, and senior nutrition program. Currently the building is utilized as the youth boxing gym.

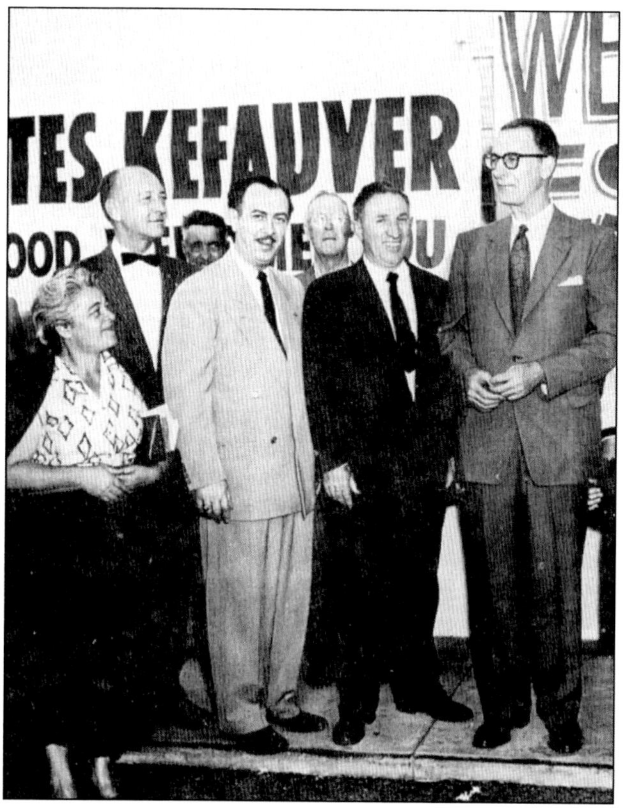

In 1952, Sen. Estes Kefauver from the State of Tennessee is shown in front of Maywood City Hall. Kefauver, the unsuccessful Democratic presidential candidate in 1952, was defeated by President Eisenhower. Kefauver was also the 1956 Democratic vice president candidate who ran with Adlai Stevenson. Former Maywood postmaster Jack Freeman is shown third from right.

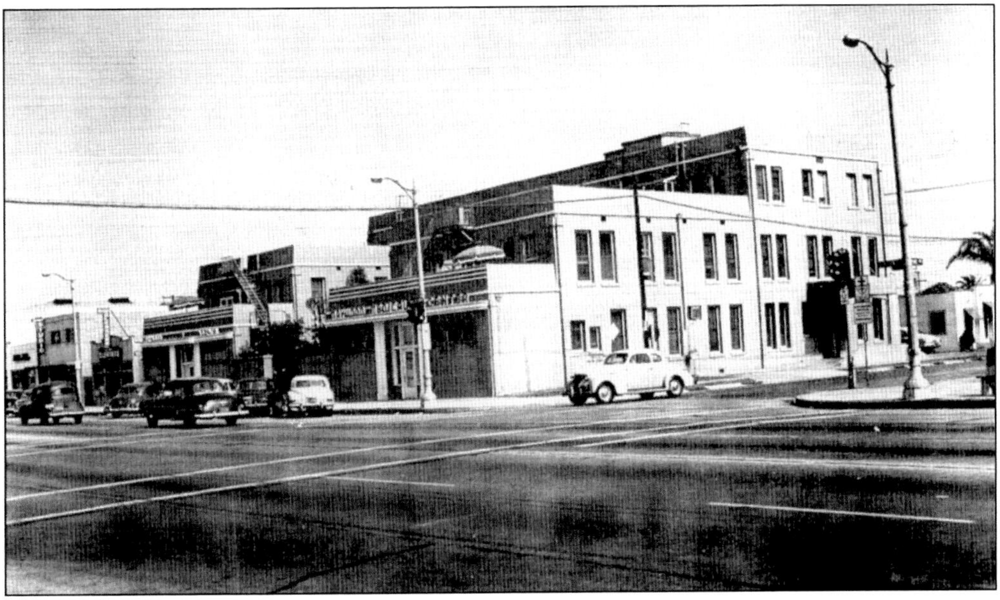

The old Maywood Hospital was located on the corner of Pine and Slauson Avenue.

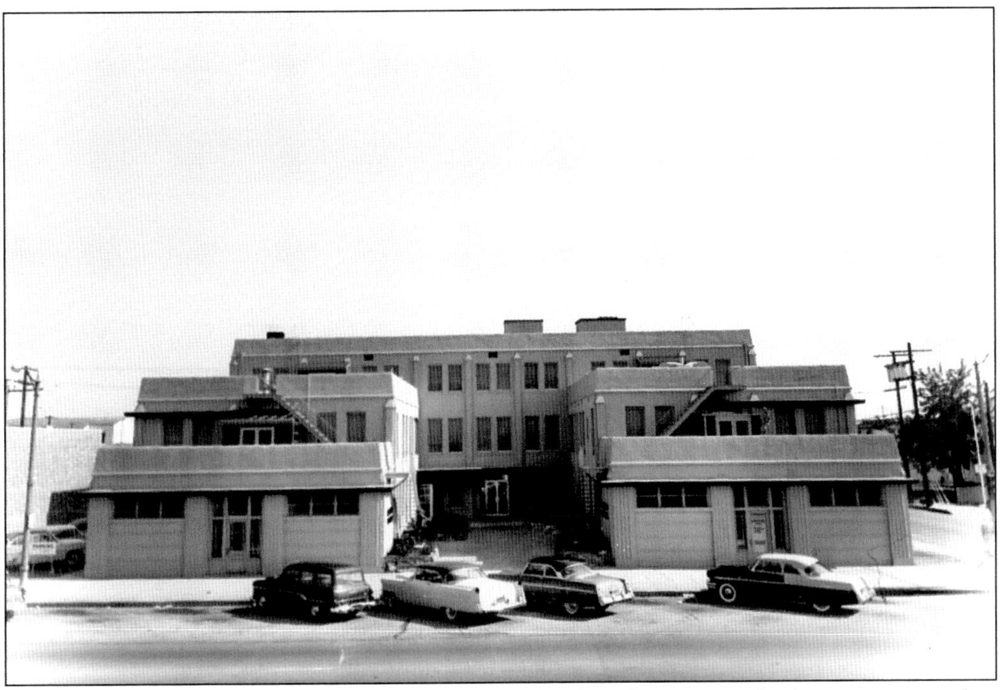

Maywood Hospital was formerly on a site that was developed into part of a shopping center that cost $11 million.

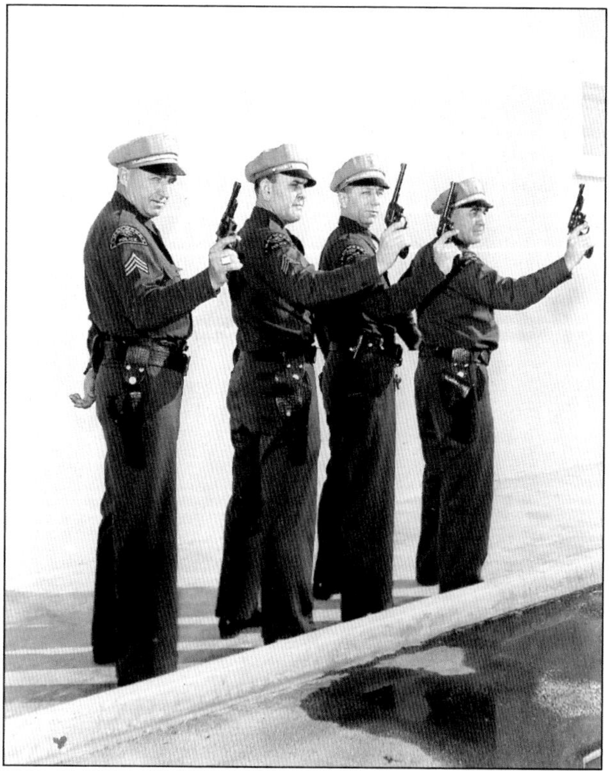

In the 1950s, Maywood's police force demonstrates its readiness at the firing range. Drawing their service revolvers, from left to right, are Ernest Flanagan, Robert Freeland, Marion Butler, and Lloyd Mauch.

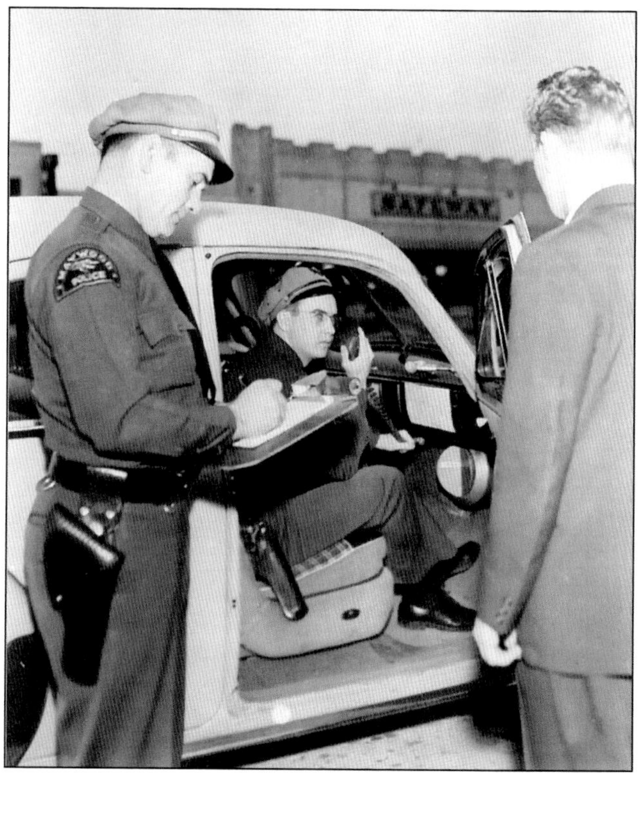

This photograph shows police officers Herman Irwin and Clem Lincicum poised for patrol duty.

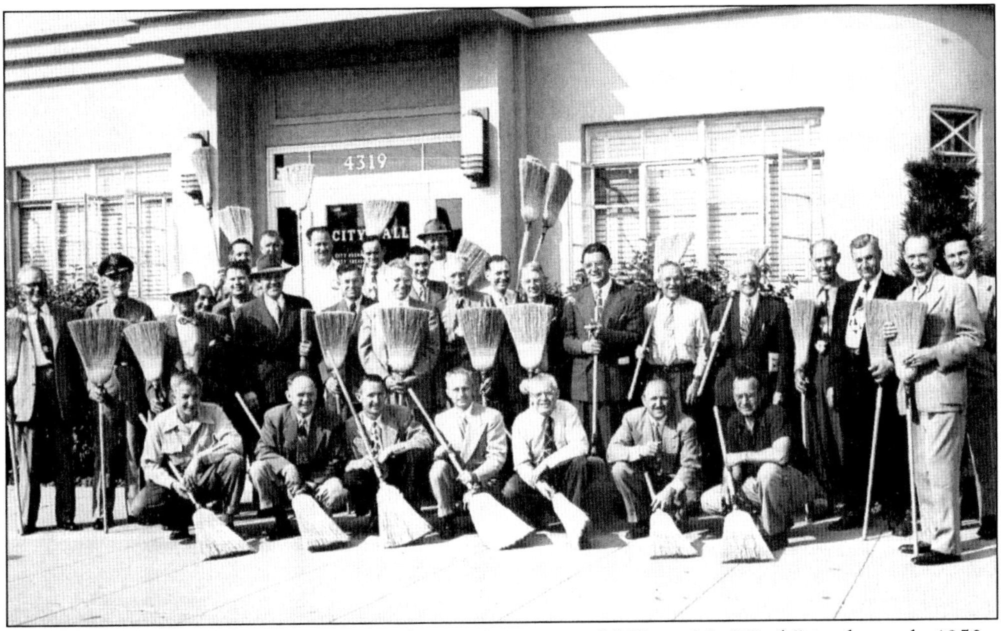

The Lions members clean up the city during their annual "Clean Up Week" in the early 1950s. The club also sold brooms to residents to help in the clean up.

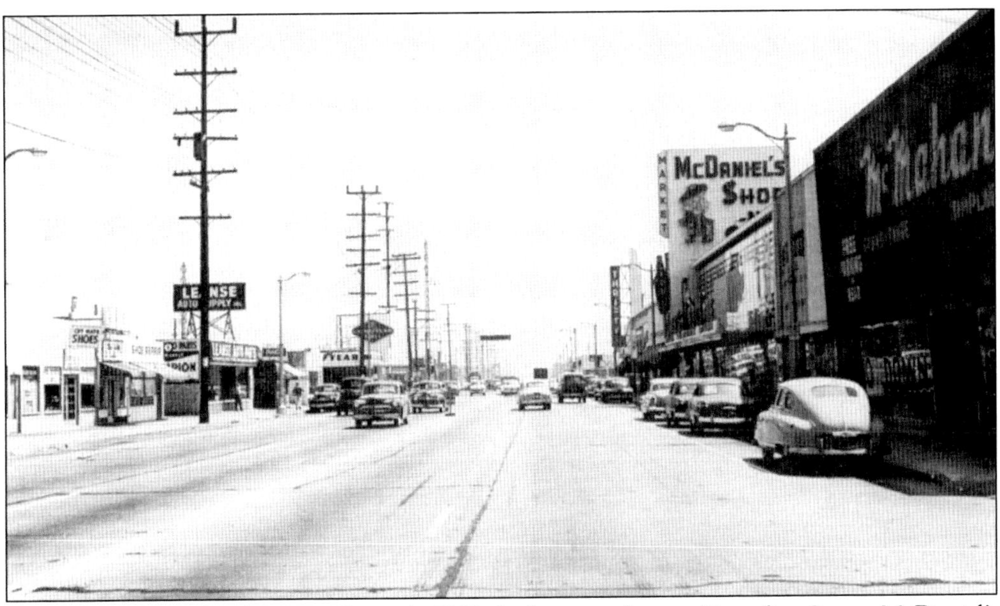

Atlantic Boulevard is shown in the early 1950s looking south near Sixty-first Street. McDaniel's later became Smith's Food King Market and is currently Liborio Market.

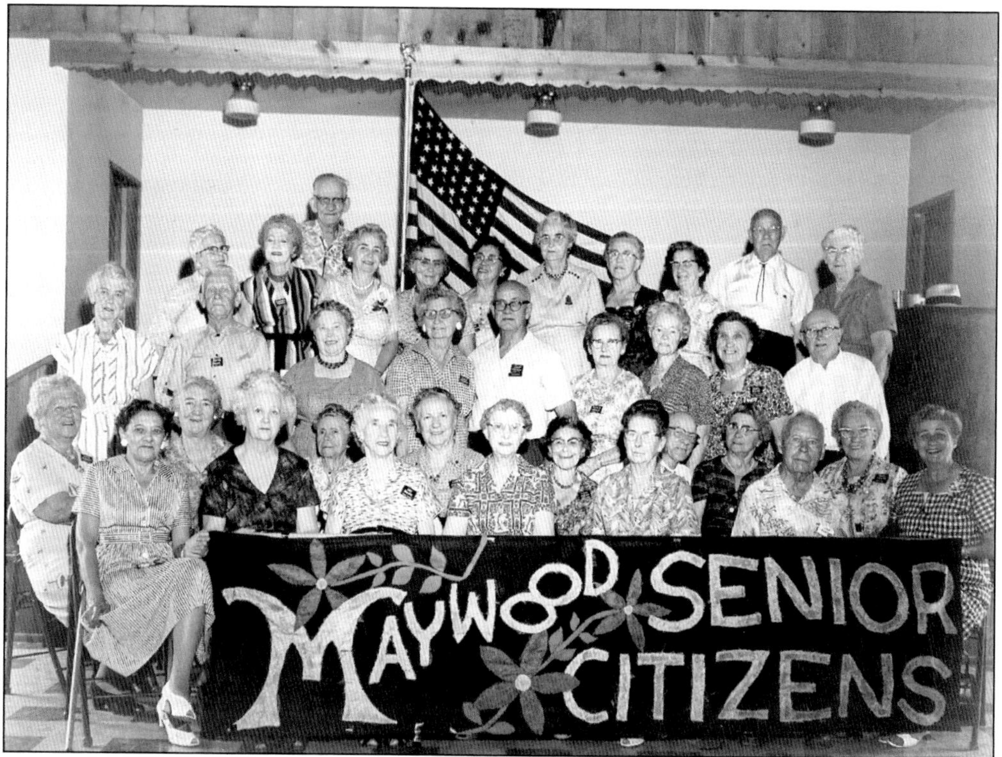

The Maywood Senior Citizens Club, proud to display the Stars and Stripes, is shown here all decked out in the early 1950s.

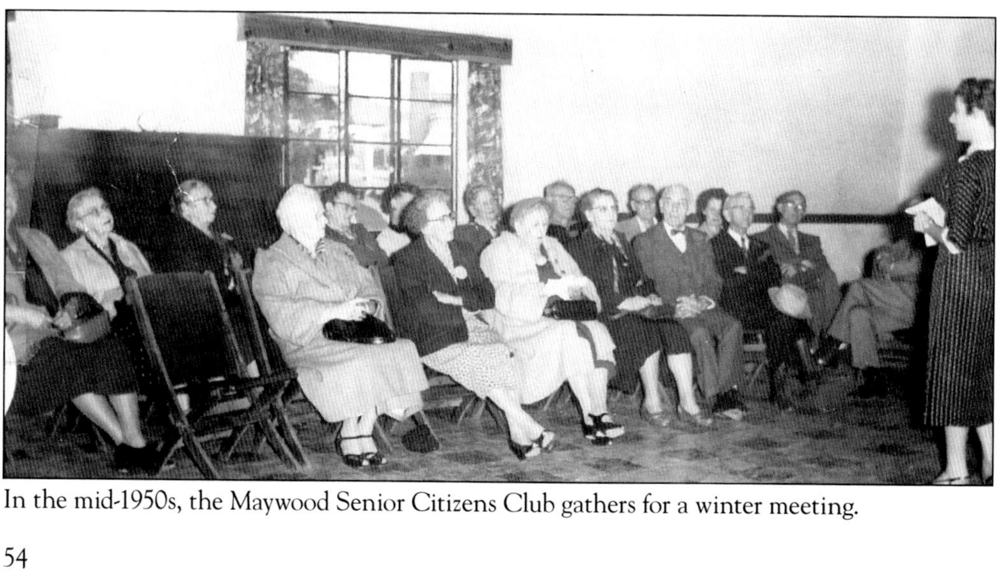

In the mid-1950s, the Maywood Senior Citizens Club gathers for a winter meeting.

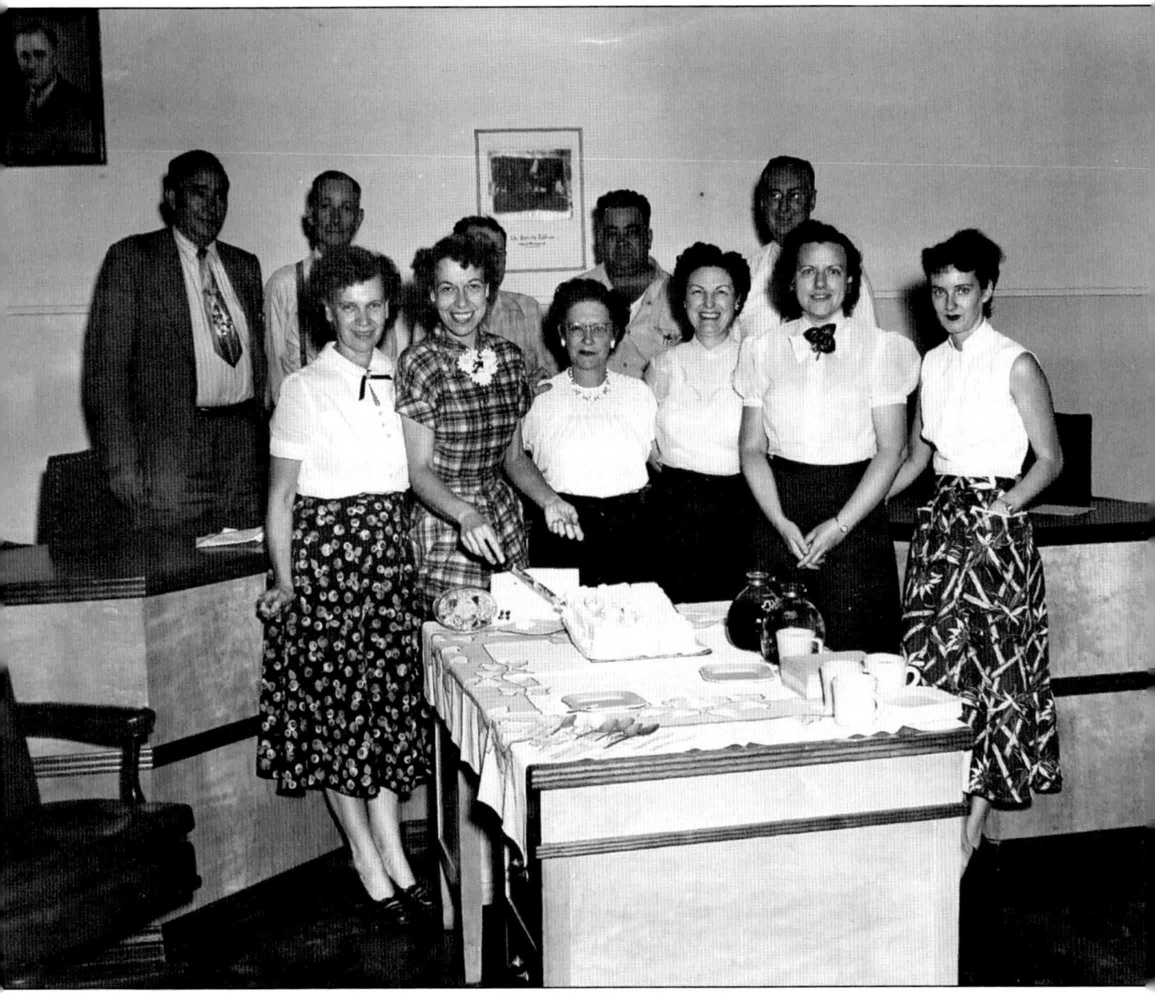

Maywood City Hall staff in the 1950s included city clerk Isabel Dedmore, front far left, and chief of police William Durham, back far right.

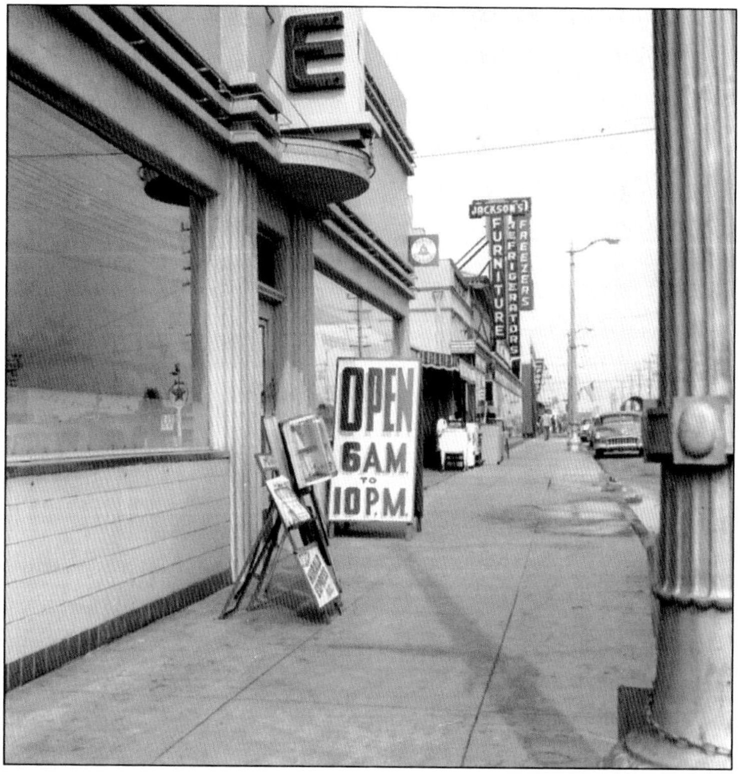

This photograph features the Biscuit Cafe on Atlantic Boulevard. It opened for 6:00 a.m. coffee and closed after a late suppertime.

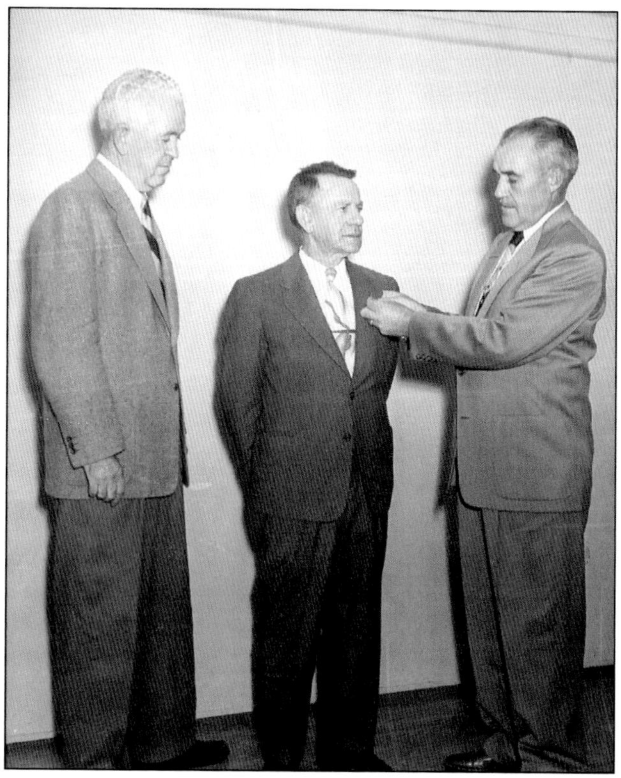

Fire chief Charles Coon received his 25-year pin in 1955 from council member Milan Canning, right, and city attorney Harold Cragin.

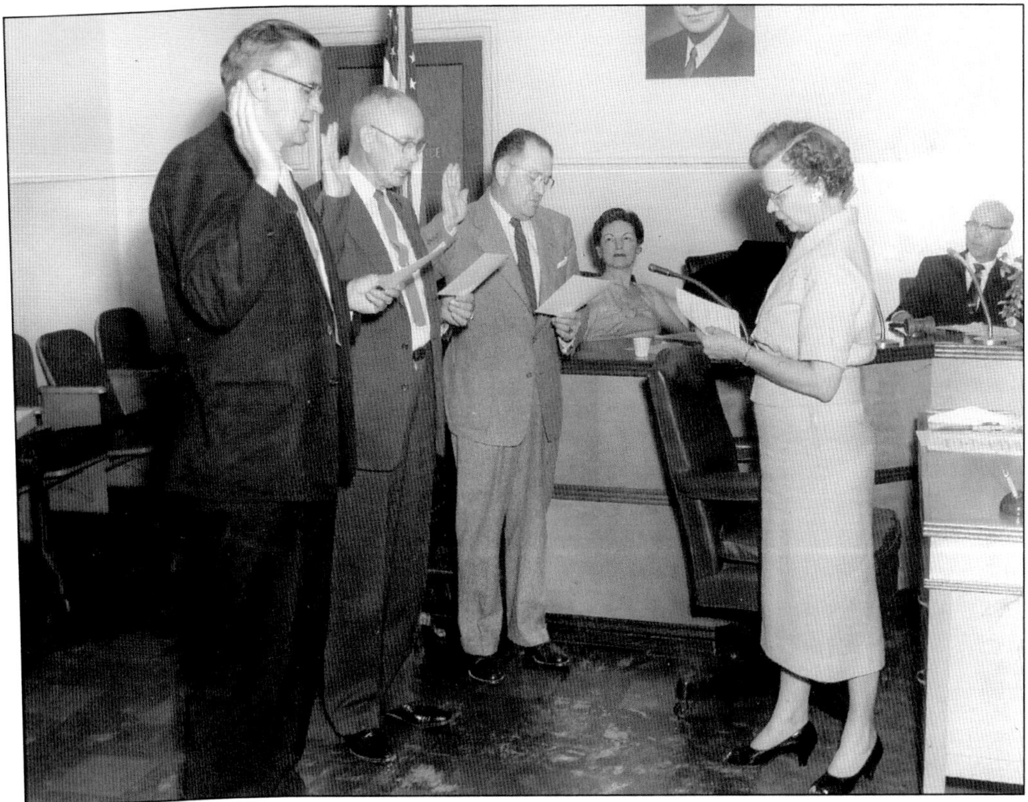

In 1958, city treasurer Milton Strauss (third from left) is sworn in by city clerk Isabel Dedmore. Maywood City Council members George Glenn and Lou Young (left to right) witness the event.

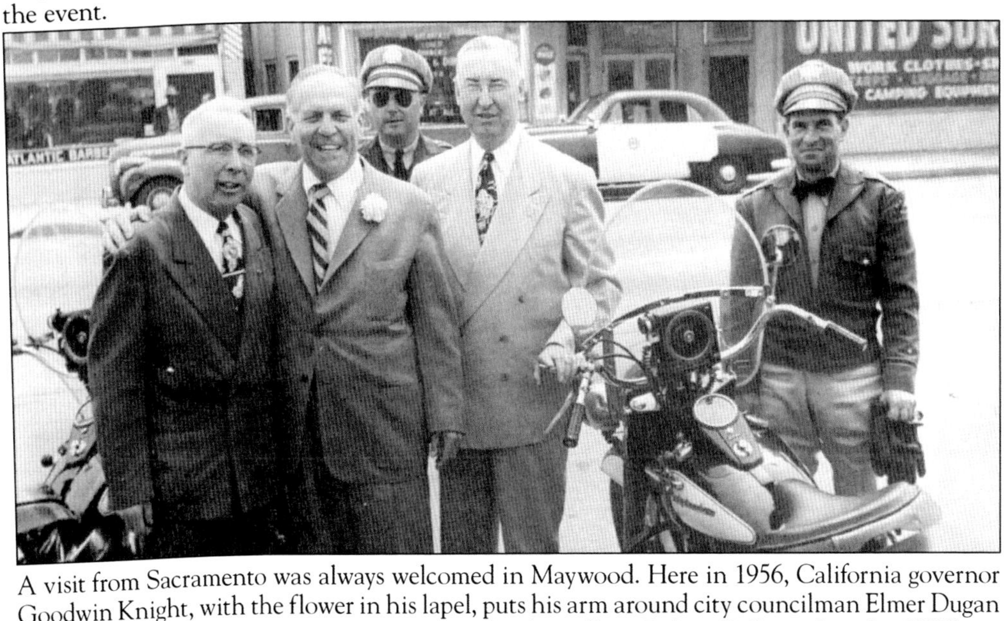

A visit from Sacramento was always welcomed in Maywood. Here in 1956, California governor Goodwin Knight, with the flower in his lapel, puts his arm around city councilman Elmer Dugan in the company of, from left to right, Maywood police officer Robert Fuller, police chief William Durham and, by the motorcycle, Officer Andy Rizzio, the force's radio technician.

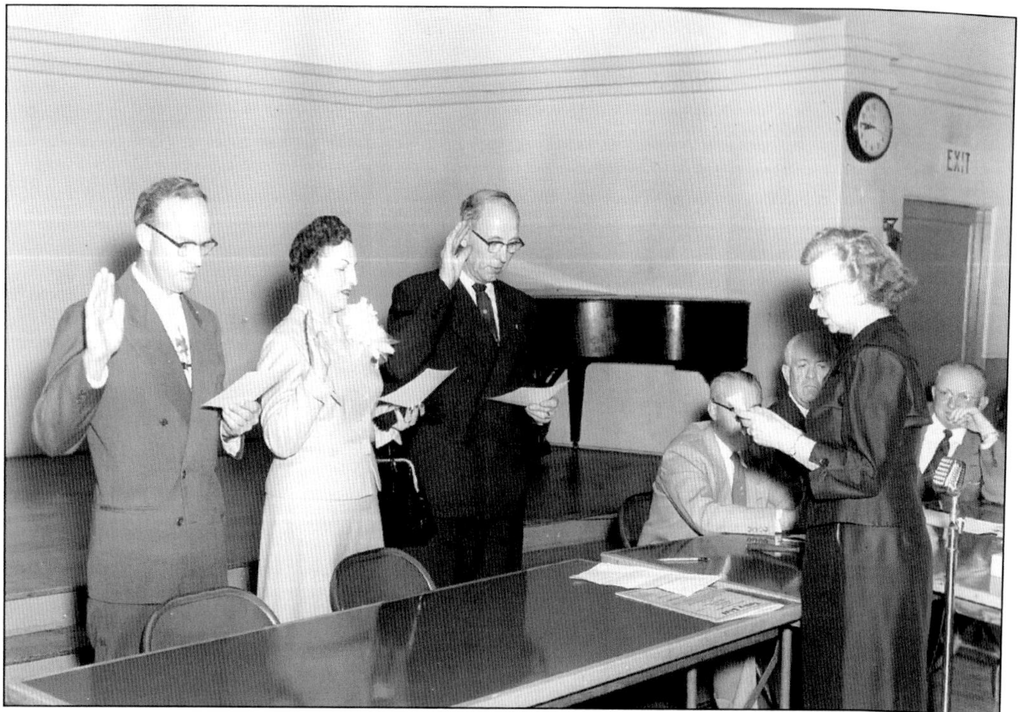

Once again, city clerk Isabel Dedmore swears in Maywood City Council members. Pictured here, from left to right, are Gifford Case, Reva Allsop, and Verne Tennis.

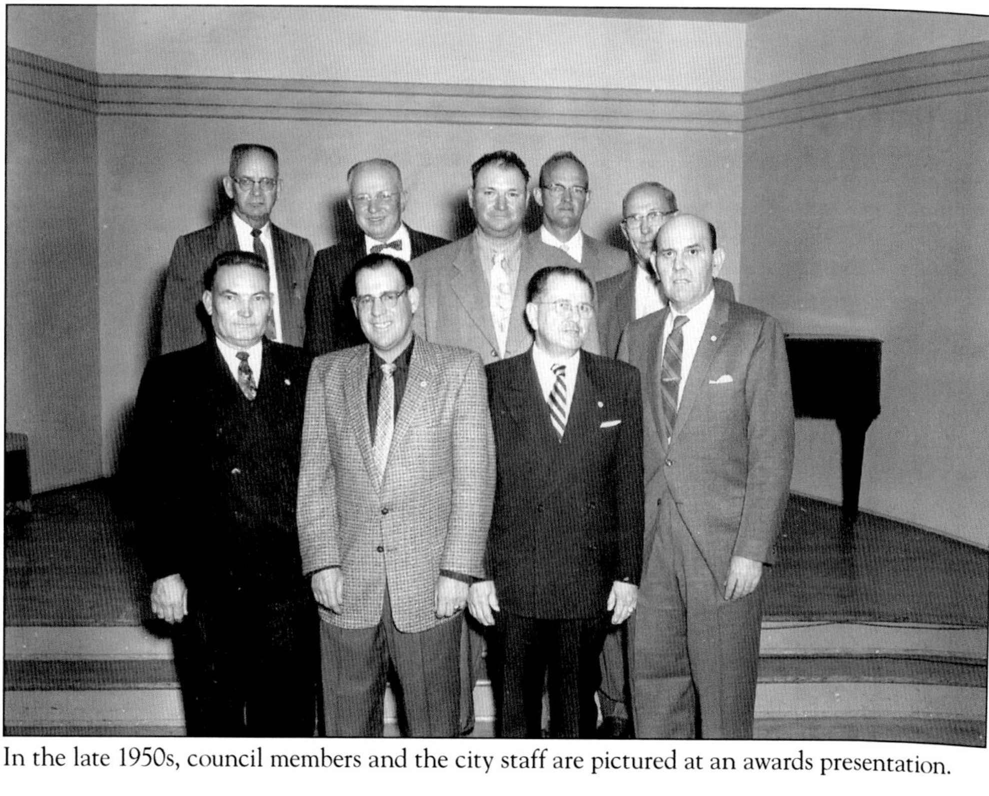
In the late 1950s, council members and the city staff are pictured at an awards presentation.

The Maywood Chamber of Commerce was as optimistic as any of its counterparts, and the cover for the Maywood, California, City Business Map concluded with certainty that this was "your future home." Among the dozens of businesses highlighted on the inside map were Dowell Cleaners and Hatters, Jaxson's Women's Fashions, Young and Strong Realtors and Insurers, The Ace Snack Bar and Tavern, McGuire's Cleaners, Helyn's Beauty Shop, Frank's Derby Cafe, Ed-Len Rug Cleaners, Maywood Five Minute Car Wash, and many more.

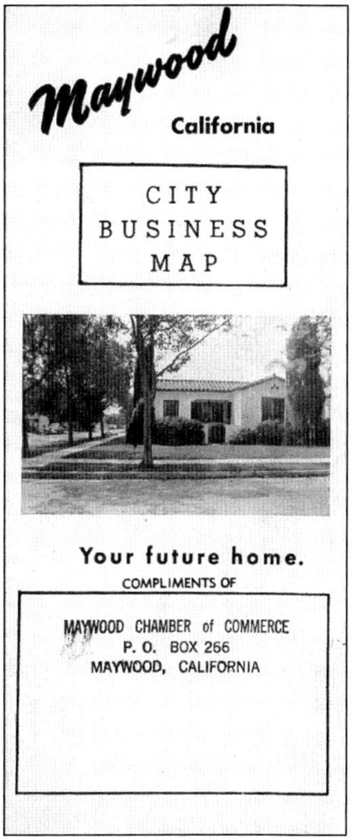

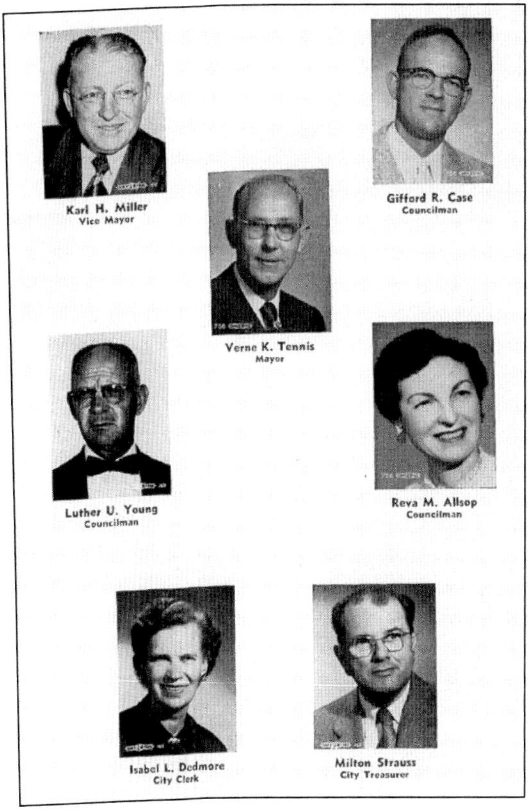

Along with the city clerk and treasurer, the Maywood City Council members are featured in the 1956–1957 edition of the city's annual report.

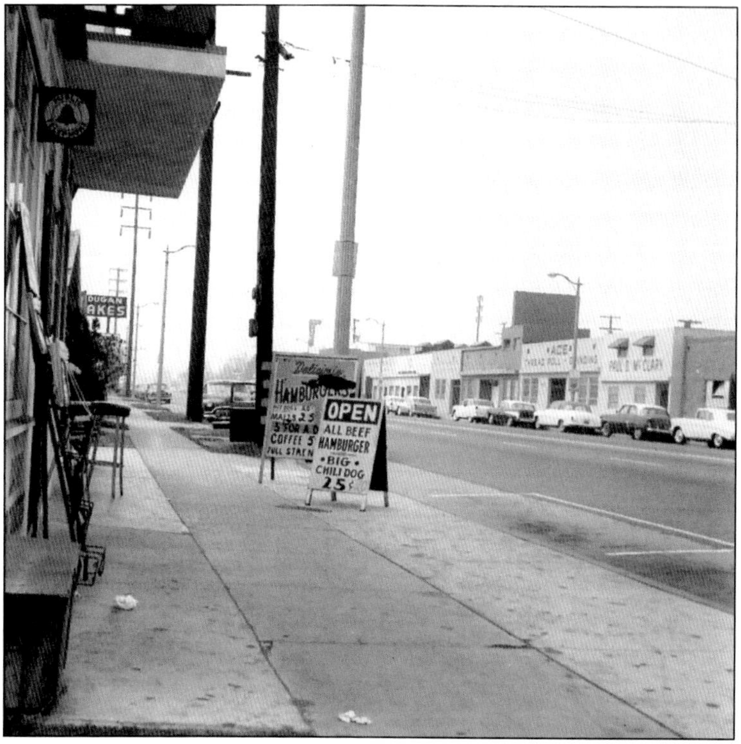

A series of 1957 cityscape snapshots begins here with a view of 4900 Slauson Avenue.

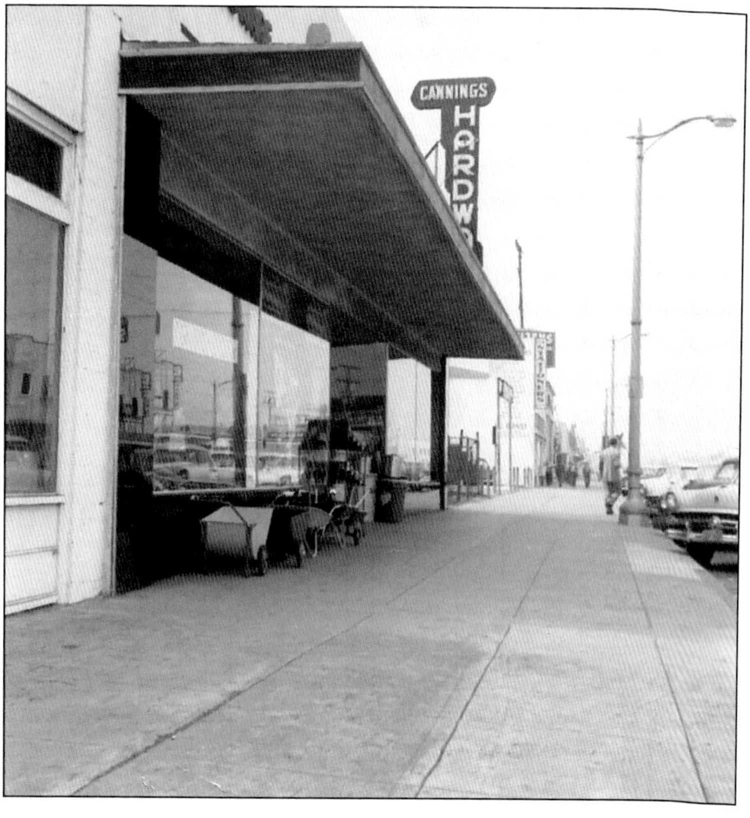

At 4524 Slauson Avenue was Cannings Hardware. A variety of light wheelbarrows and spreaders for lawn improvement were situated on the sidewalk.

Levine's Furniture and Appliances, at 4542 Slauson Avenue, sold both new and used models of chairs, mattresses, tables, and other home items.

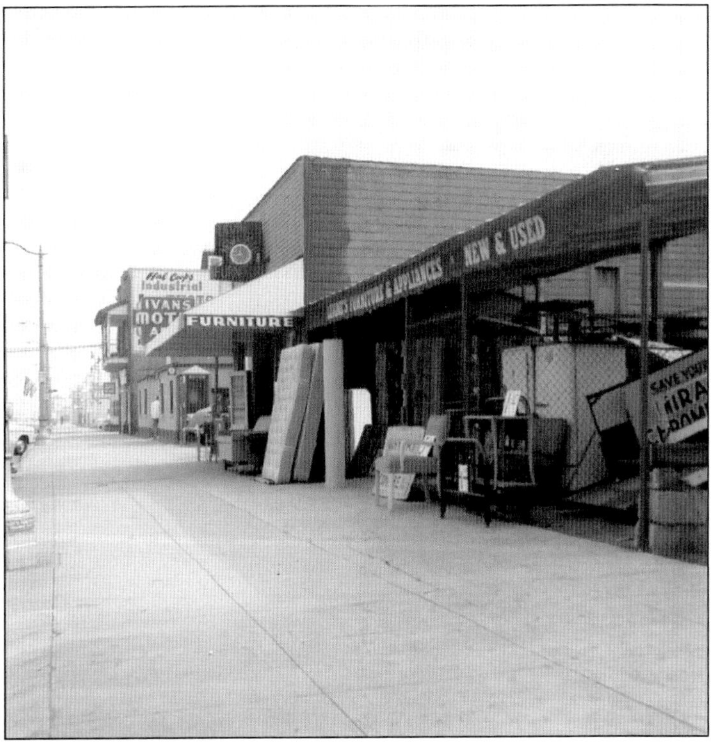

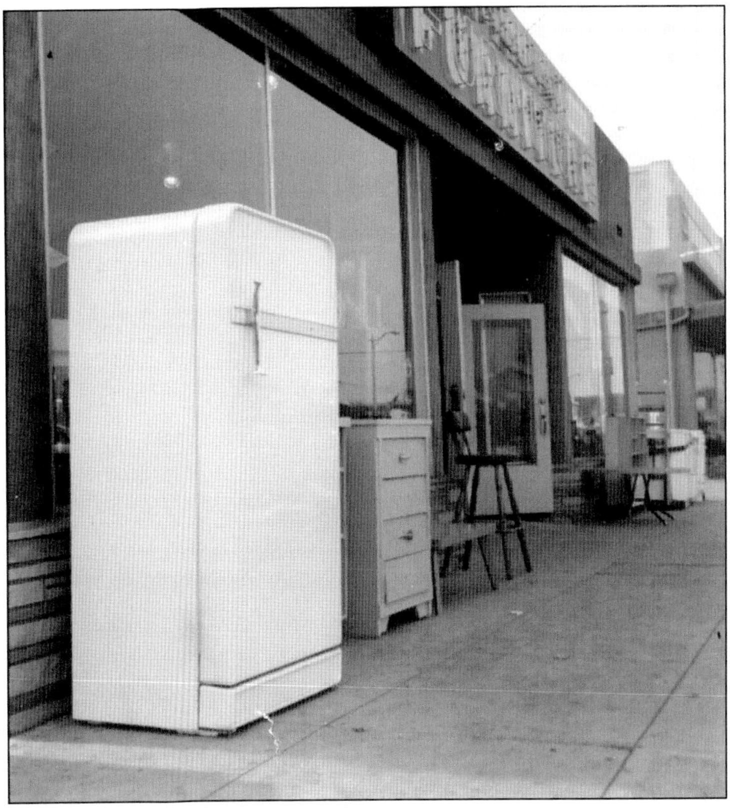

At Farland Furniture, located at 4118 Slauson Avenue, one could find this 1957-era, classic (non-automatically defrosting) refrigerator.

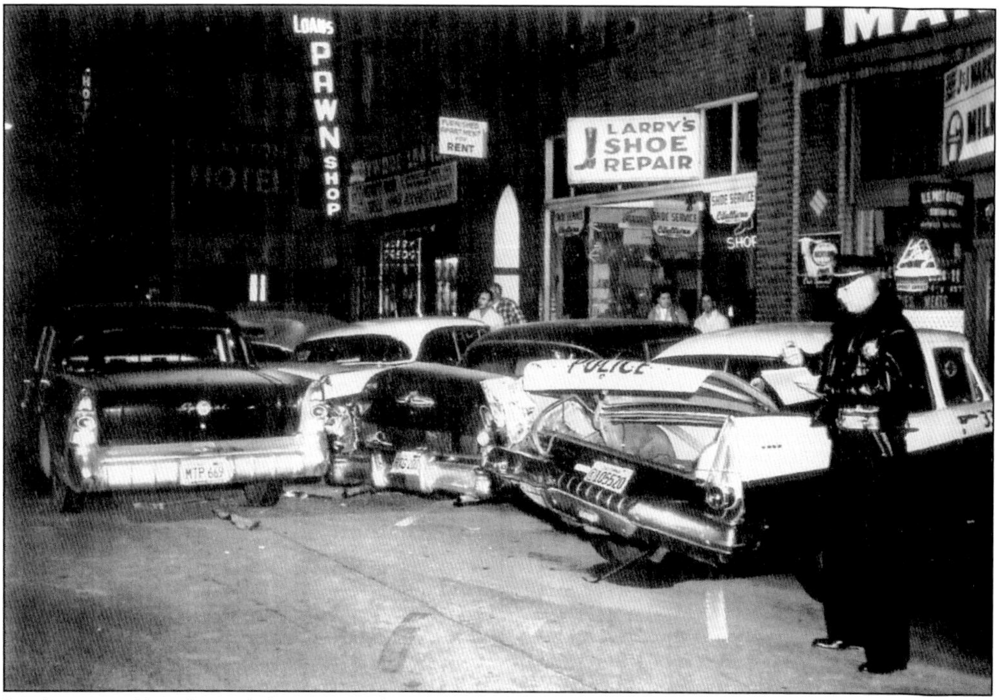

In the era of big-finned, heavy-steel American cars, a high-impact crash could twist a lot of metal. And when one of the cars involved was a police cruiser, such as in this 1957 (or 1958) wreck in front of Larry's Shoe Repair in Maywood, sorting out the culprit(s) was done with the optimum care.

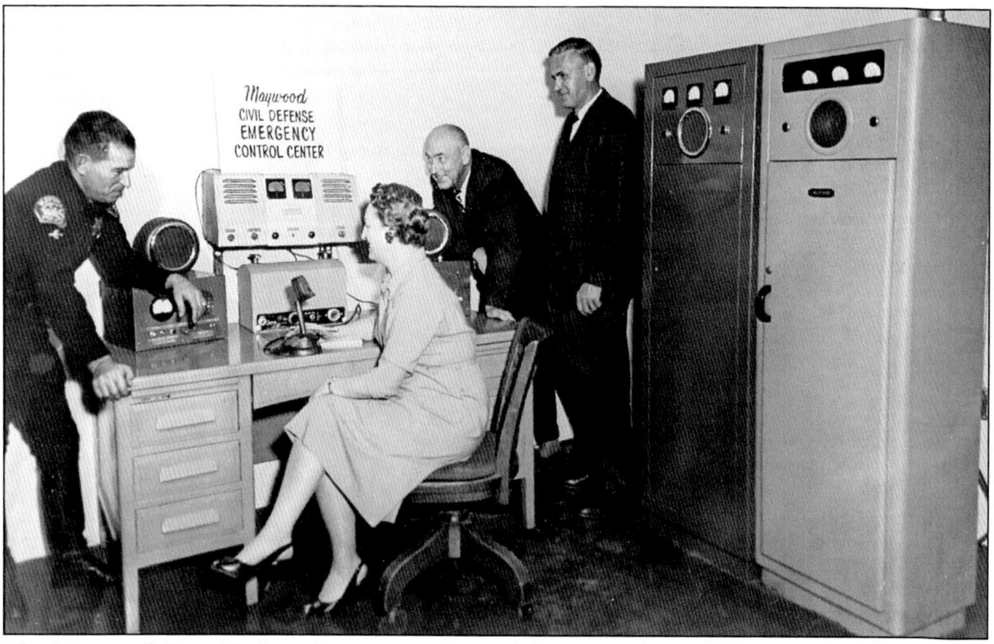

The Maywood Civic Defense Emergency Control Center is depicted here in the 1950s. Police officer Andy Rizzio, who worked for the city for an amazing 45 years, is seen at the far left. Police chief Ed Bray is second from right.

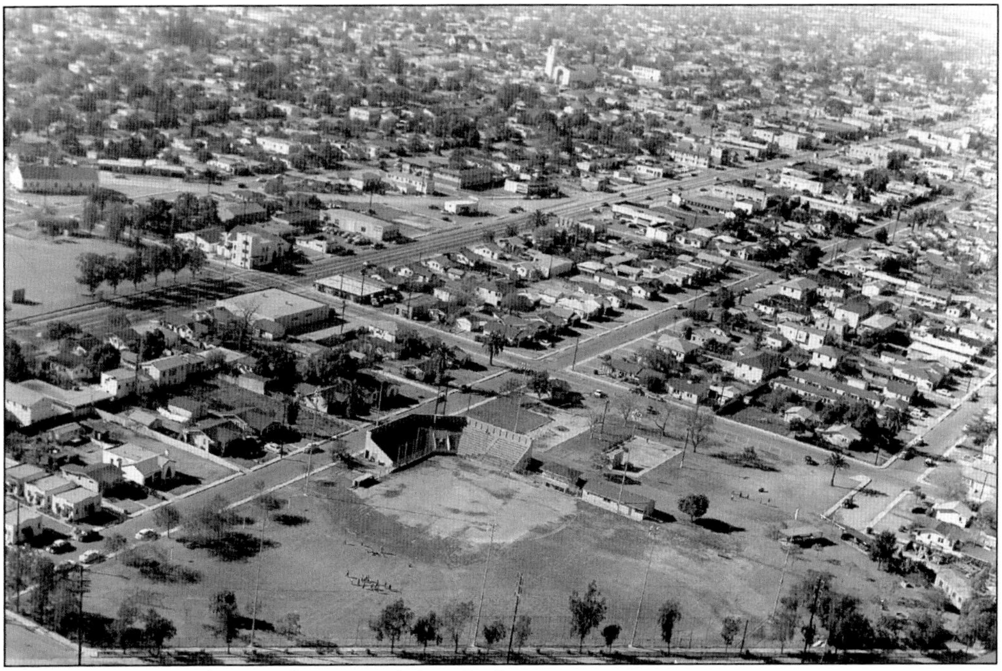

This is a 1956 aerial view of Maywood City Park.

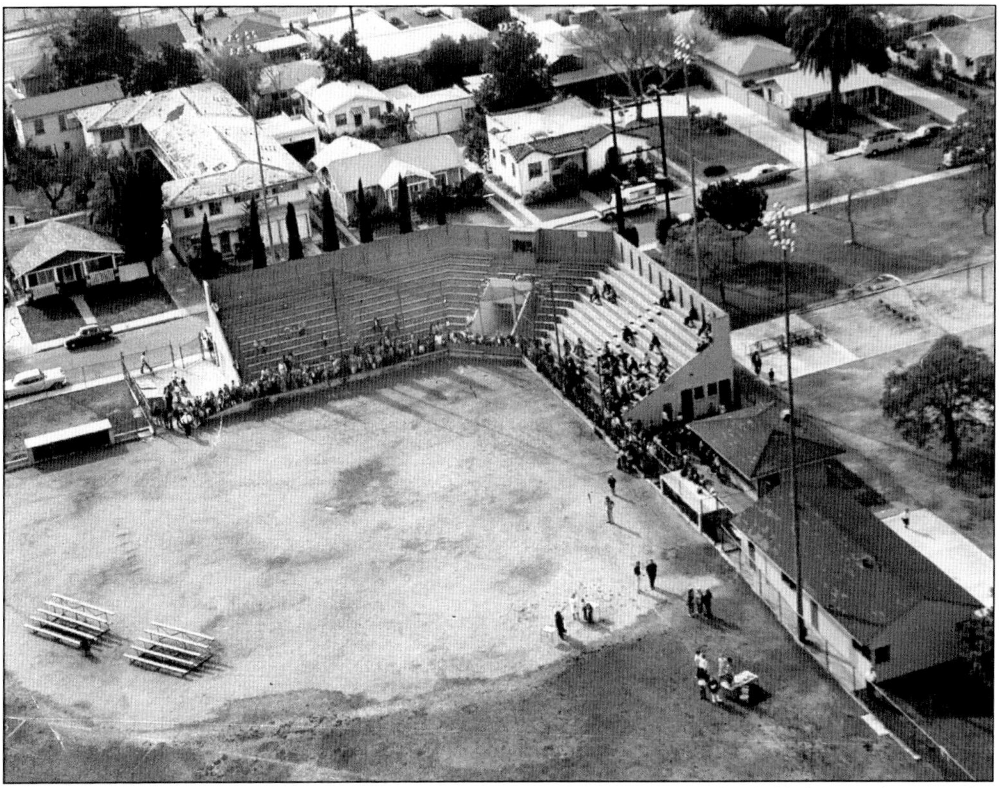

Another aerial view of Maywood City Park, in 1957, focuses in on the ball diamond. Note the stadium-style raised bleachers.

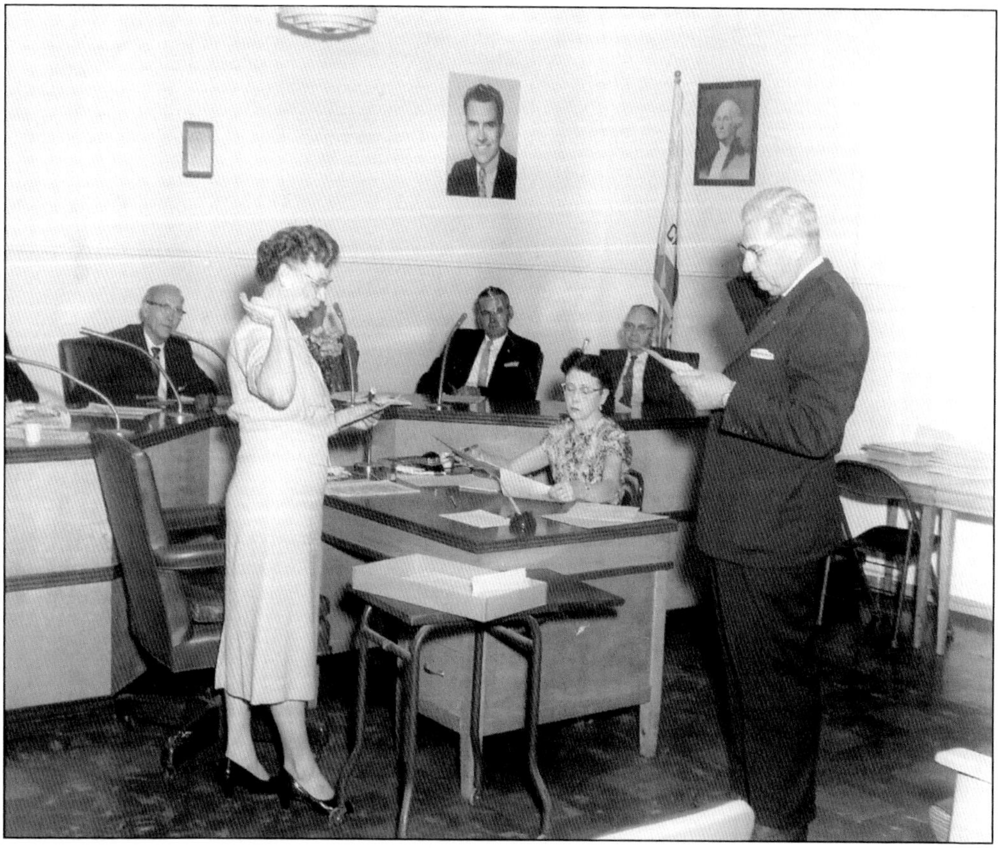

For this 1958 loyalty oath, city clerk Isabel Dedmore is, for once, on the other end of the process. Judge Mullendore administers the oath.

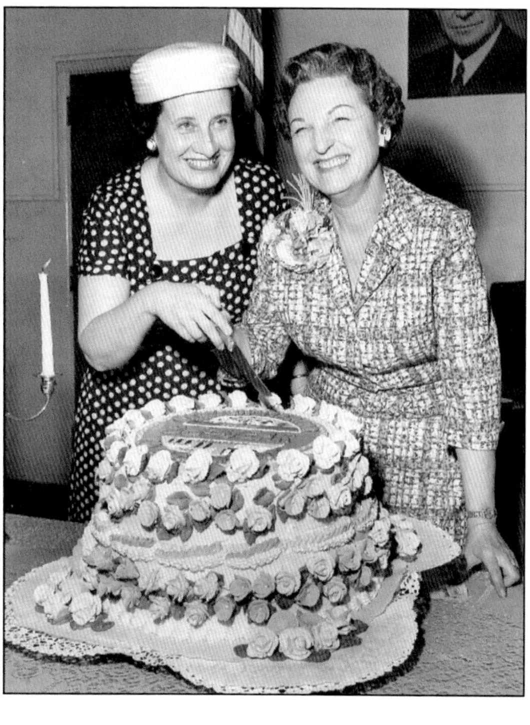

On September 2, 1959, Mayor Reva M. Allsop, right, celebrates Maywood's 35th anniversary. Happy enough to provide the cake was Mercedes Bates, left, from Duncan Hines.

Five

The 1960s

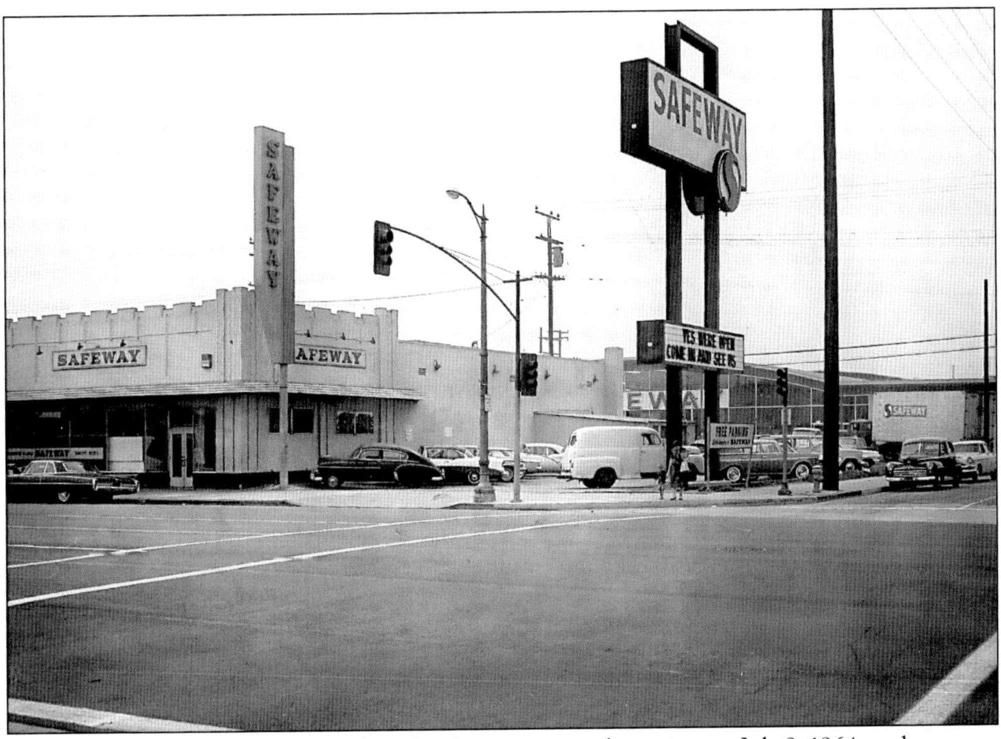

The Safeway Market had a full parking lot during its grand opening on July 8, 1964, at the corner of Slauson Avenue and Fishburn.

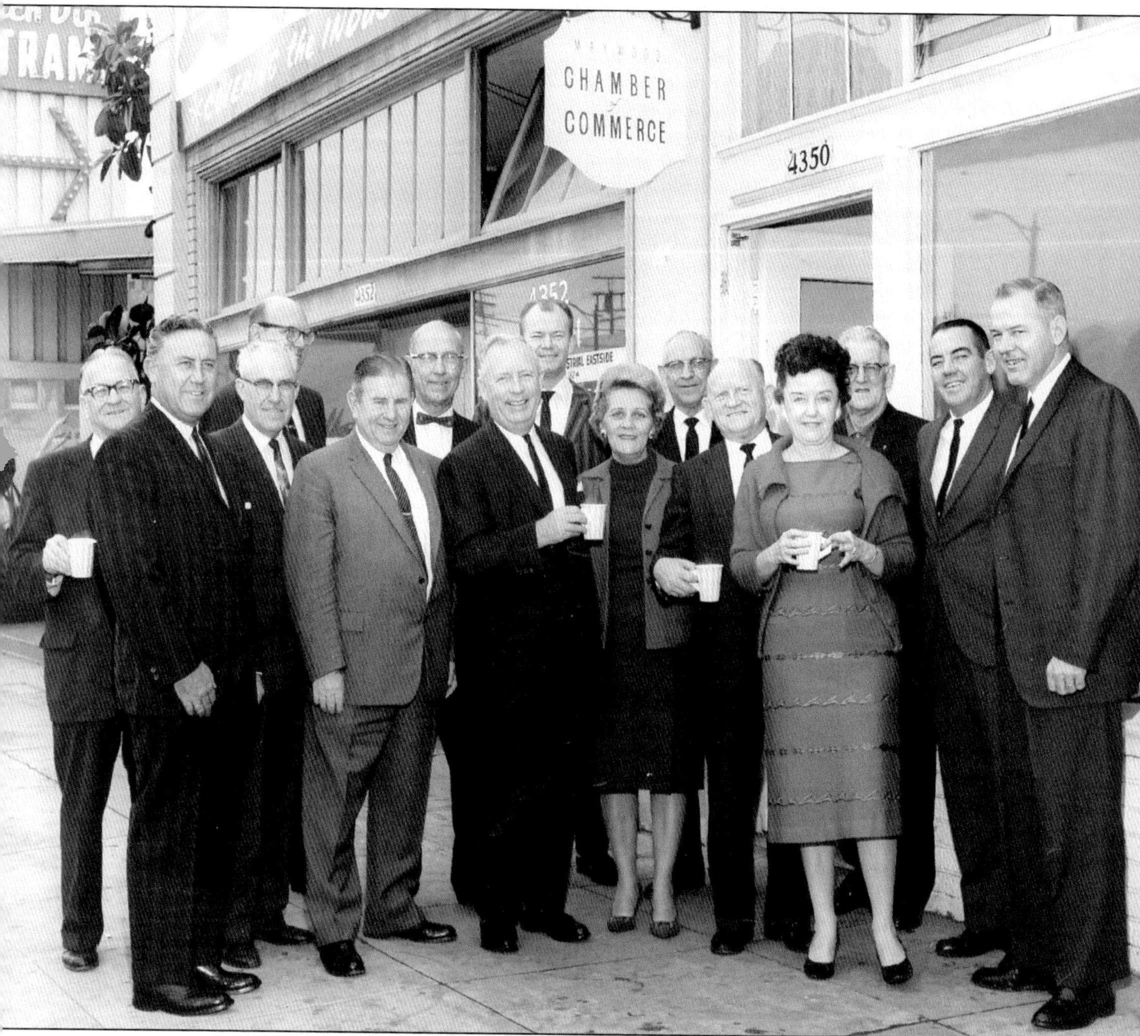

The Maywood Chamber of Commerce steps outside of the chamber's offices at 4350 East Slauson Avenue to celebrate during a monthly board meeting.

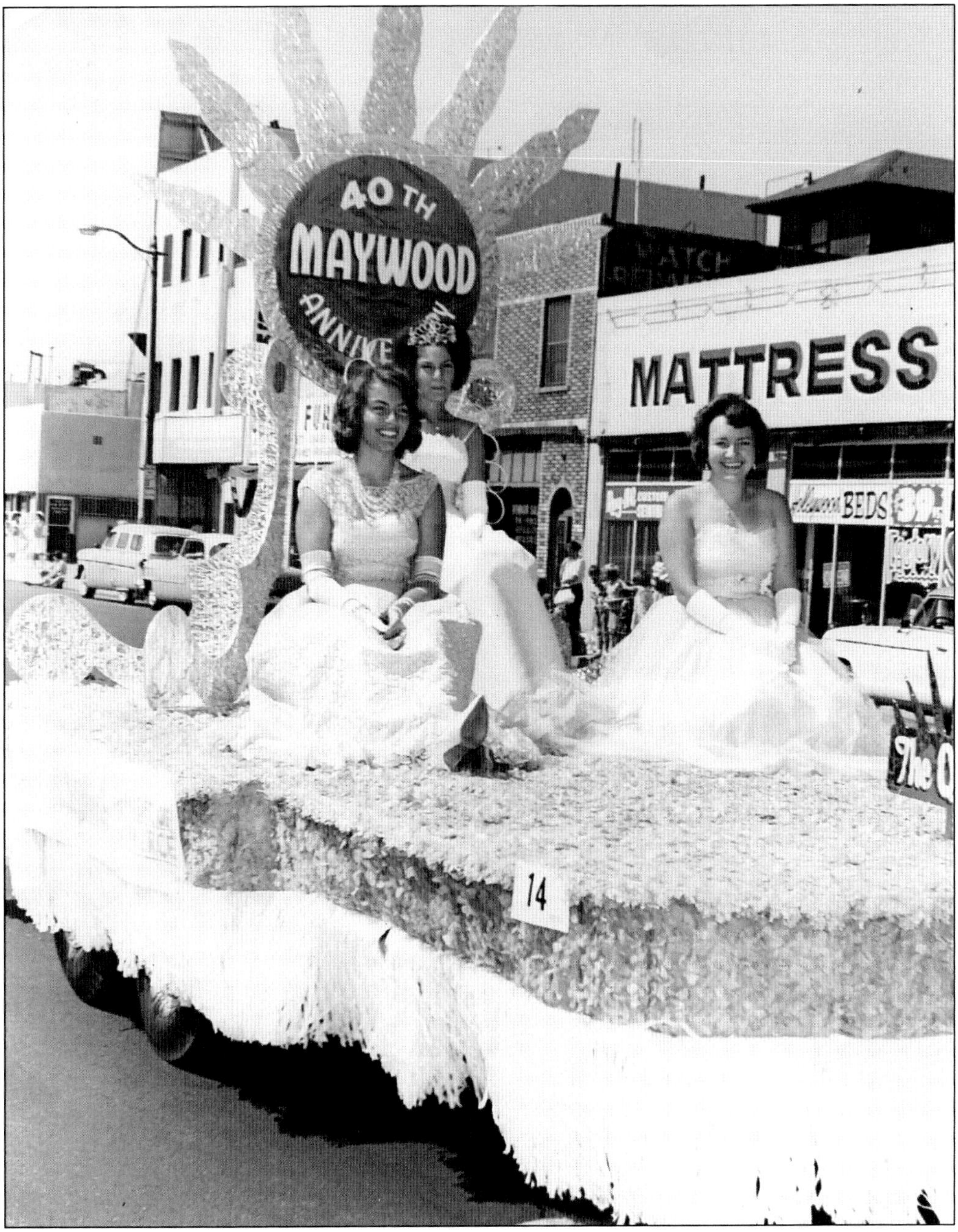

In 1964, at Maywood's 40th anniversary celebration parade, the queen and her court ride on one of the many gorgeous floats.

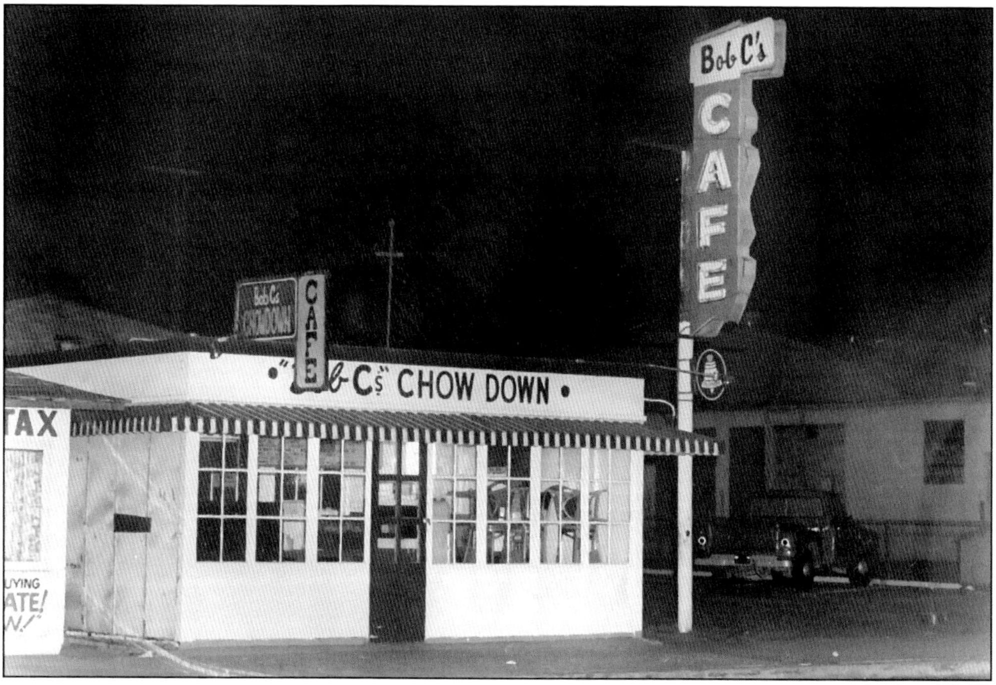

Chowing down was never quite so "direct and to the point" as it was to the many return patrons at Bob C's Chow Down on Slauson Avenue and Corona in Maywood.

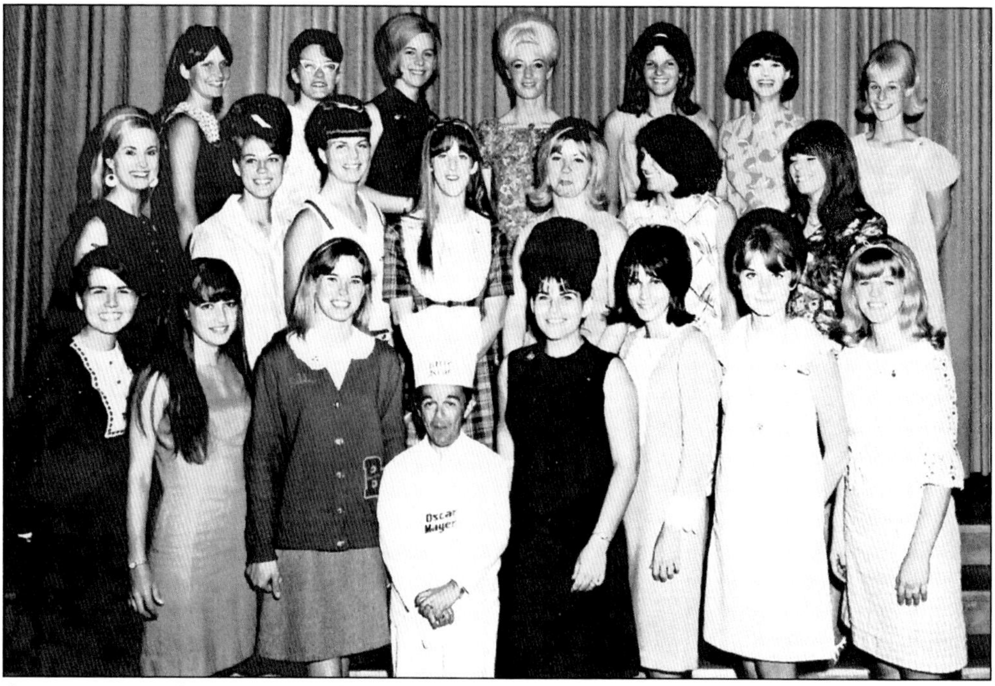

Oscar Mayer and Company sold all the wurst, mainly bockwurst and liverwurst, in Chicago through the turn of the 20th century. It is doubtful that many of the company's representatives were quite so happy as this one here, surrounded by all of the lovely contestants for one of Maywood's 1960s parades.

Somebody had to string up the Stars and Stripes. Ignoring any signs of vertigo, Pete Lombardo, on October 20, 1961, gets ready for the opening of the new Maywood branch of the Los Angeles County Public Library, located right next to city hall. Fire chief Floyd is pointing at the photographer, and librarian Esther Goldsmith can be seen, left of the truck, entering her domain.

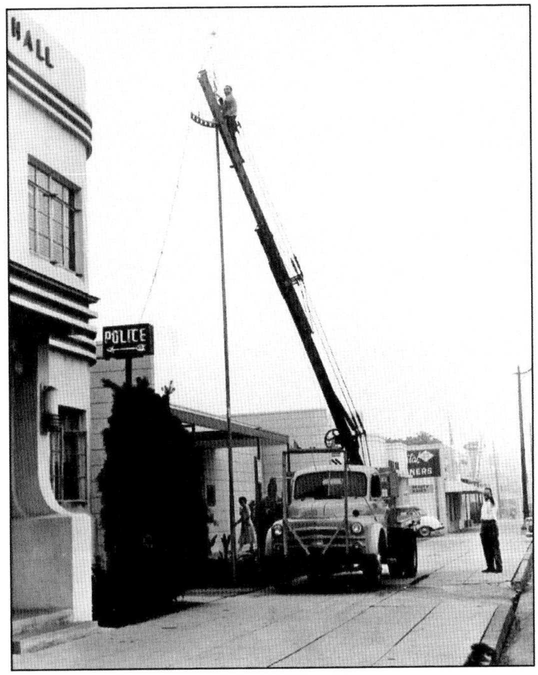

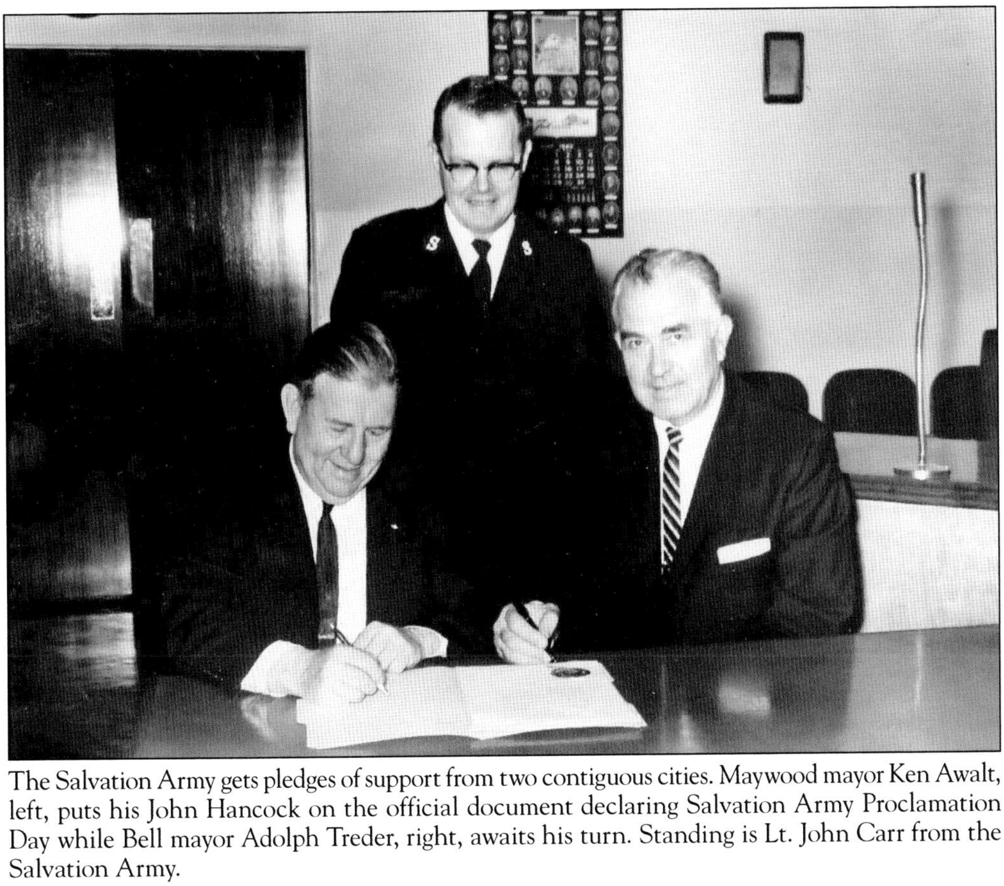

The Salvation Army gets pledges of support from two contiguous cities. Maywood mayor Ken Awalt, left, puts his John Hancock on the official document declaring Salvation Army Proclamation Day while Bell mayor Adolph Treder, right, awaits his turn. Standing is Lt. John Carr from the Salvation Army.

Food Giant Market In Maywood Starts Month Long Grand Opening

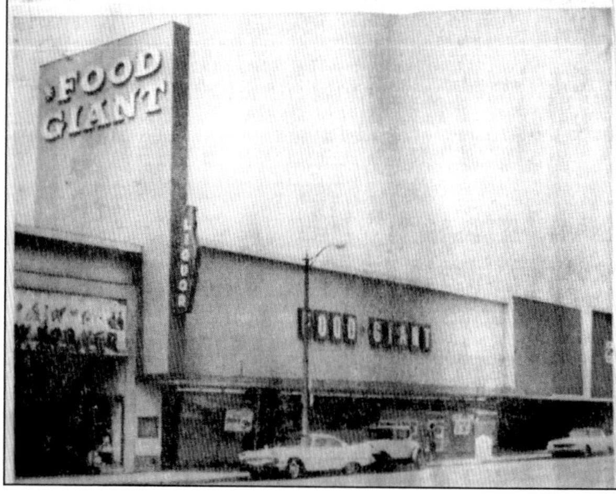

Food Giant's newest market at 6135 Atlantic Boulevard in Maywood sparkled with an attractive, modern front. Formerly McDaniels, the building had been completely redecorated and restored, inside and out, for this grand opening, reported in the tri-cities *Industrial Post* on April 5, 1962. The tri-cities, by the way, are Bell, Maywood, and Cudahy.

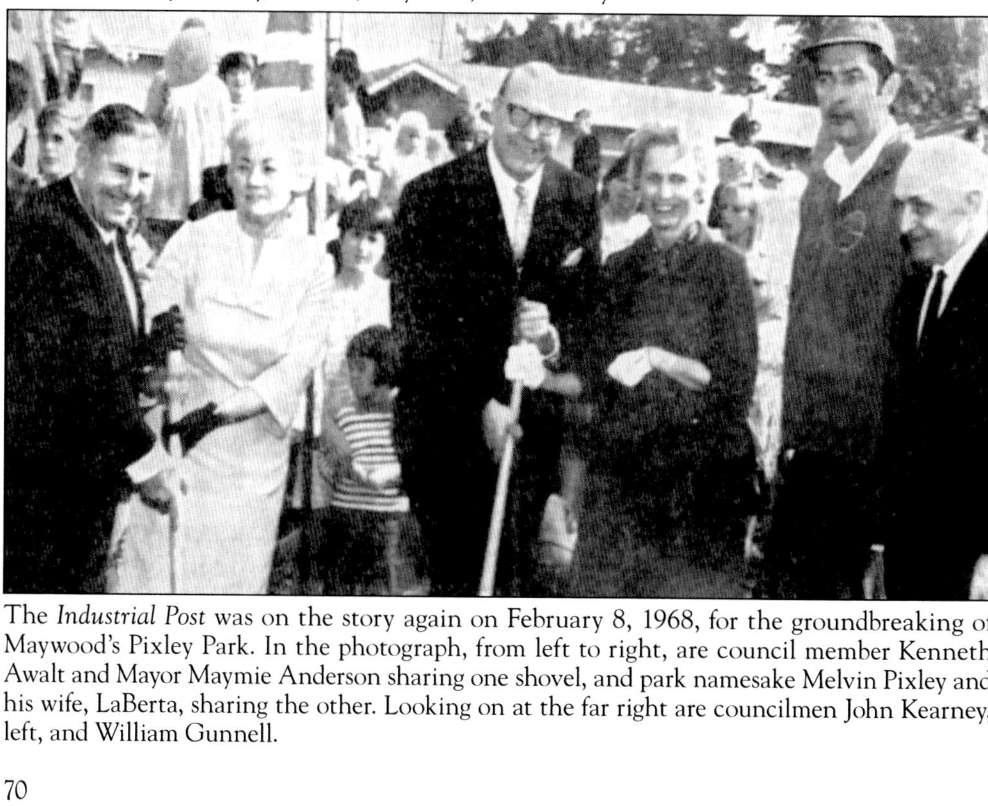

The *Industrial Post* was on the story again on February 8, 1968, for the groundbreaking of Maywood's Pixley Park. In the photograph, from left to right, are council member Kenneth Awalt and Mayor Maymie Anderson sharing one shovel, and park namesake Melvin Pixley and his wife, LaBerta, sharing the other. Looking on at the far right are councilmen John Kearney, left, and William Gunnell.

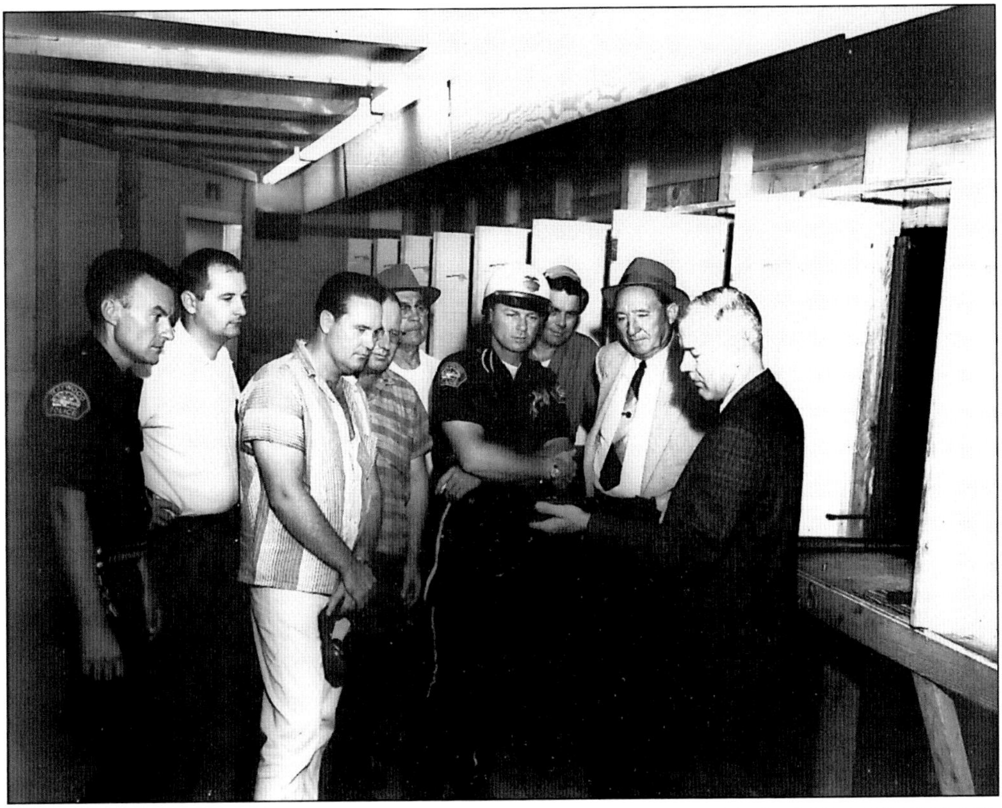

Police chief Wilford Sparks demonstrates the use of what appears to be a shotgun to both on-duty and off-duty Maywood officers.

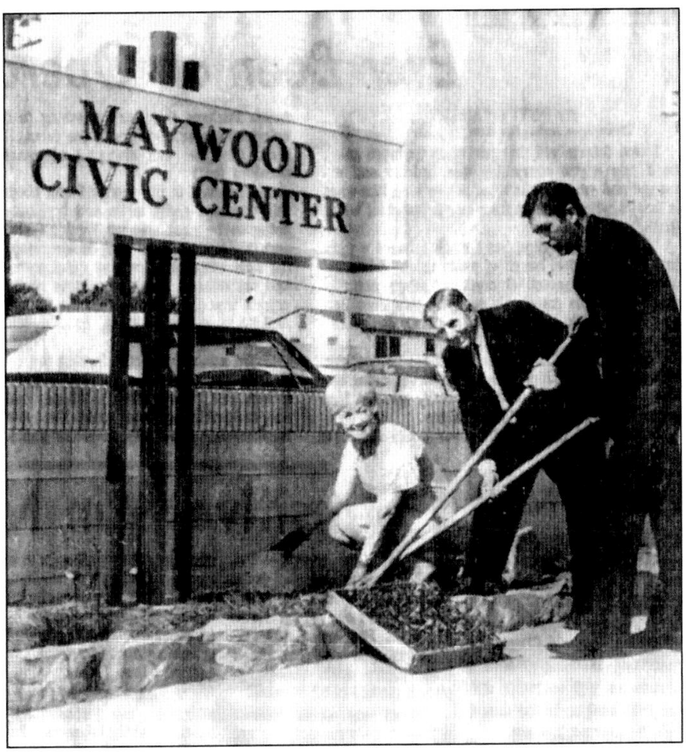

This clipping from the July 17, 1967, *Daily Signal* shows Mayor Maymie Anderson and councilmen Ken Awalt and John Kearney planting snapdragons at Maywood Civic Center.

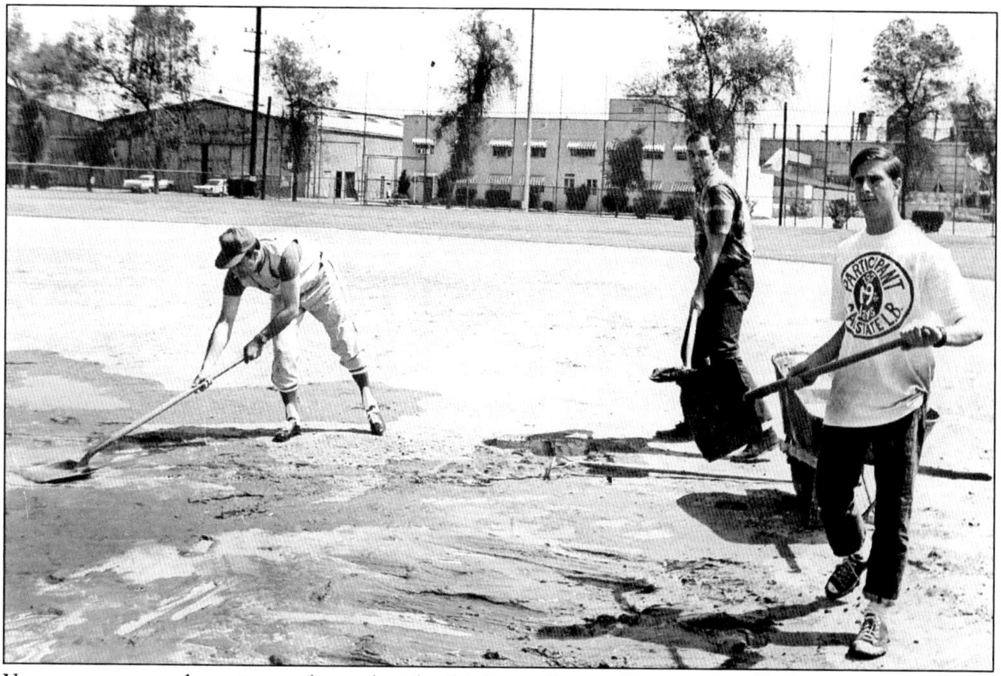

You can never underestimate the zeal with which sandlot rivalries are instilled. In an unsuccessful attempt to sabotage a game, this Maywood baseball field was flooded. This photograph shows recreation leaders and the Golden State team coach cleaning up the infield diamond.

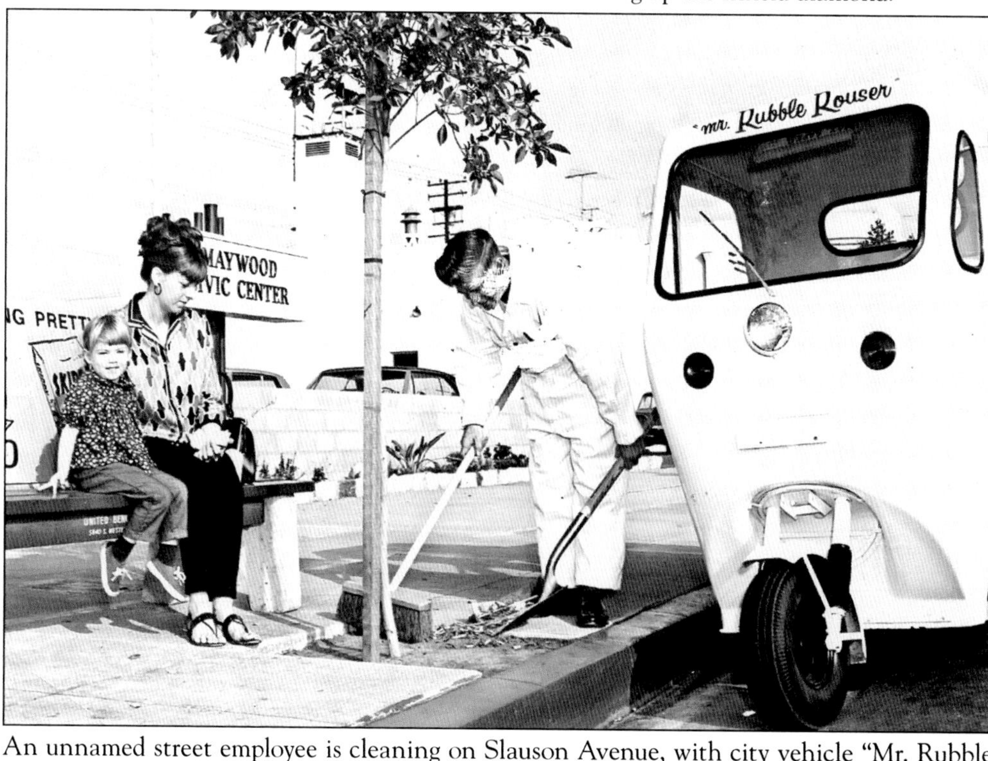

An unnamed street employee is cleaning on Slauson Avenue, with city vehicle "Mr. Rubble Rouser" parked at right.

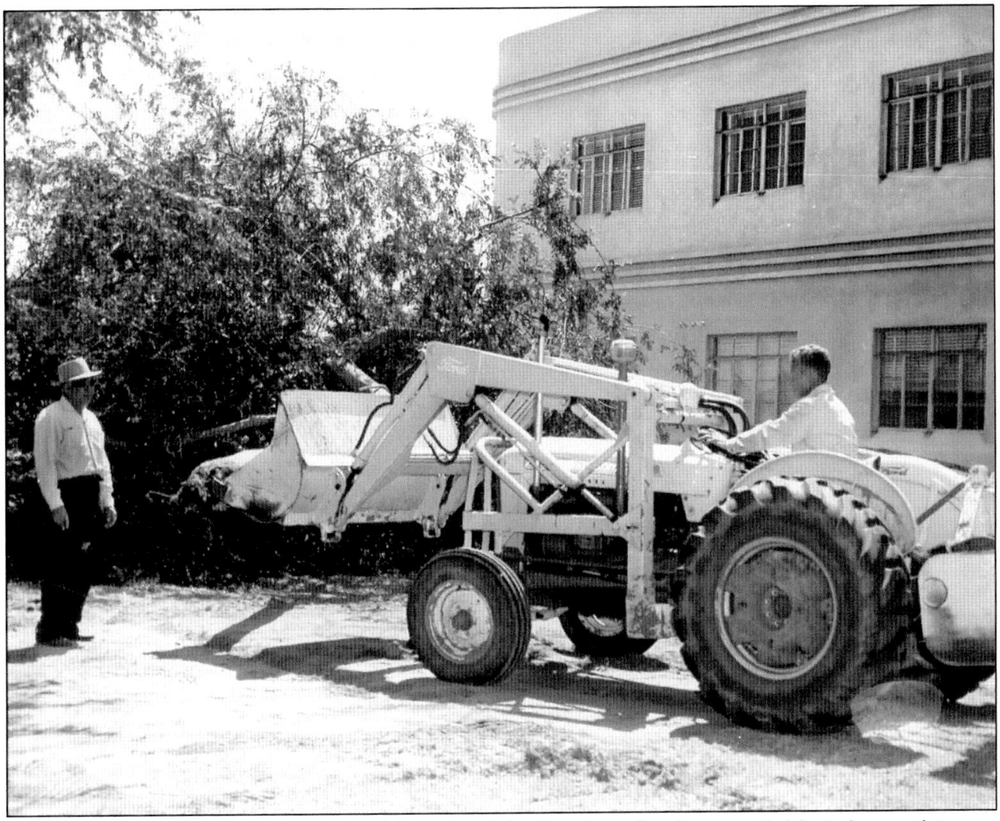

To make room for the new Maywood branch of the Los Angeles County Public Library, this tree was uprooted near city hall.

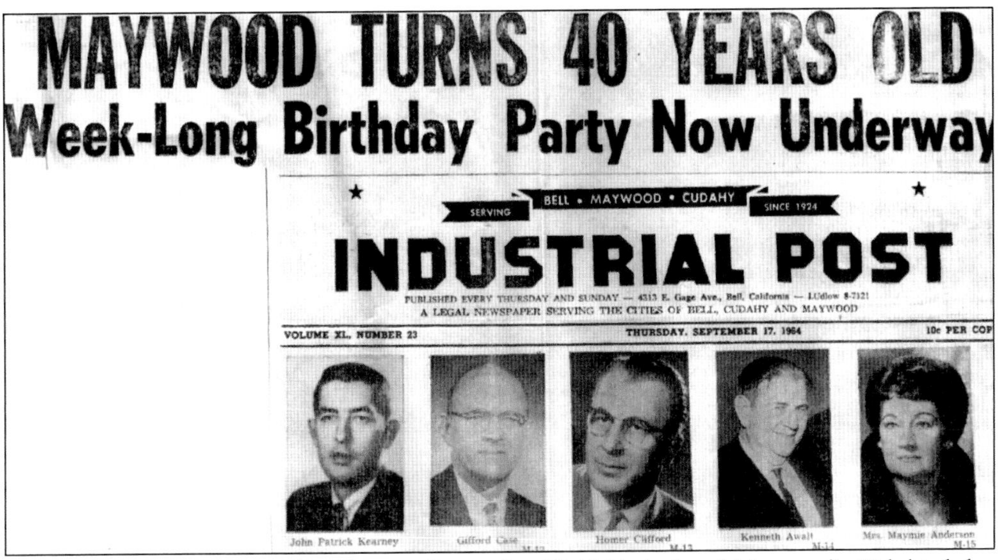

MAYWOOD TURNS 40 YEARS OLD

Week-Long Birthday Party Now Underway

SERVING BELL • MAYWOOD • CUDAHY SINCE 1924

INDUSTRIAL POST

PUBLISHED EVERY THURSDAY AND SUNDAY — 4313 E. Gage Ave., Bell, California — LUdlow 8-7121
A LEGAL NEWSPAPER SERVING THE CITIES OF BELL, CUDAHY AND MAYWOOD

VOLUME XL, NUMBER 23 THURSDAY, SEPTEMBER 17, 1964 10c PER COP

John Patrick Kearney — Gifford Case — Homer Clifford — Kenneth Awalt M-14 — Mrs. Maymie Anderson M-15

The *Industrial Post*'s banner headline on September 17, 1964, declared Maywood's 40th birthday celebration, a week-long series of events. Pictured, from left to right, were city council members John Kearney, Gifford Case, Homer Clifford, Kenneth Awalt, and Maymie Anderson.

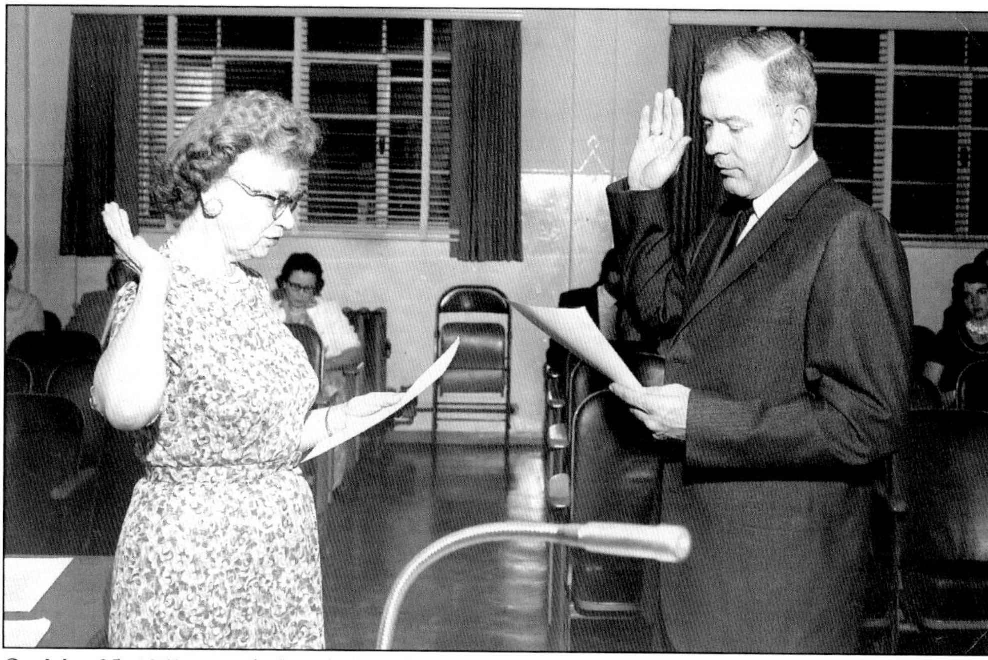

On May 25, 1962, city clerk Isabel Dedmore swears in Chief Wilford Sparks, City of Maywood Police Department.

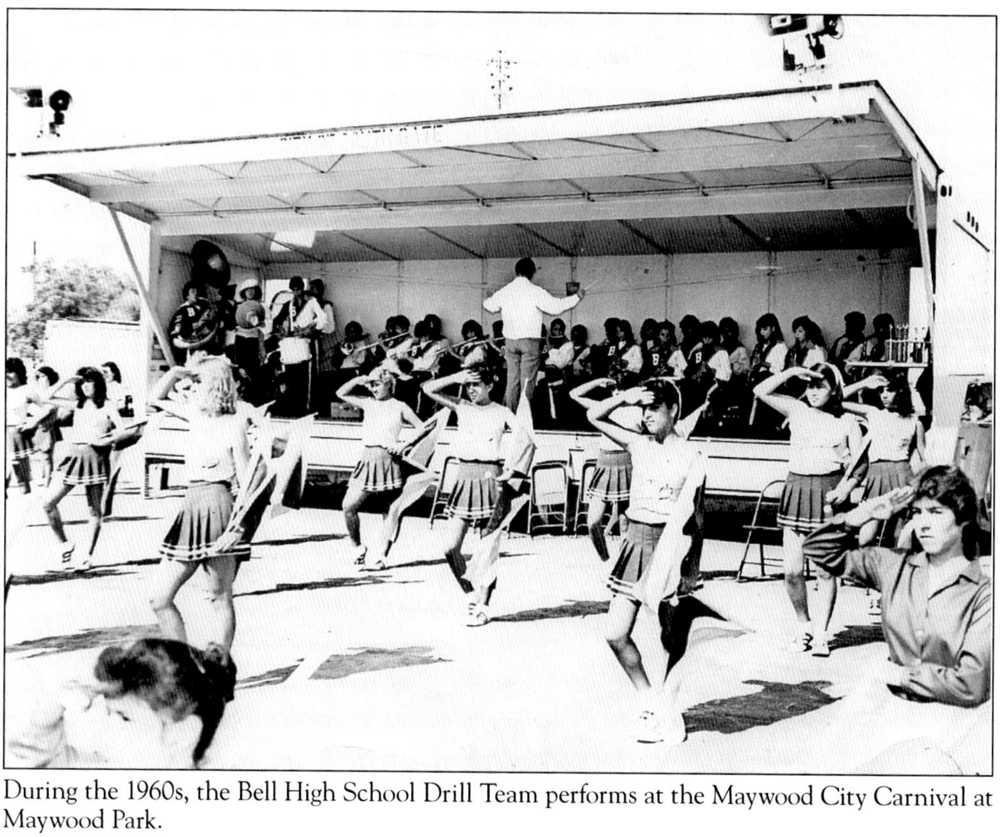

During the 1960s, the Bell High School Drill Team performs at the Maywood City Carnival at Maywood Park.

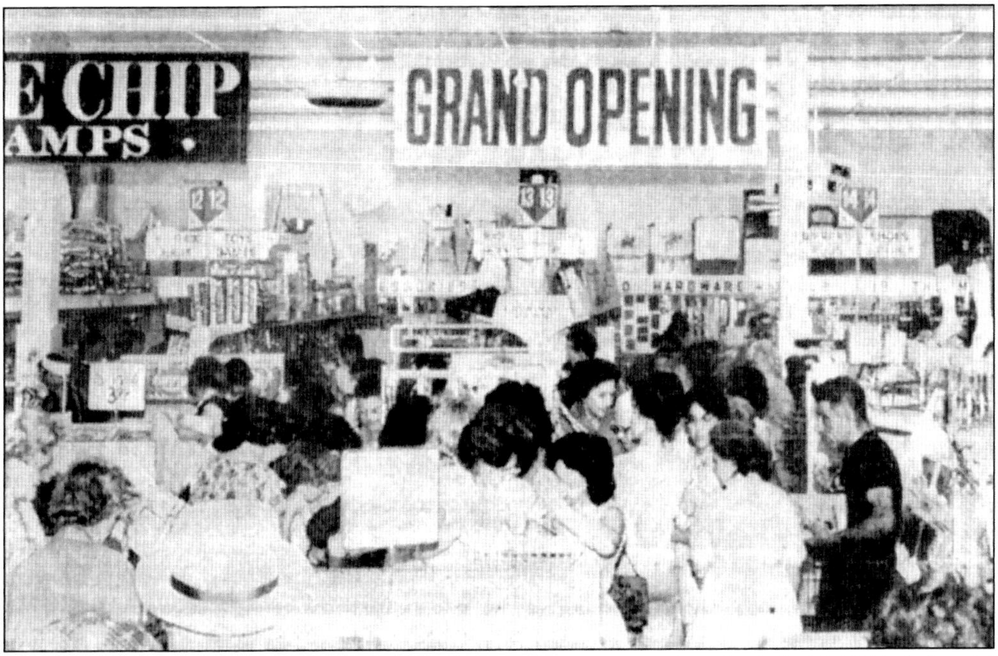

The Thrifty Drug Store reopening lured huge crowds, as reported in the July 16, 1964, *Industrial Post*. Thousands of orchids were presented to women shoppers, and thousands of balloons and gift items were distributed. An array of prizes were offered as part of the grand reopening sale two days later.

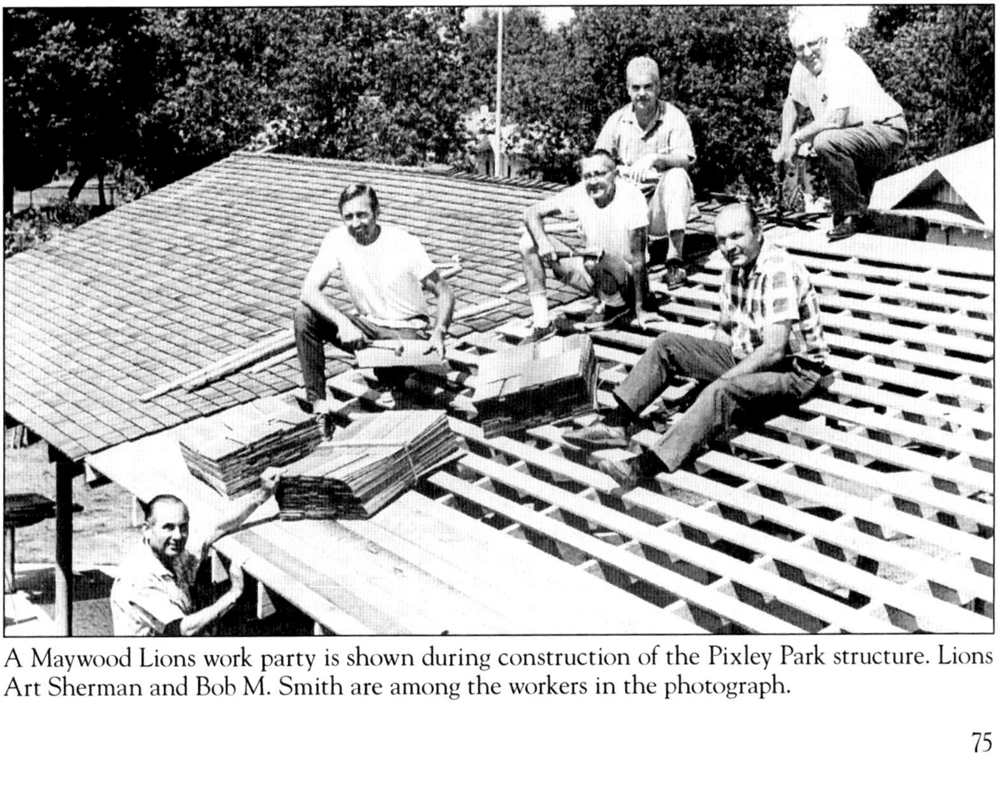

A Maywood Lions work party is shown during construction of the Pixley Park structure. Lions Art Sherman and Bob M. Smith are among the workers in the photograph.

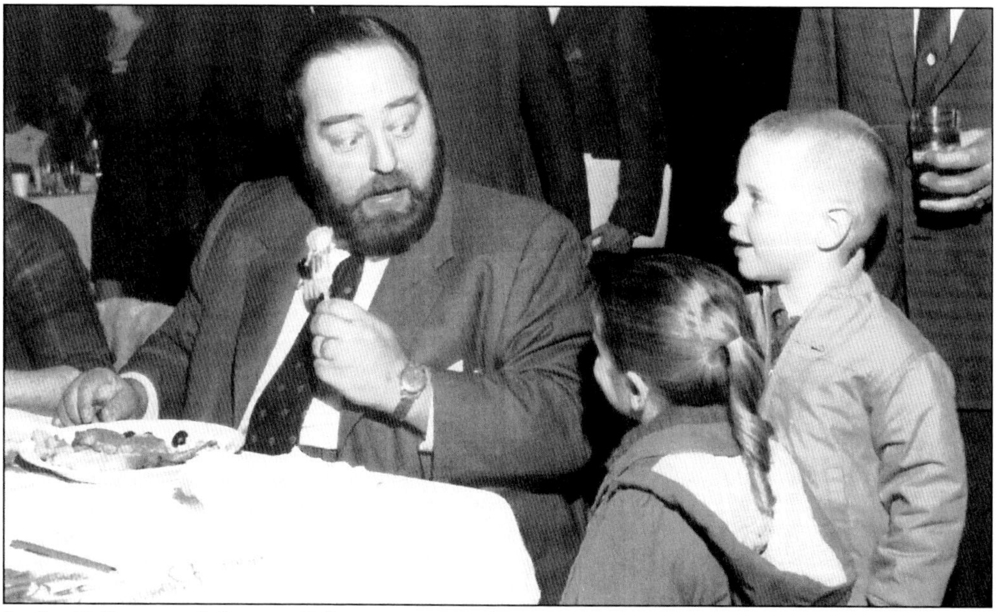

In the 1960s, actor Sebastian Cabot entertains the youngsters at the Maywood Moose Lodge. The portly Cabot most notably costarred in the television series *Checkmate* and *Family Affair*, and also dozens of films including *Ivanhoe* (1952), *Romeo and Juliet* (1954), and *The Time Machine* (1960).

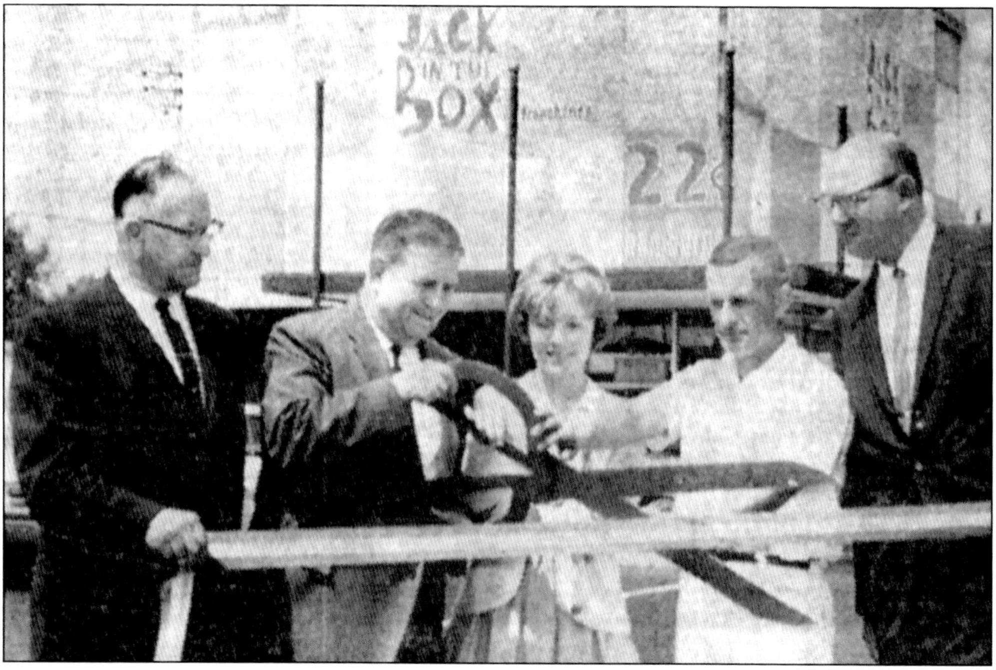

Maywood welcomes a new business. Maywood dignitaries were on hand when ribbon-cutting ceremonies were held for a Jack in the Box hamburger stand at 3700 East Slauson Avenue, near Loma Vista. Pictured, from left to right, in the *Industrial Post* coverage of August 1, 1963, are P. A. Yerian, Maywood Chamber of Commerce secretary; Mayor Kenneth Awalt; Sandra Leatherman, Maywood's reigning queen; Daniel N. Southard Jr., manager of the new business, and William Matters, chamber president.

Mike Lee, a 21-year-old Southeast baseball star, signed with the San Francisco Giants for an estimated $80,000 bonus. In 1960, Lee pitched in the American League for the Cleveland Indians and, in 1963, for the Los Angeles Angels.

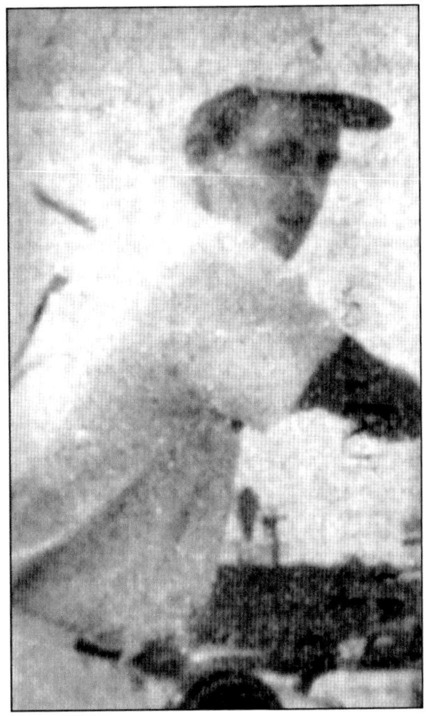

In a hit-them-on-the-head demonstration, Bell and Maywood policemen get a practical understanding—if you can call this a practical understanding—of the difference between the new safety helmets and the standard felt jobs. Sgt. Paul A. Suttle, left, of the Bell Police Department, sports the modern headgear and "doesn't feel a thing." Officer Charles Malatacca, right, of the Maywood Police Department, makes with a painful look. Providing the nightstick lesson, purely in the interests of safety and the *Industrial Post*, is Officer Victor Logrecco, also a Maywood policeman.

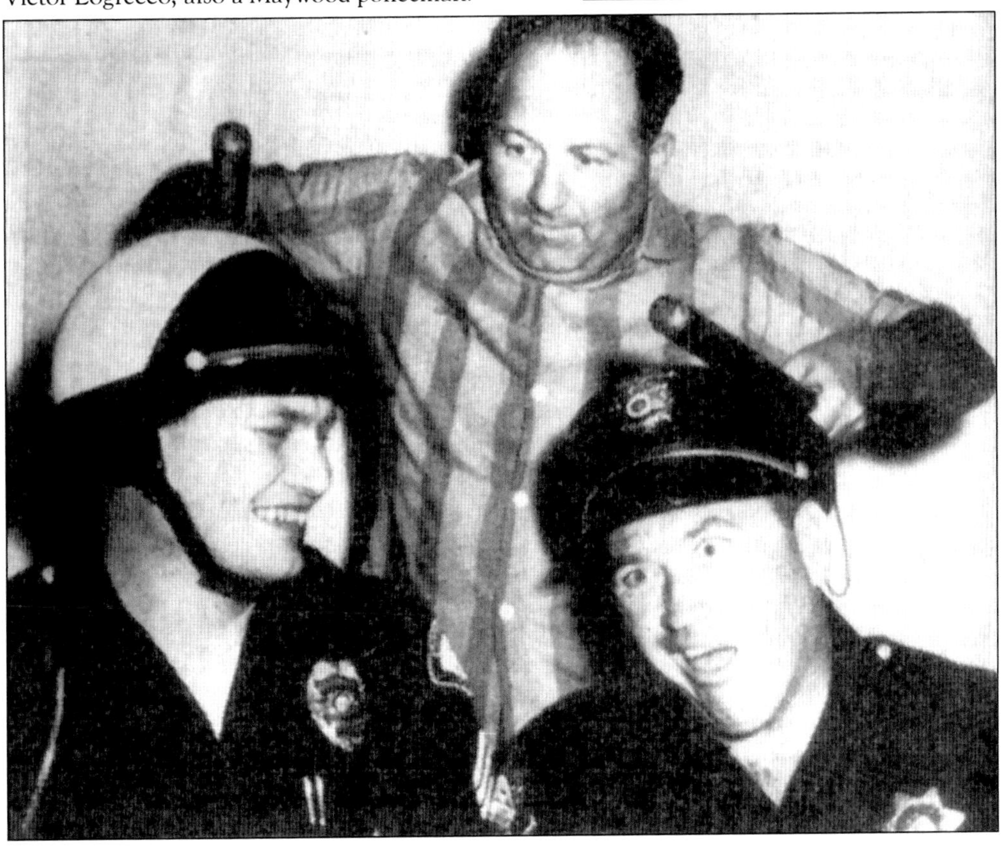

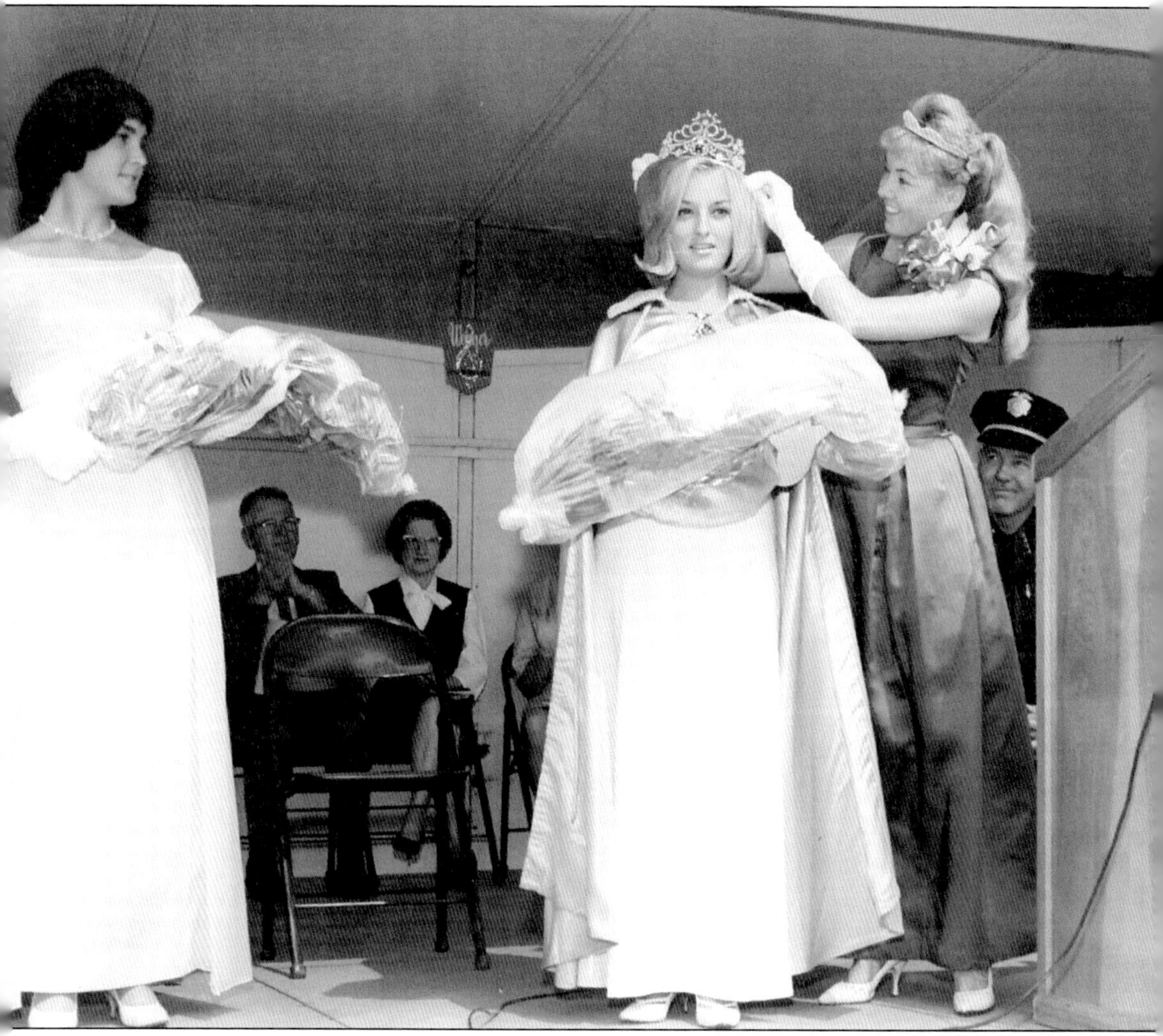

Queen Sherry Upton gets her crown in 1965 from Linda Lohman, while Rebecca Hanson looks on.

Six

The 1970s

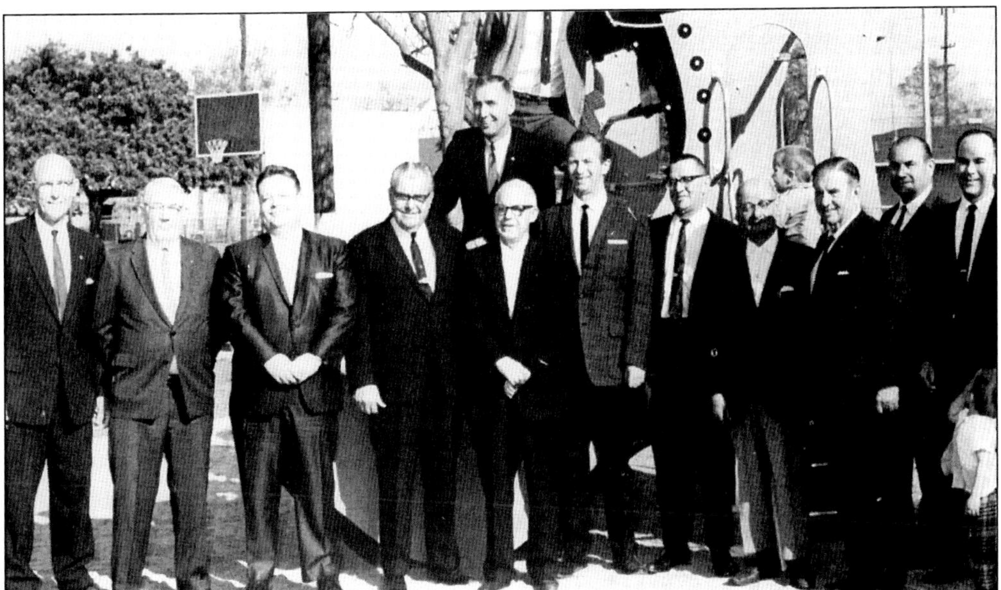

One of the many donations to the city's parks took place in the early 1970s when the Lions Club donated the Old Woman in a Shoe, a combination slide and climbing apparatus, to Maywood Park.

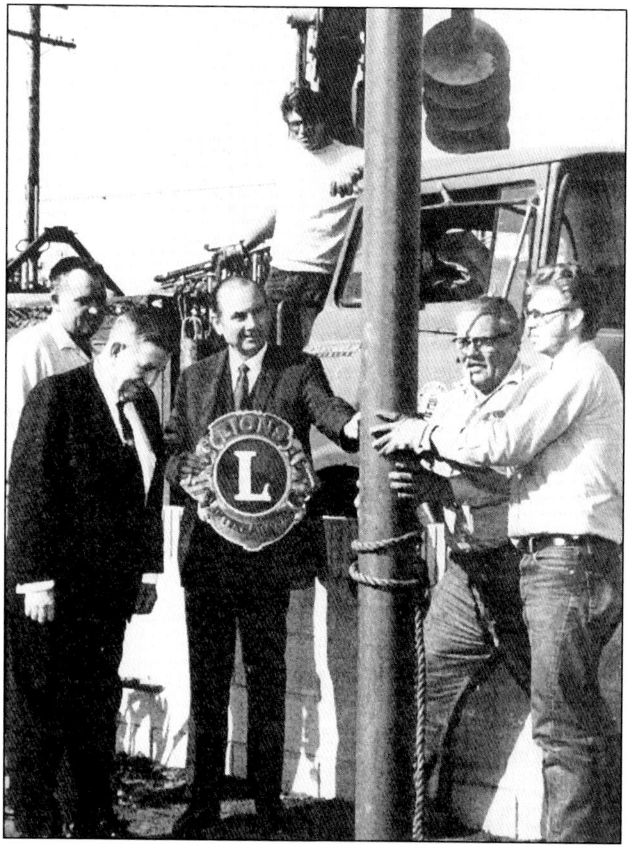

In the early 1970s, at the base of the new Maywood City Hall sign, are several of the Lions Club members.

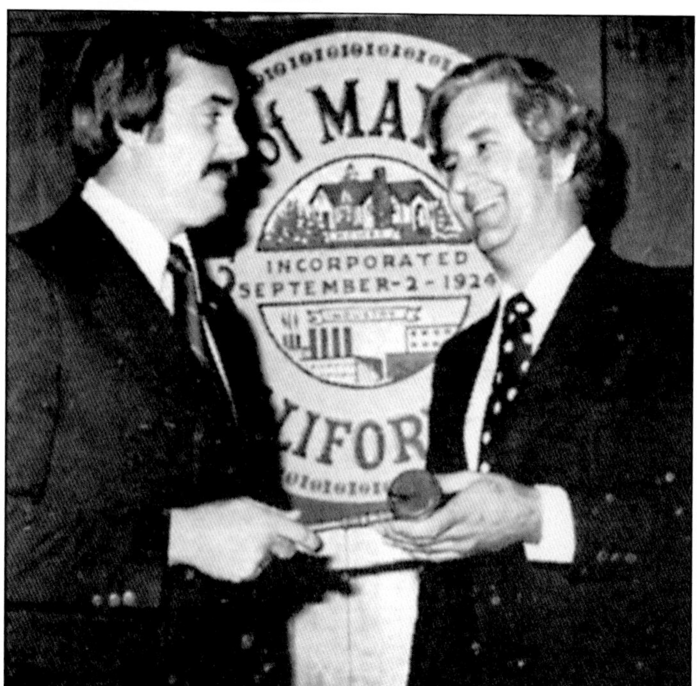

In 1979, the newly installed mayor, Stephen Hegstrom (left) receives a gavel from former mayor James Awalt.

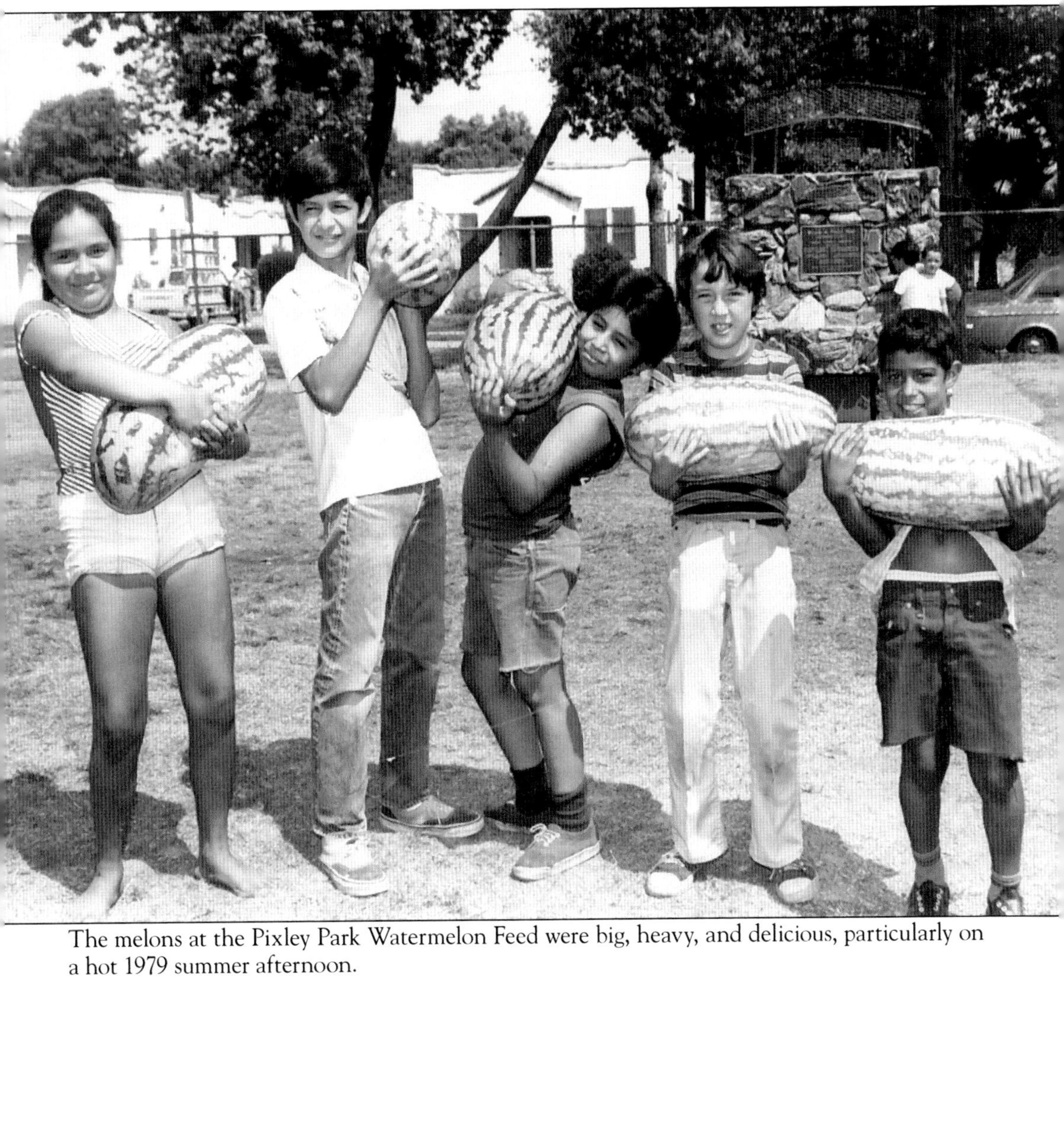

The melons at the Pixley Park Watermelon Feed were big, heavy, and delicious, particularly on a hot 1979 summer afternoon.

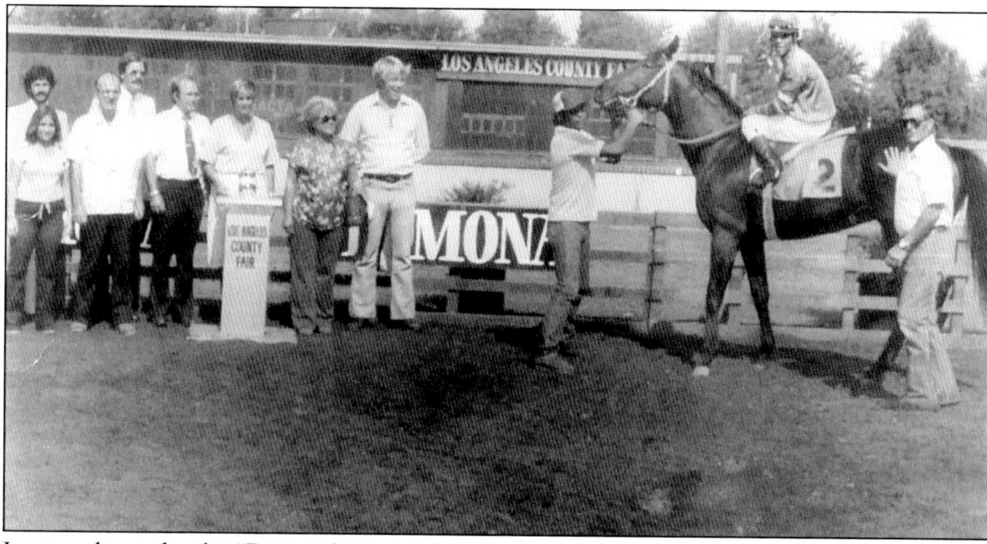

In attendance for the "Day at the Races 1979" at the Los Angeles County Fair at the county fairgrounds in Pomona are city administrative officer Edward Ahrens, and city council members Rose Busciglio and Terry Fallesen. Jockey John Bombek is riding the winning horse, Bert J.

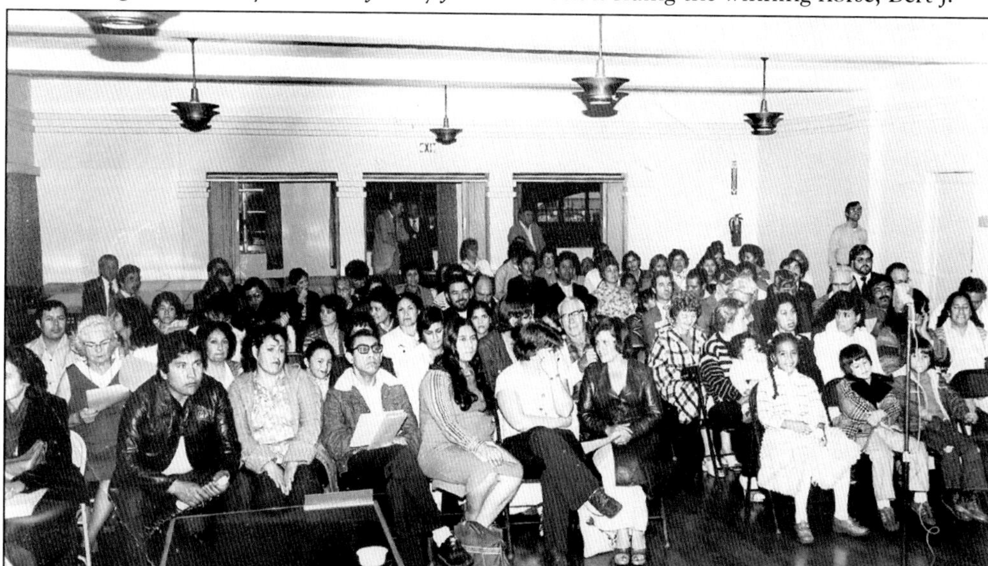

As in this November 1979 photograph, Maywood residents would occasionally rally at monthly city council meetings around specific issues, such as the widening of Fishburn Avenue, located west of the city hall parking lot. The issue being discussed here, unfortunately, has been obscured with the passage of time.

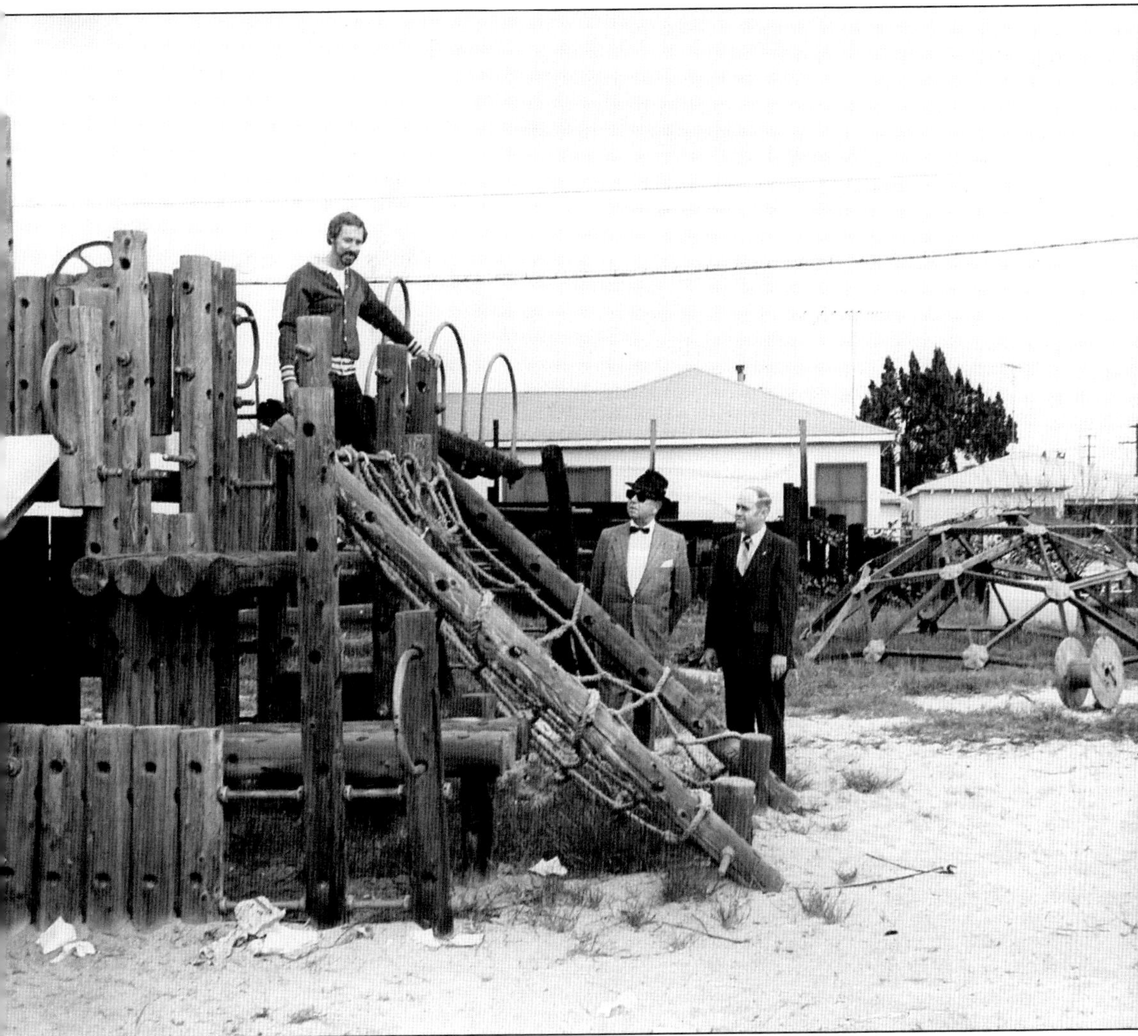

In the 1970s, recreation supervisor Vic Heintzman inspects newly donated, fort-like climbing equipment. City administrator Leonard Locher, far right, looks on.

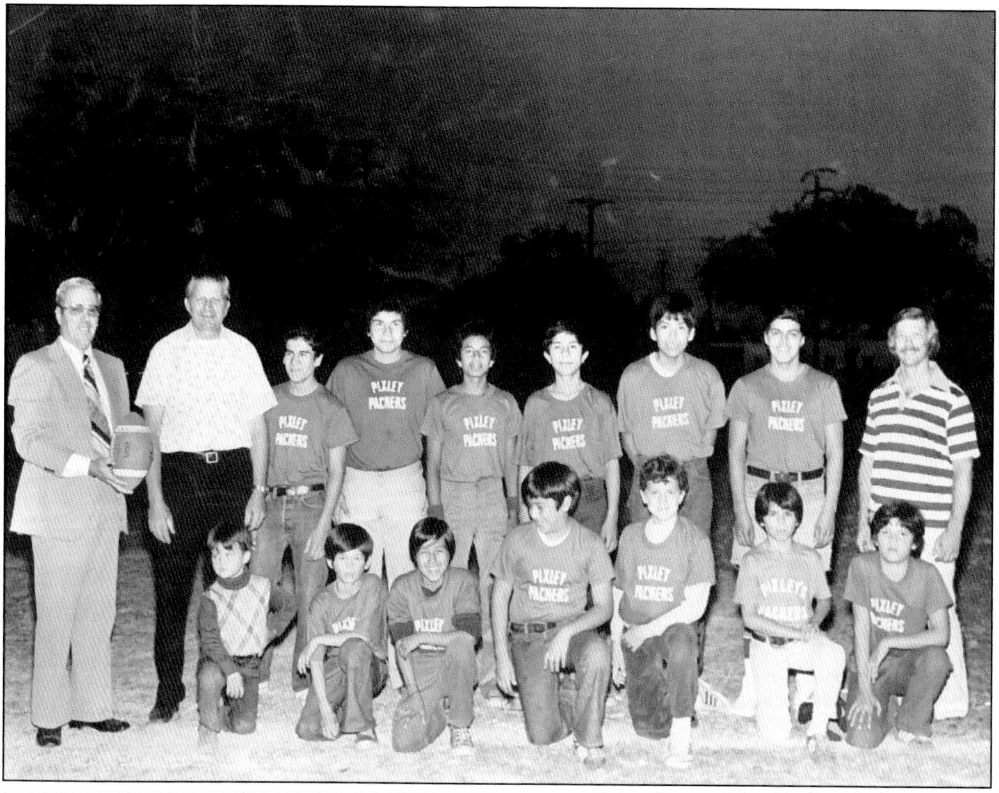

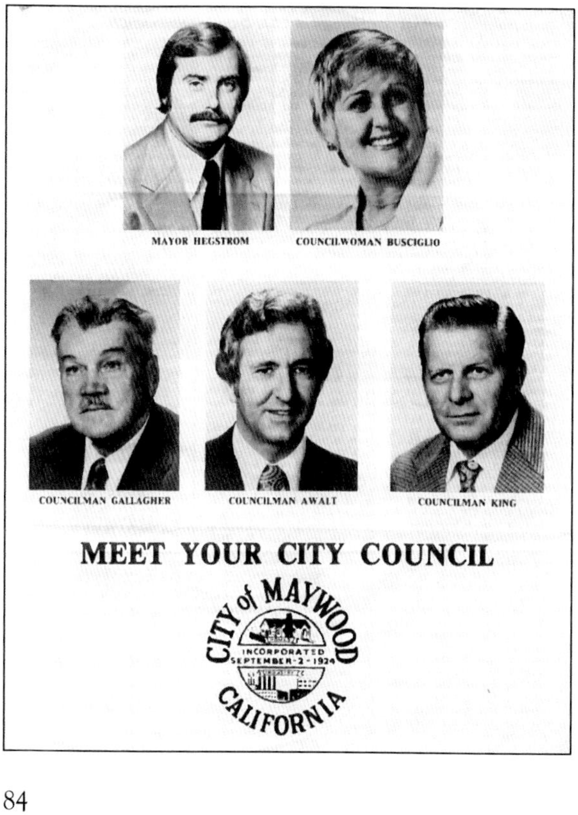

Members of the Pixley Packers flag football team are pictured in 1978. Council members William Hamilton, far left with the pigskin, and William King, beside him, show their support. Recreation supervisor Vic Heintzman is at the far right.

The Maywood City Council, pictured in 1979, from left to right, are (first row) Mayor Stephen Hegstrom and Rose Busciglio; (second row) Gallagher, Awalt, and King.

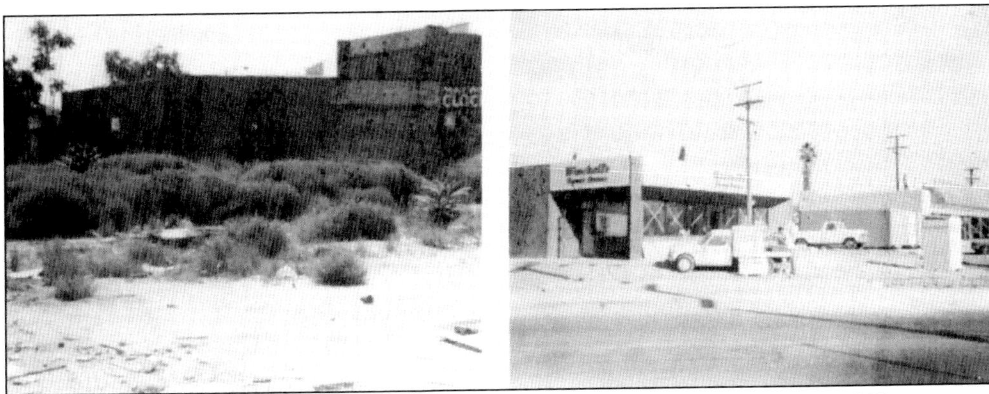

These before and after photographs show the redevelopment on the corner of Slauson and Maywood Avenues.

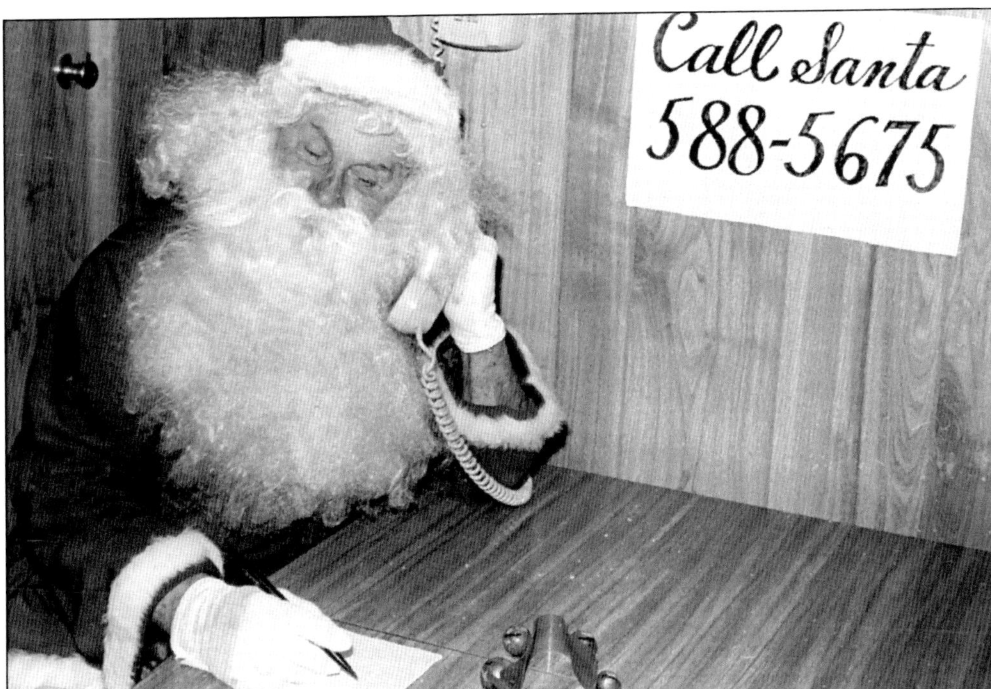

The beloved Ed Fraser always got busy in December as orders stacked up for Santa. Modern wood paneling and AT&T finally made it to the North Pole by the 1970s, and Santa always made sure the kids didn't have to call long distance. While changes came to Santa, Ed was a Maywood mainstay for the kids.

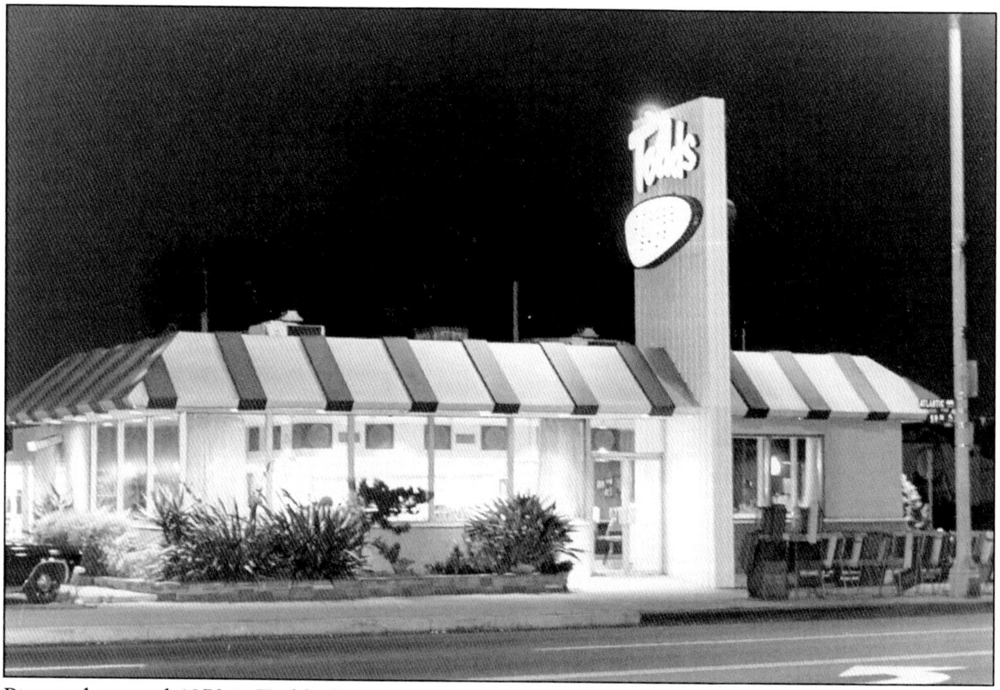

Pictured around 1973 is Todd's Restaurant on Atlantic Boulevard. A neighborhood favorite in Maywood, Todd's always had a cup of coffee ready for the regulars, including the city's police force. The restaurant was demolished in the late 1980s.

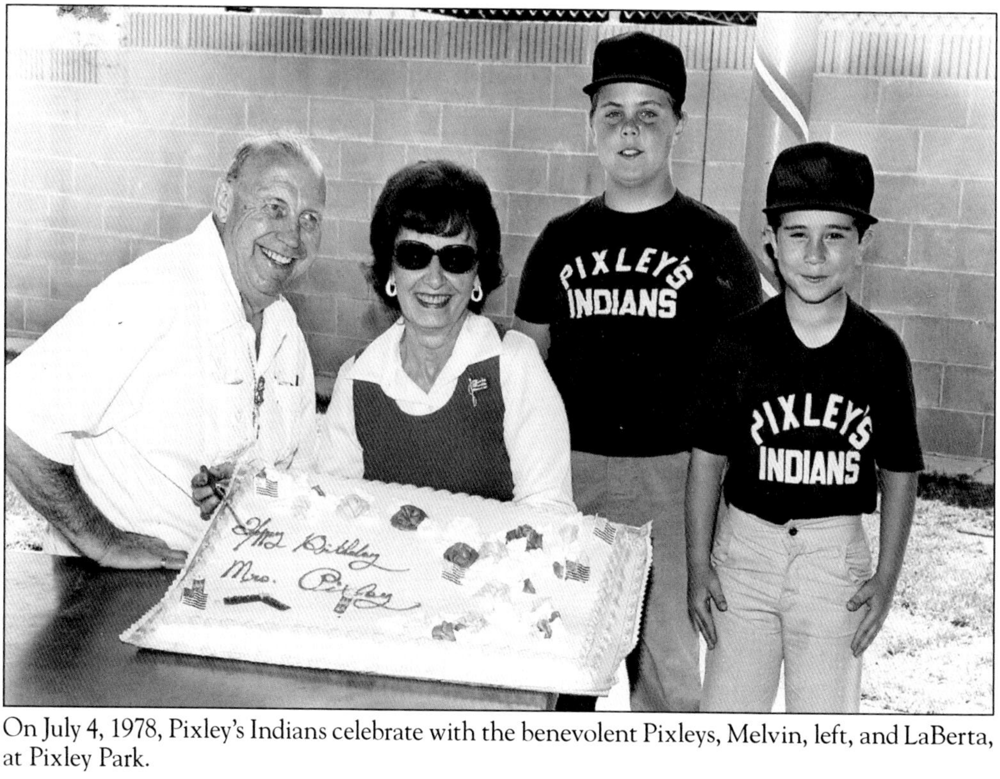

On July 4, 1978, Pixley's Indians celebrate with the benevolent Pixleys, Melvin, left, and LaBerta, at Pixley Park.

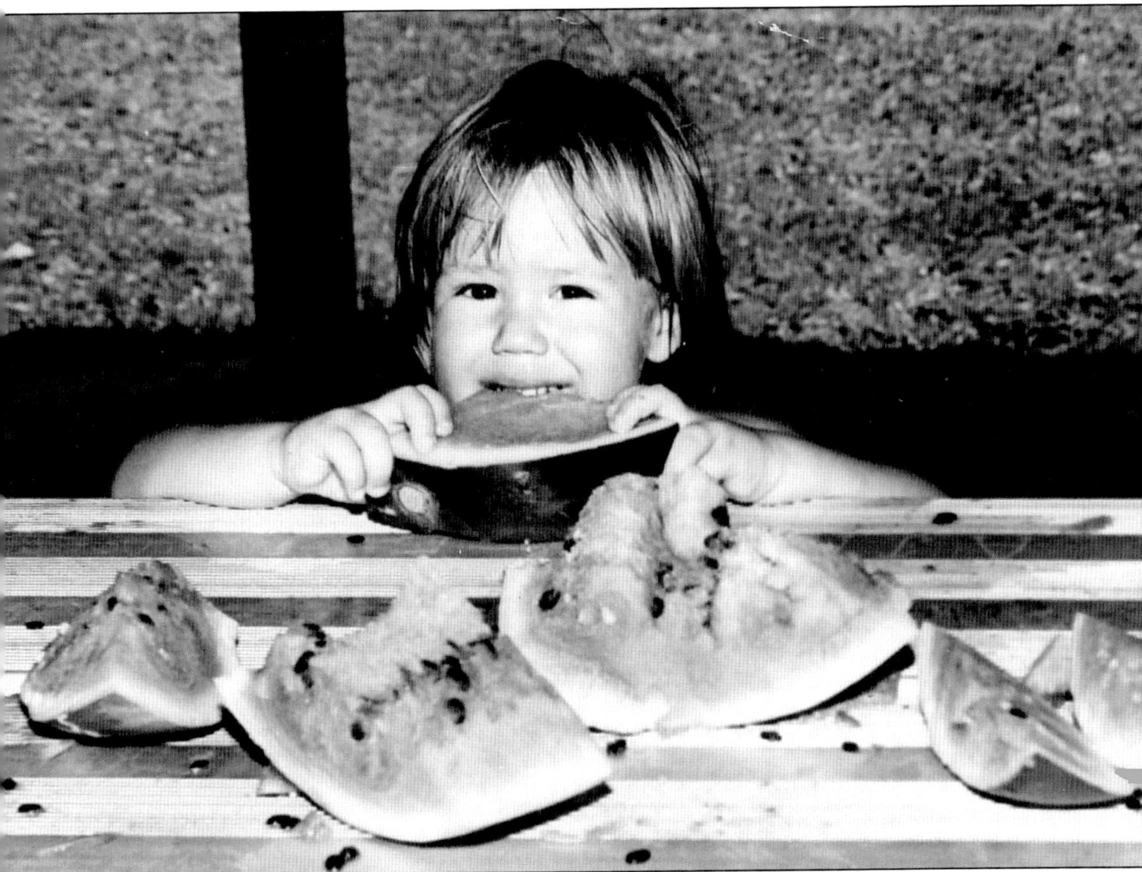

A lot of damage has been done at the Maywood Park Watermelon Feed, and there appears to be plenty more to do. Seed swallowing and spitting was optional.

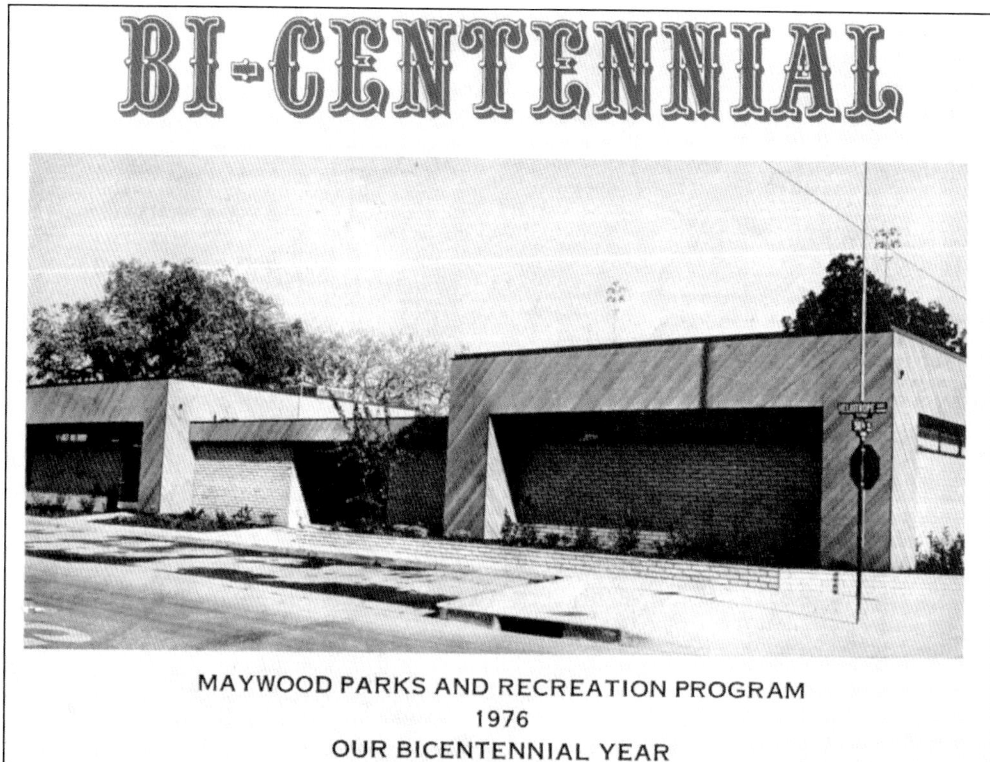

Maywood's new park building at Heliotrope Avenue and Fifty-eighth Street is depicted on the cover of the Maywood Parks and Recreation Program Bi-Centennial Program.

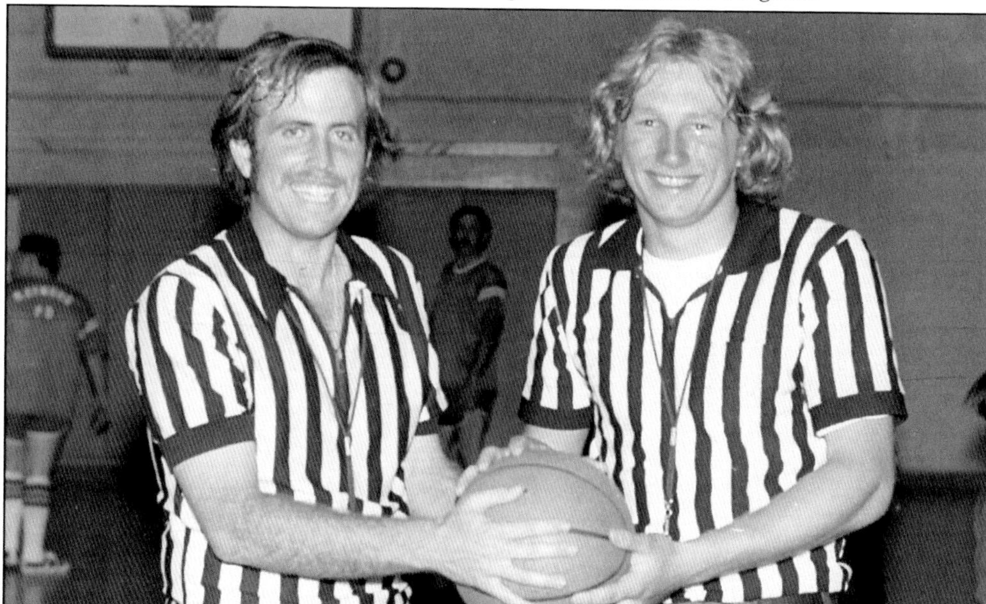

Maywood's recreation supervisors—John De Mooy, left, and Tom Martin—broke out the grins in March 1977 before refereeing a benefit game between the Maywood Police Department and the Los Angeles Rams.

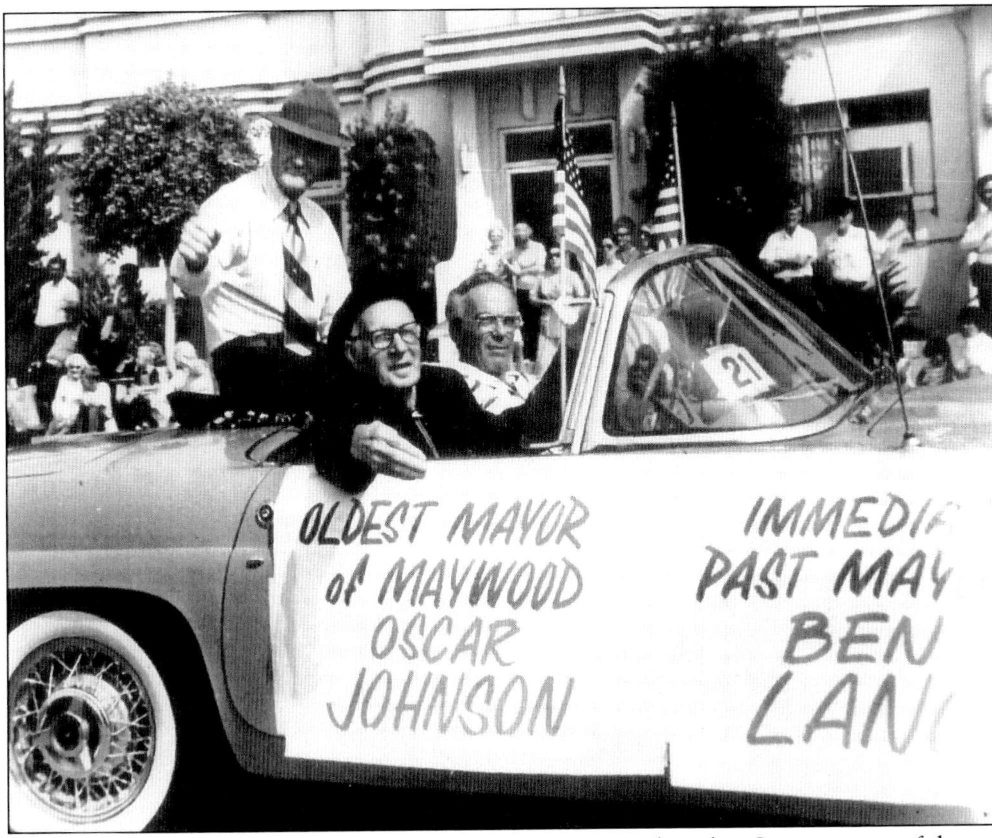

During the Maywood parade in 1974, past luminaries receive their due. Sitting on top of the car is Ben Lang, a 24-year councilman who also served as mayor, and, in the passenger seat, Oscar Johnson, a Maywood mayor in the early 1930s.

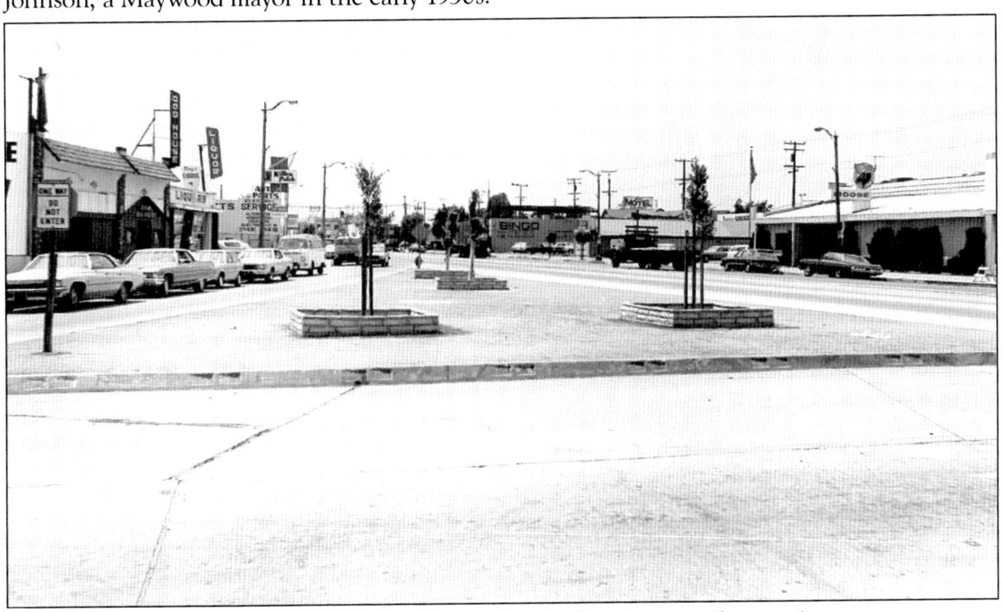

Pictured here in the 1970s is the "island beautification" project on Slauson Avenue.

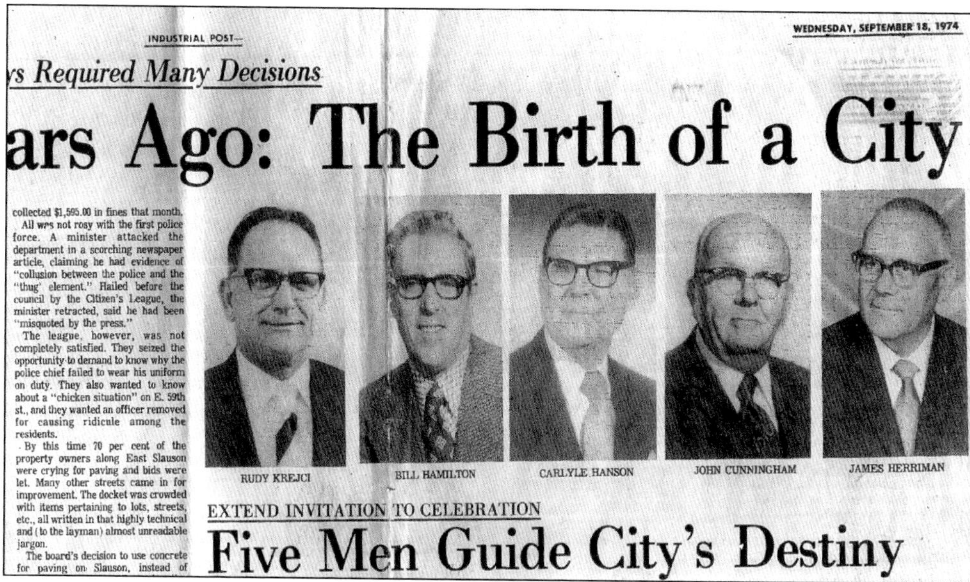

INDUSTRIAL POST—

WEDNESDAY, SEPTEMBER 18, 1974

ʹs Required Many Decisions

ars Ago: The Birth of a City

collected $1,595.00 in fines that month.

All wrs not rosy with the first police force. A minister attacked the department in a scorching newspaper article, claiming he had evidence of "collusion between the police and the "thug' element." Hailed before the council by the Citizen's League, the minister retracted, said he had been "misquoted by the press."

The league, however, was not completely satisfied. They seized the opportunity to demand to know why the police chief failed to wear his uniform on duty. They also wanted to know about a "chicken situation" on E. 59th st., and they wanted an officer removed for causing ridicule among the residents.

By this time 70 per cent of the property owners along East Slauson were crying for paving and bids were let. Many other streets came in for improvement. The docket was crowded with items pertaining to lots, streets, etc., all written in that highly technical and (to the layman) almost unreadable jargon.

The board's decision to use concrete for paving on Slauson, instead of

RUDY KREJCI BILL HAMILTON CARLYLE HANSON JOHN CUNNINGHAM JAMES HERRIMAN

EXTEND INVITATION TO CELEBRATION

Five Men Guide City's Destiny

This 1974 clipping from the *Industrial Post* celebrated the city's silver anniversary. The City of Maywood's 1974 council members, from left to right, are Rudy Krejci, Bill Hamilton, Carlyle Hanson, John Cunningham, and James Herriman.

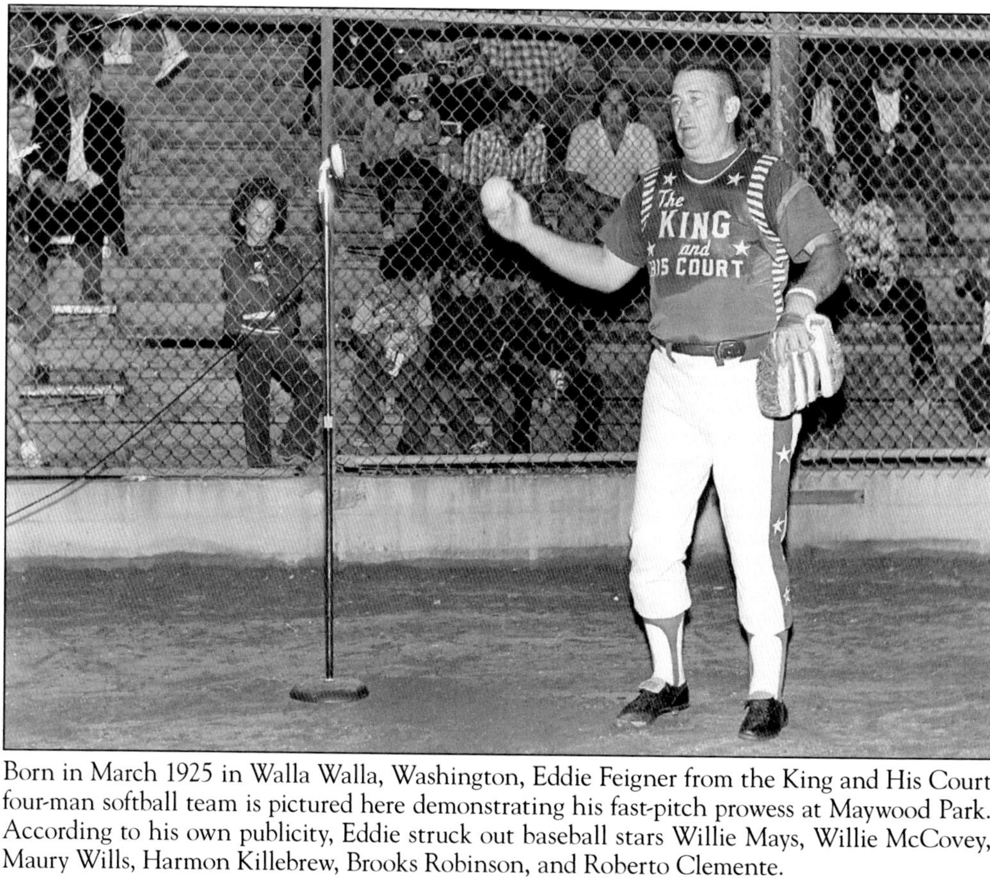

Born in March 1925 in Walla Walla, Washington, Eddie Feigner from the King and His Court four-man softball team is pictured here demonstrating his fast-pitch prowess at Maywood Park. According to his own publicity, Eddie struck out baseball stars Willie Mays, Willie McCovey, Maury Wills, Harmon Killebrew, Brooks Robinson, and Roberto Clemente.

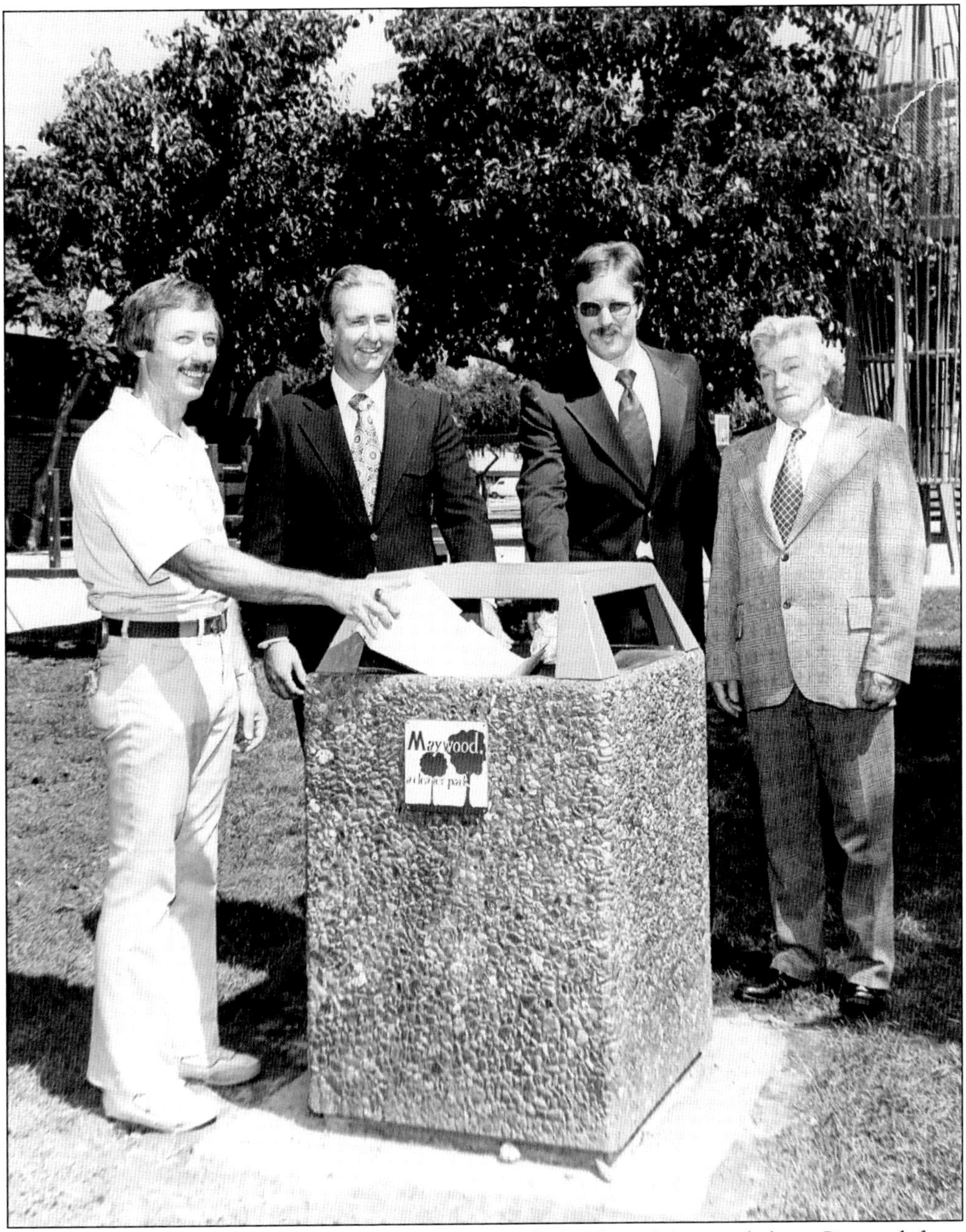

In September 1979, new trash receptacles were installed to keep Maywood clean. Pictured, from left to right, are recreation supervisor Vic Heintzman, Mayor James Awalt, city administrative officer Edward Ahrens, and councilman Ray Gallagher.

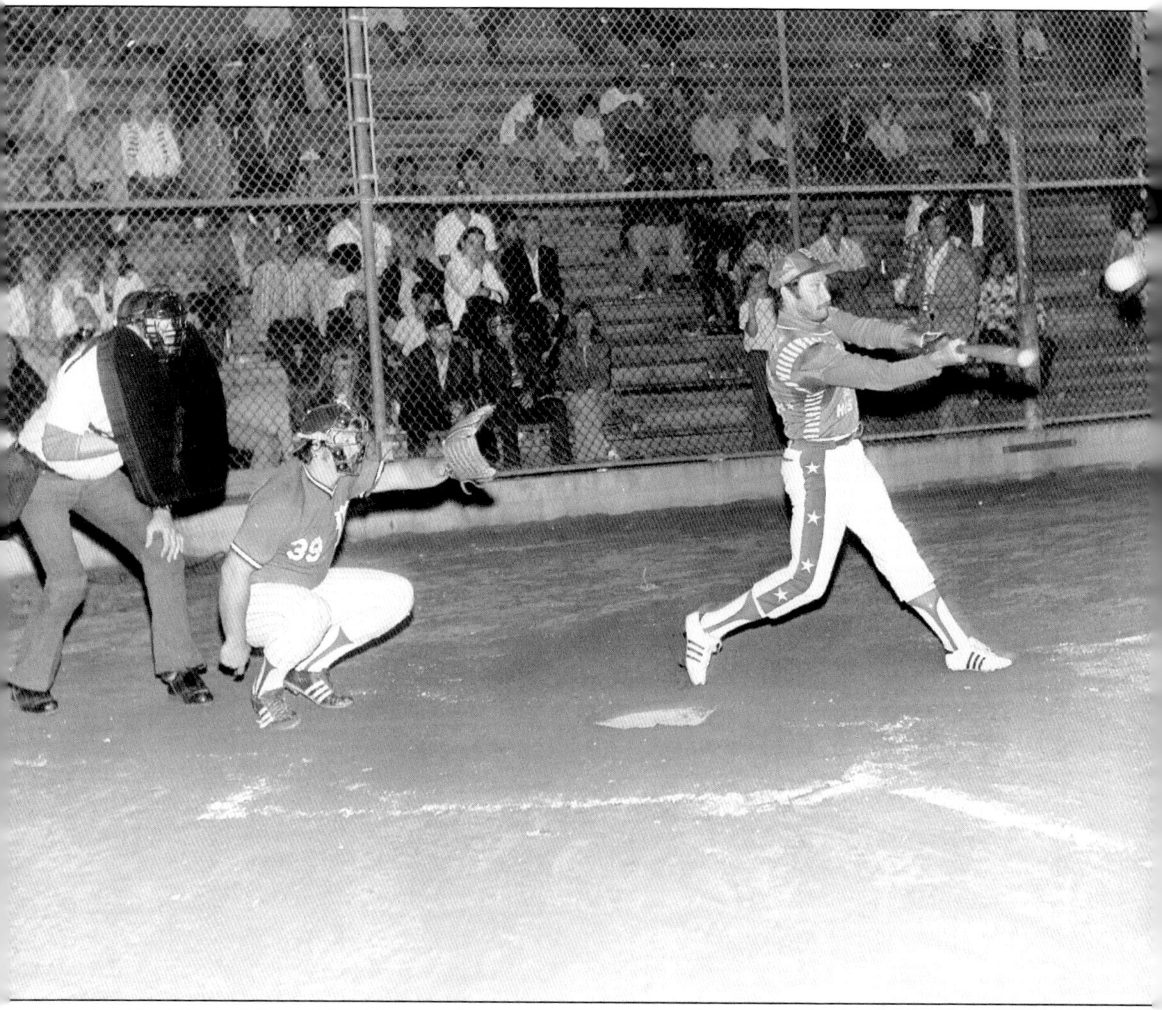

In 1977, Gary West of the King and his Court rips a hit at Maywood Park. The court performed twice in Maywood—1976 and 1977.

Seven

The 1980s

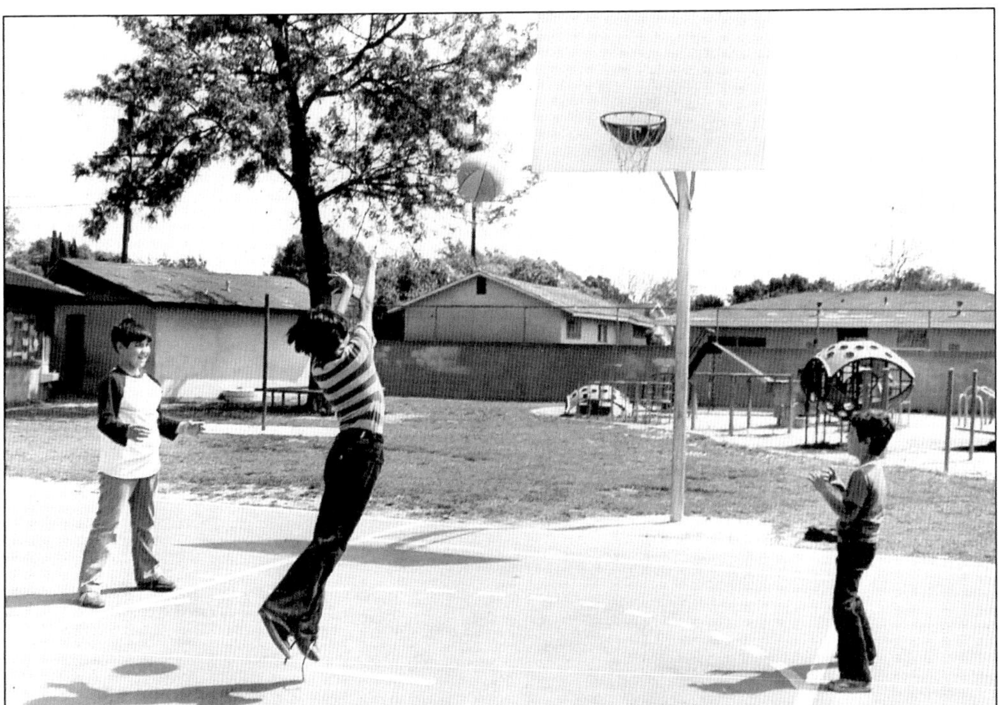

Youngsters play on the newly installed basketball court at Pixley Park.

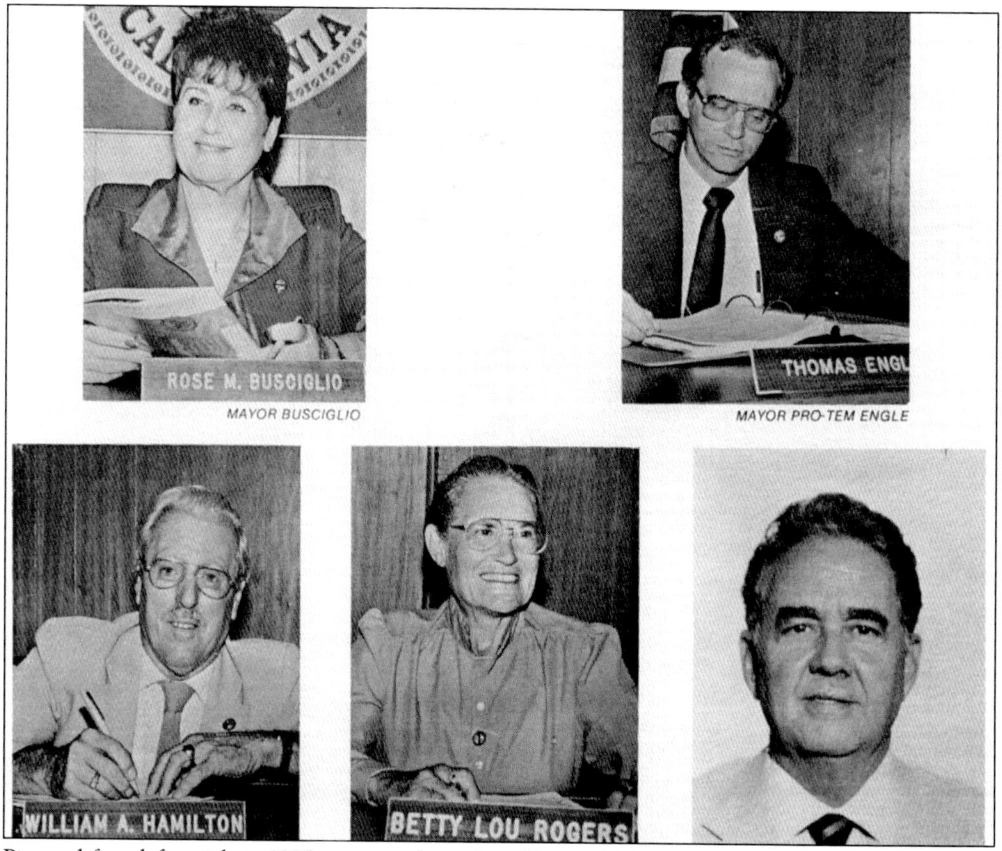

Pictured, from left to right in 1985, are council members (first row) Mayor Rose Busciglio and mayor pro tem Thomas Engle; (second row) William Hamilton, Betty Lou Rogers, and Henry Santiago.

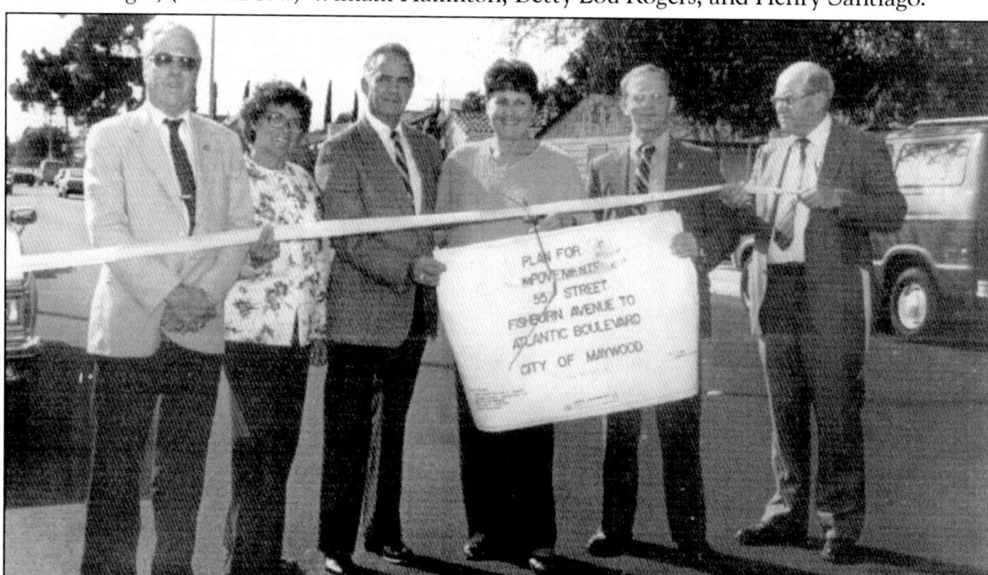

Pictured are council members and city administrative officer Leonard Locher, far right, celebrating the widening of Fifty-fifth Street in the mid-1980s.

This council, which directed Maywood's progress in the late 1980s, was comprised of William Hamilton, Rose Busciglio, Mayor Thomas Engle, Betty Lou Rogers, and Henry Santiago, all seated in the first row. Maywood Chamber of Commerce members and city attorney Cary Reisman, second from right, are standing.

CITY GOVERNMENT

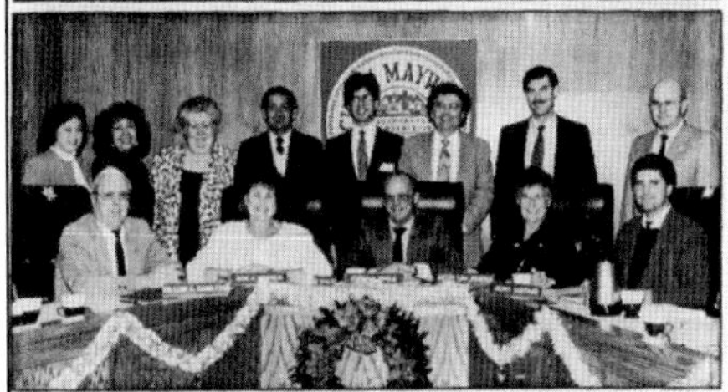

The City Council is comprised of (L to R), William Hamilton, Rose Busciglio, Mayor Thomas Engle, Betty Lou Rogers and Henry Santiago, who have directed Maywood's progress in recent years and look forward to the 90's.

Pictured standing are Maywood Chamber of Commerce members (L to R), Carmen Rivera, Director; Carmen Mirabal, Past Director; Claire Beard, Chamber Manager; Jorge Mansilla, Past Director, Manuel Chacon, President; Sig Freidman, Past-President; Cary Reisman, Maywood City Attorney; Leonard Locher, Chamber Director and CAO, City of Maywood.

CITY OF MAYWOOD

Incorporated September 2, 1924

Population - 24,576 estimated

MAYOR .... Thomas H. Engle
MAYOR PRO-TEM .... Henry Santiago Jr.
Council .... William Hamilton
Betty Lou Rogers
Rose Marie Busciglio

POLICE CHIEF .... Ted Heidke
CHIEF ADMINISTRATIVE OFFICER/
CITY CLERK .... Leonard R. Locher
CITY TREASURER .... Michael Williams
DIRECTOR OF BUILDING & PLANNING .... Ronald Lindsey
DIRECTOR OF COMMUNITY SERVICES .... Edward Ahrens
CITY ATTORNEY .... Cary Resiman
CITY ENGINEER .... Matt Binder

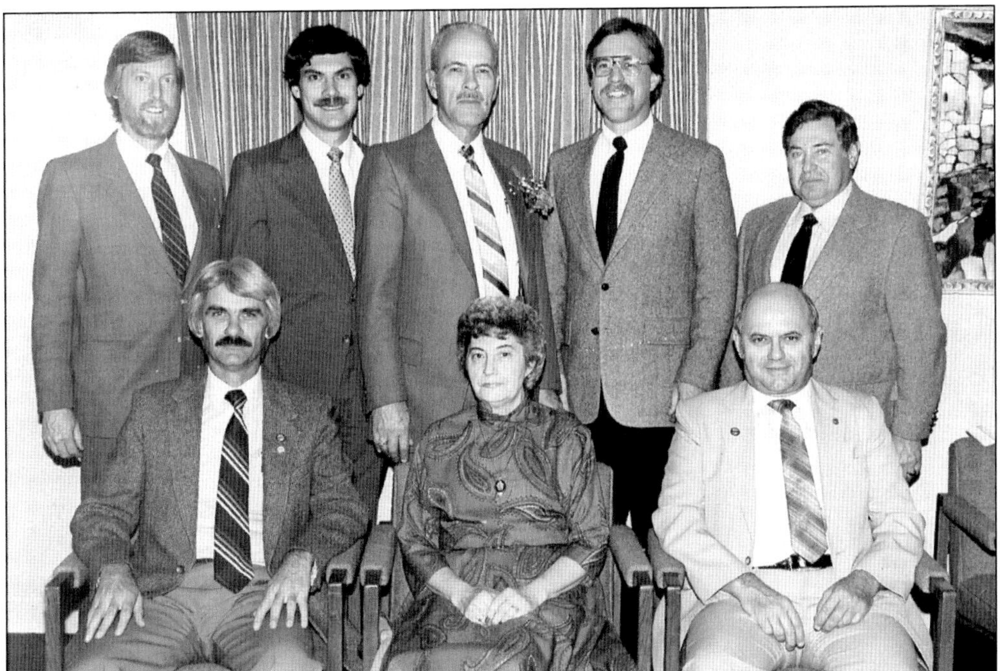

The city hall staff, pictured in the mid-1980s, from left to right, are (first row) Ron Lindsey, the director of the Building and Planning Department; city treasurer Ruth Hogrefe; and chief administrative officer Leonard Locher; (second row) city attorney Edward Dilkes; Cary Reisman, chief of police Ted Heidke; director of community services Edward Ahrens; and city engineer Matt Binder.

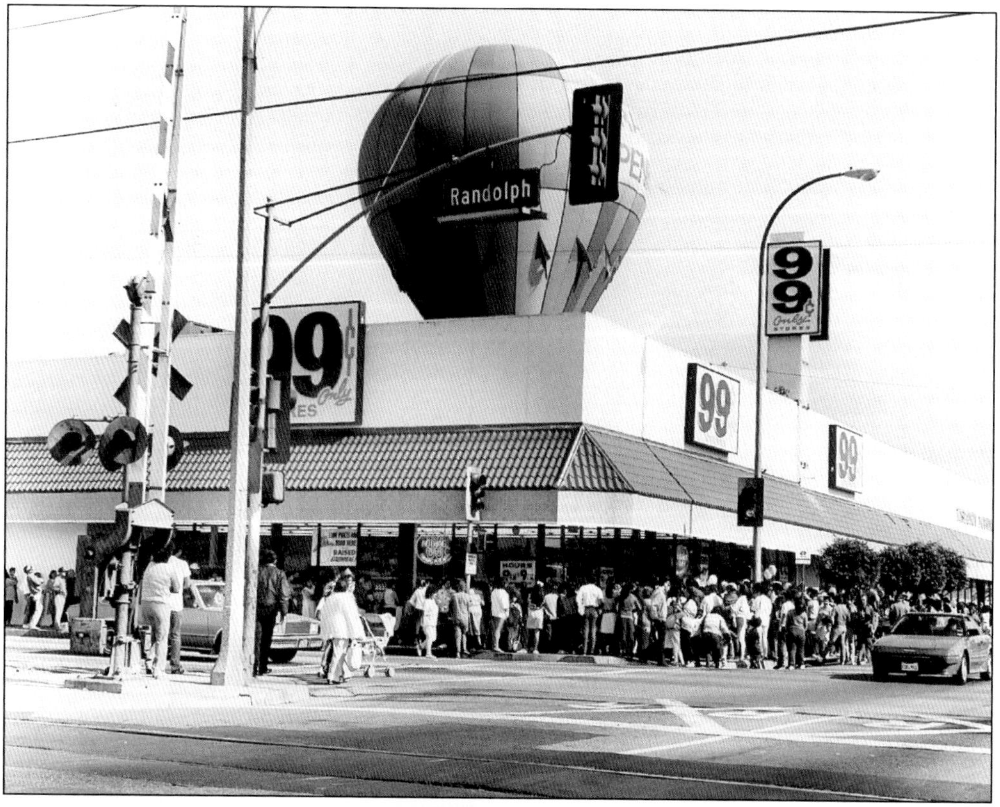

In May 1988, the grand opening of the 99¢ Store drew a huge crowd. The clientele overflowed on Atlantic Boulevard at Randolph.

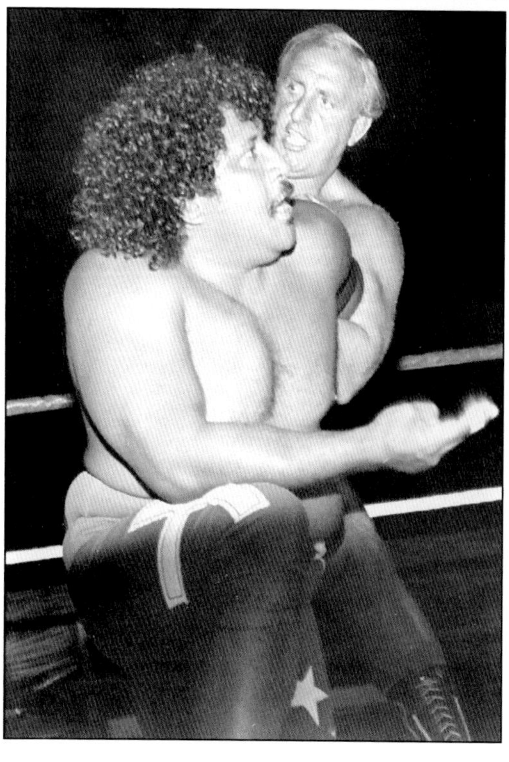

Professional wrestling has been a big draw in Maywood over the years, and these gentlemen would certainly tell you that it's a rough and very legitimate sport. Here Antonio Rocca works over the arm of Samoan Joe.

Pictured in 1986 is pro wrestler Handsome Harry with current Maywood chief of police Bruce Leflar on their way to the ring. As you can see, Harry understood that handsomeness was in the eye of the beholder, if the beholder, of course, was him.

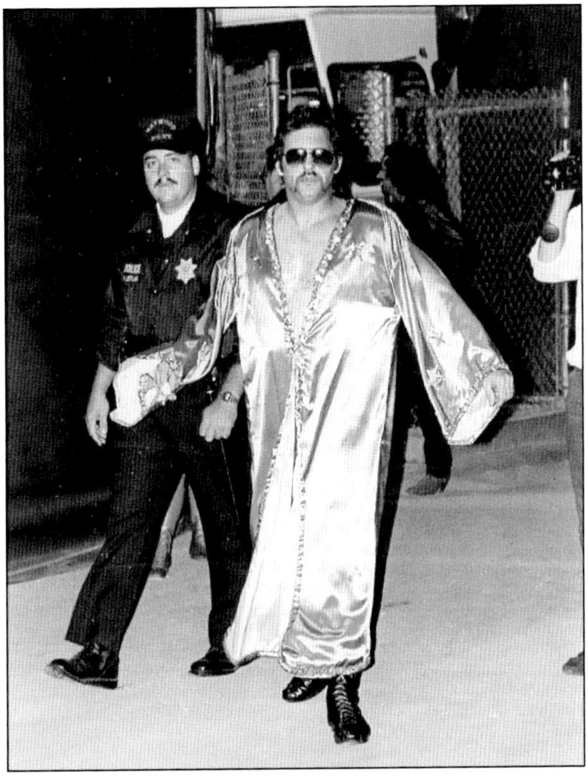

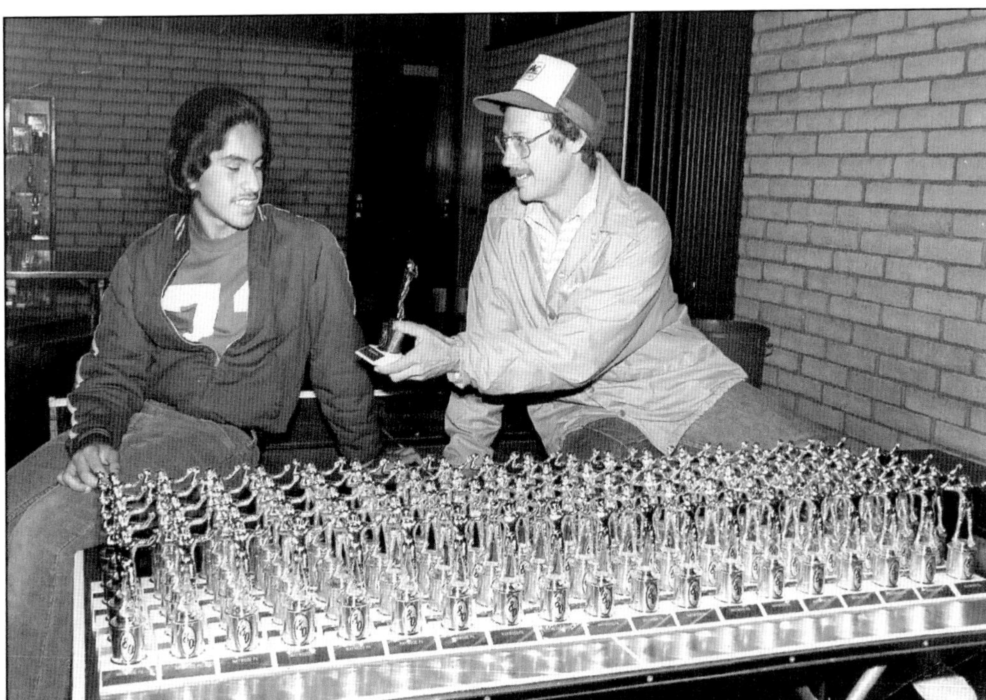

Recreation supervisor Vic Heintzman sits amid a treasure trove of trophies that he presented to deserving gridiron players.

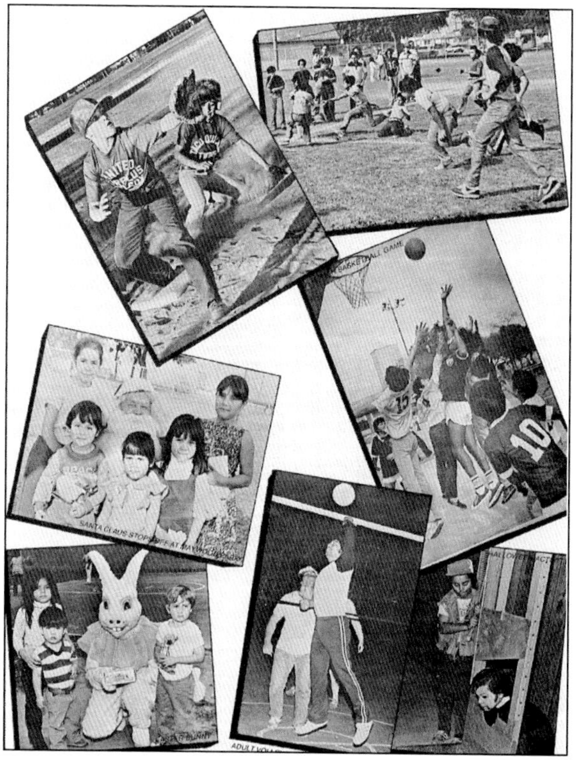

Some of the events and activities offered at Maywood Park include baseball, basketball, and volleyball. Activities for the smaller kids to enjoy during such holidays as Easter and Halloween are also offered.

The 1987 tri-cities parade and its ancillary events involved this foursome, from left to right, Pete Parra, Edward Ahrens, Mike Henry, and Ron Lindsey. Henry was a Bell High School graduate who played linebacker for the USC Trojans, then six years in the National Football League for the Pittsburgh Steelers and Los Angeles Rams. Henry and Jackie Gleason costarred as inept lawmen chasing Burt Reynolds in the *Smokey and the Bandit* movies.

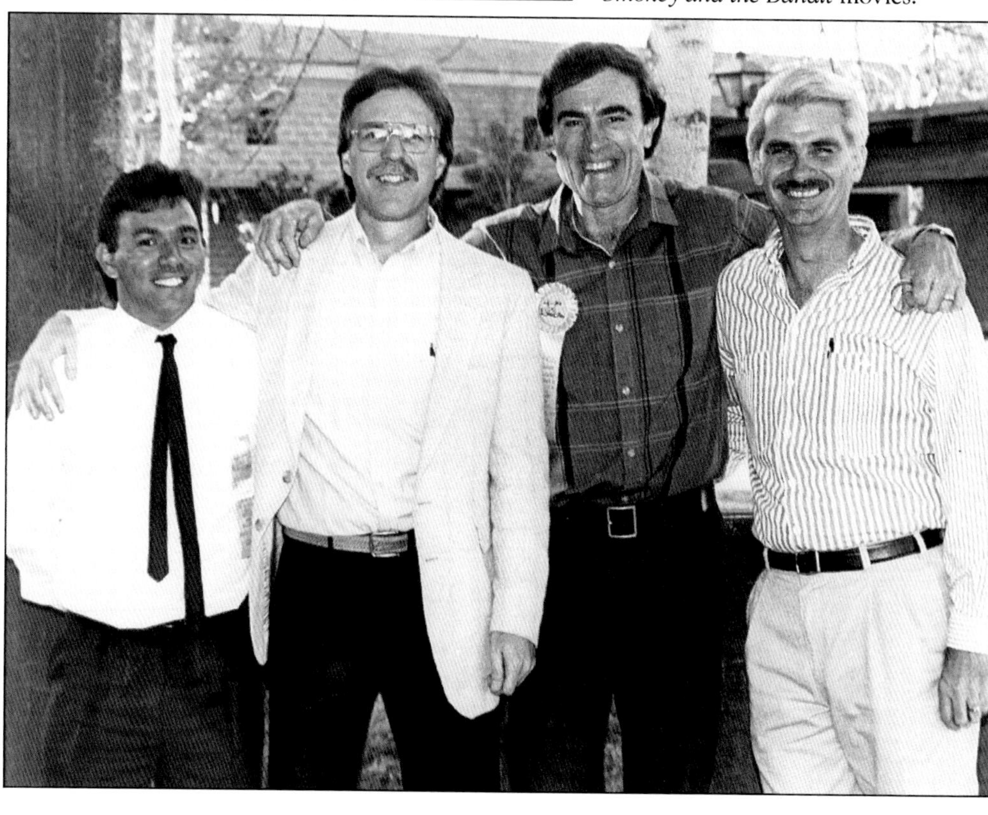

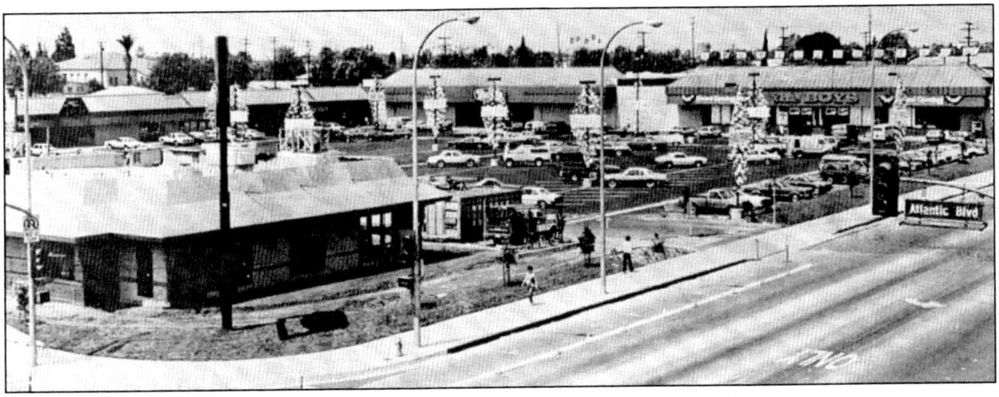

The opening of the Maywood Towne Center took place in August 1985.

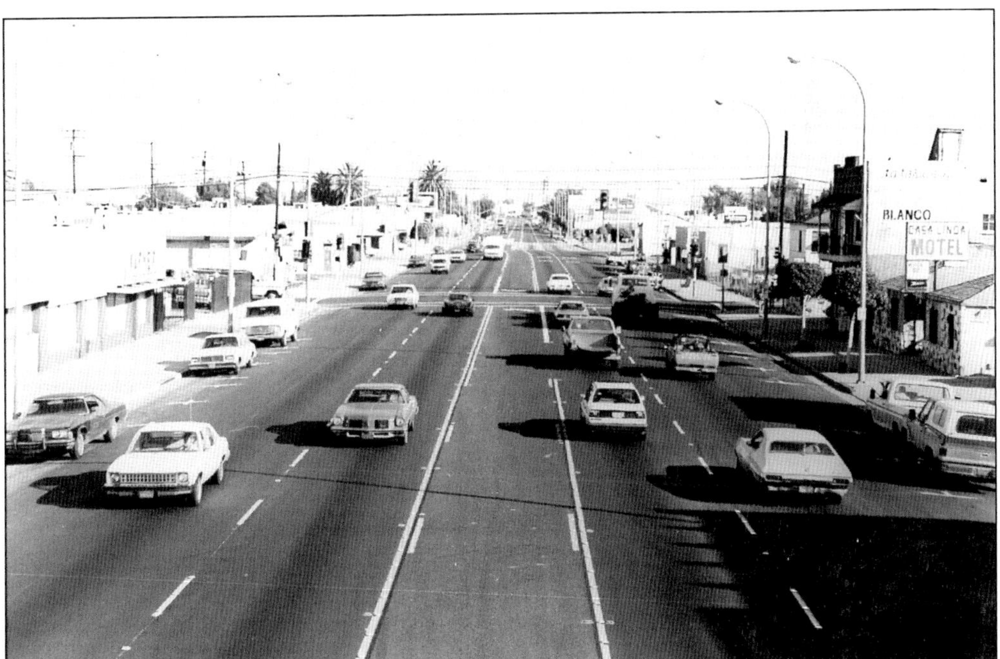

This December 1986 view looks east at Slauson Avenue after its resurfacing.

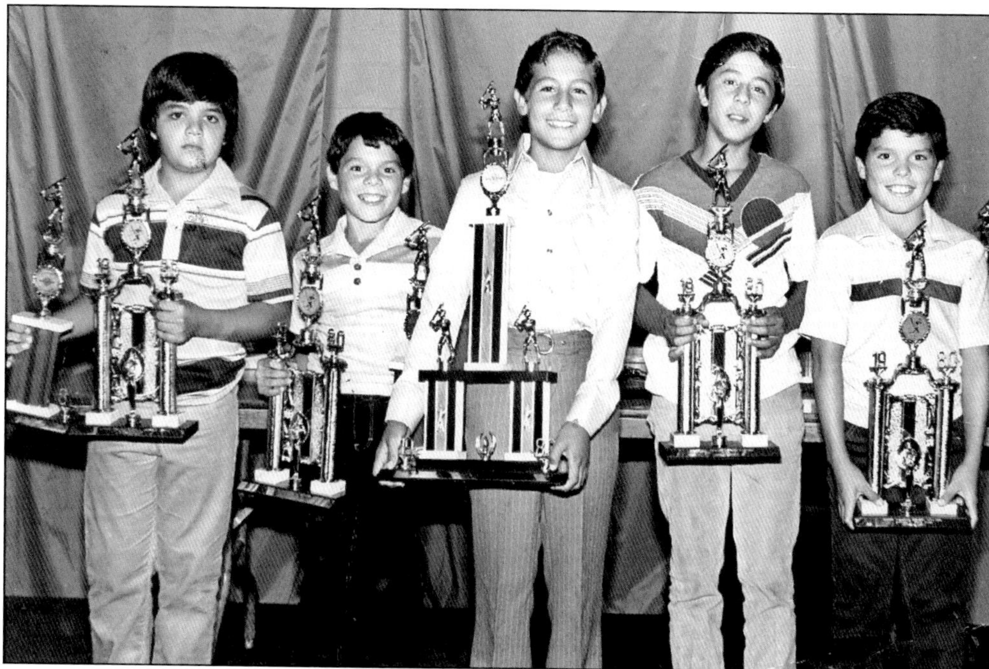

Pictured, from left to right, these triumphant Golden State baseball players from the 1980 season are Gus Mungaray, Mark Alvarez, Bobby Magallanes, Mauricio Montoya, and Manny Alvarez. Magallanes played minor league baseball and is currently a manager in the Los Angeles Angels organization.

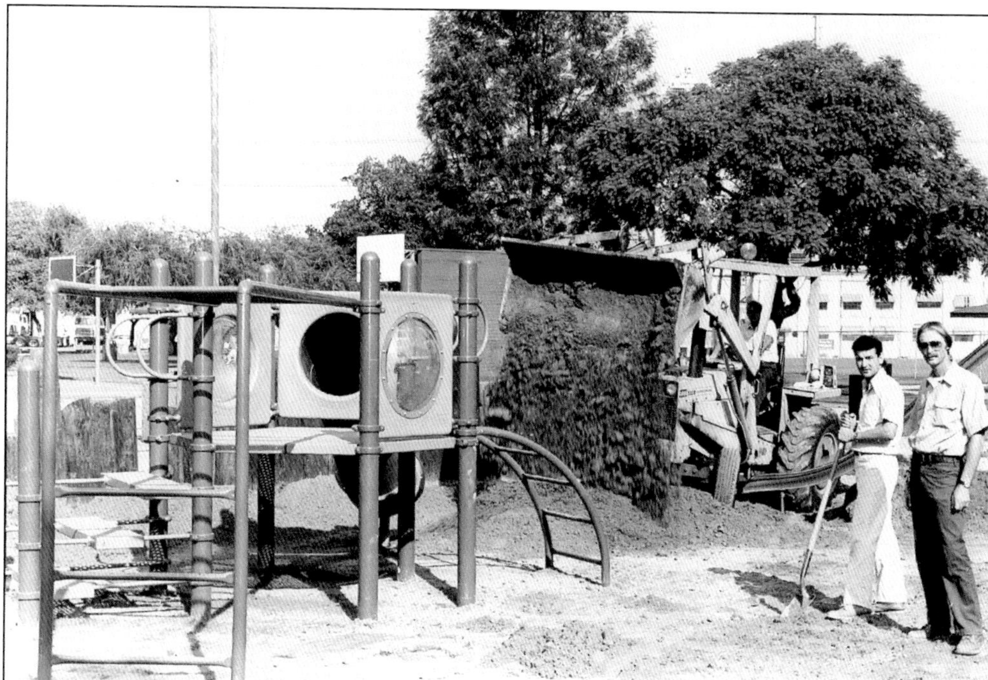

A new playground is being installed at Maywood Park. Standing at the far right is Brad McDade, who was a city employee at that time.

At a carnival in Maywood Park, several kids are very intent on a ring-toss game involving empty soda bottles. The girl on the right holds both the rings to toss and the tickets to get more.

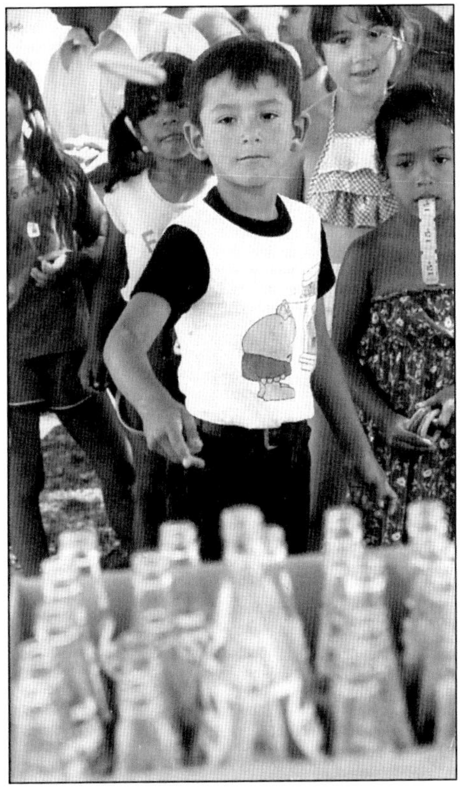

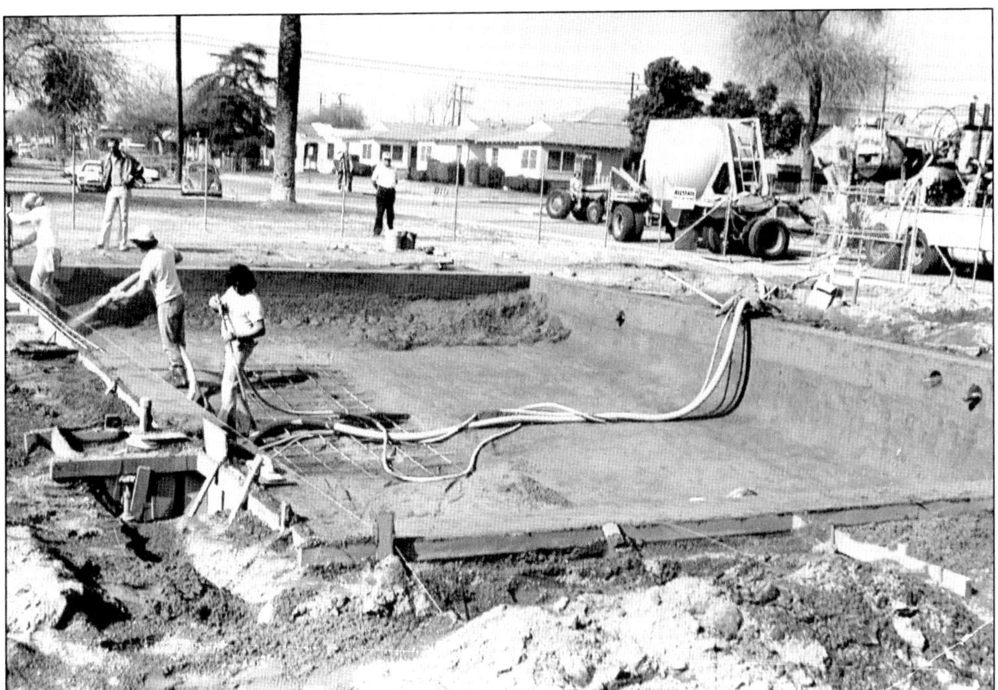

This photograph depicts the construction of what became a summertime necessity to some—the Maywood Swimming Pool.

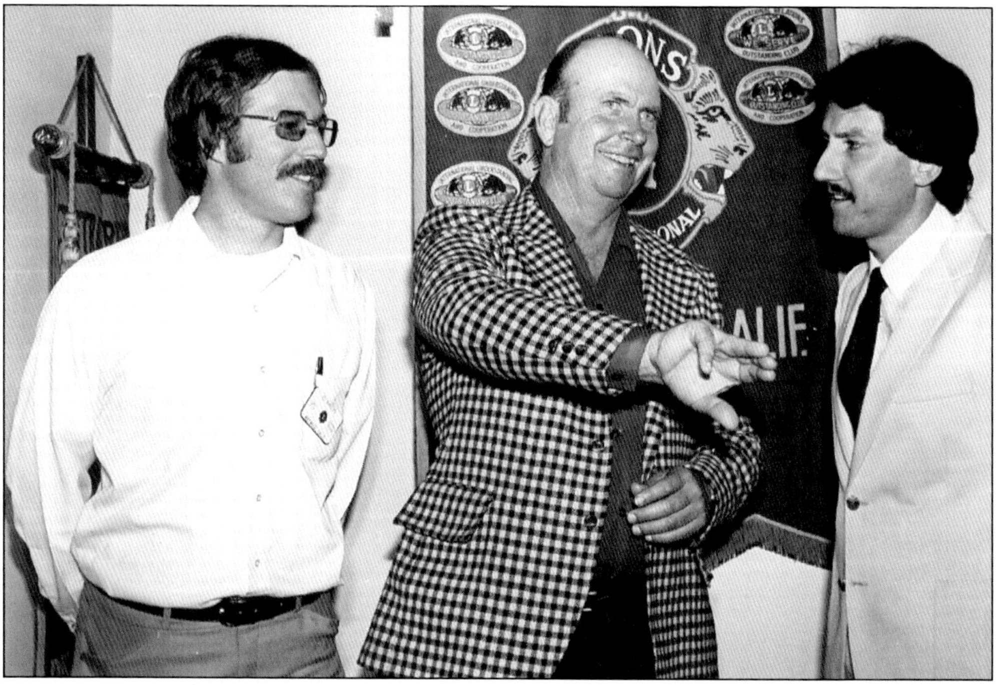

In 1982, Maywood official Edward Ahrens, left, and Dr. Al Najera watch a brief demonstration of pitching form by former Los Angeles Dodgers pitcher Ed Palmquist. Palmquist, a Los Angeles native who closed out his major league career with the Minnesota Twins, also appeared at the 1967 opening day ceremony for Maywood's baseball program.

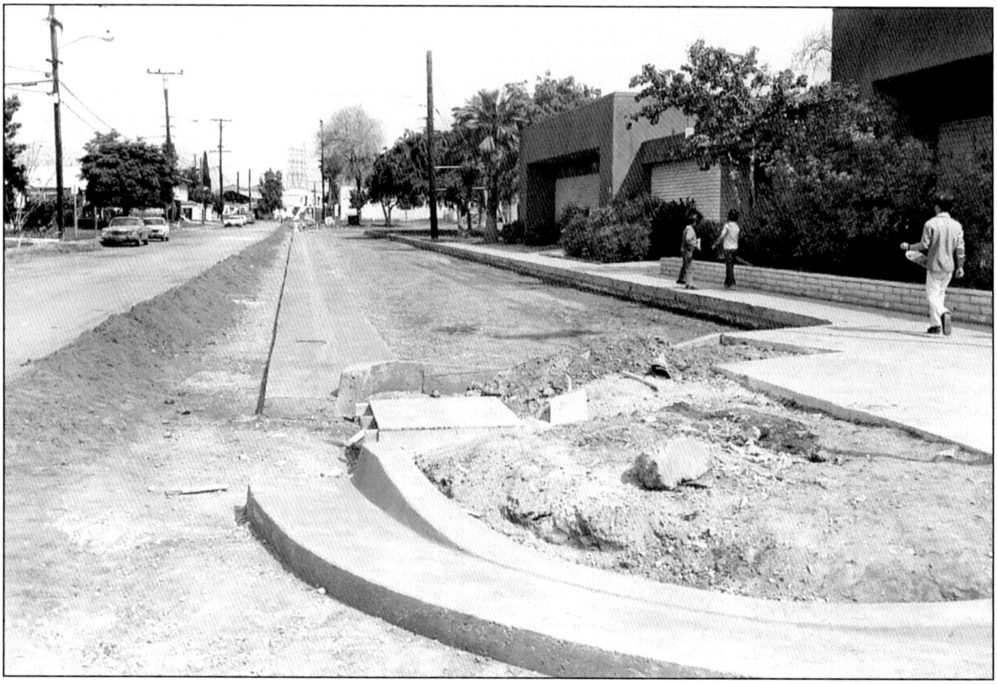

The widening of Heliotrope Avenue became necessary to handle the 1980s traffic and parking needs at Maywood Park.

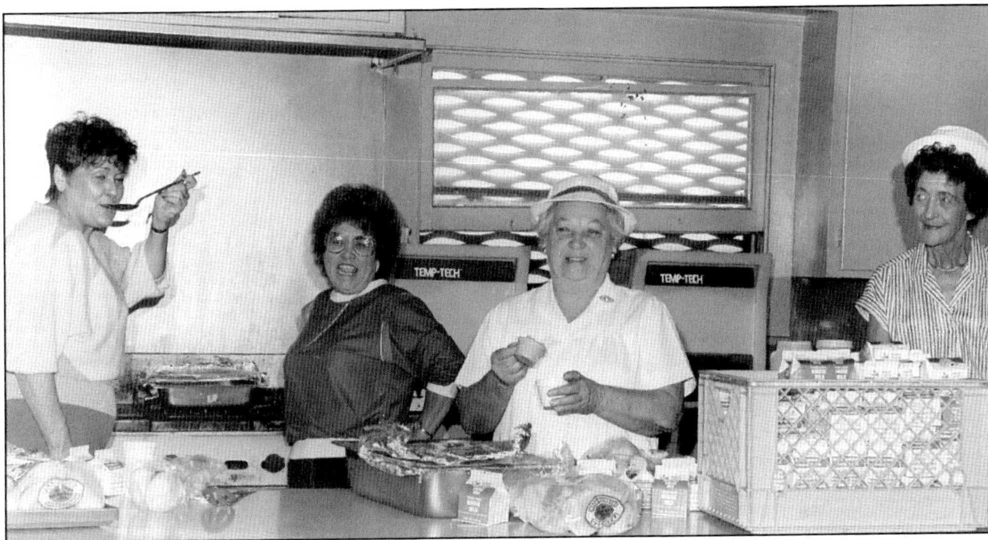

Maywood mayor Rose Busciglio, far left, tastes the victuals in the Maywood Park kitchen. Mickey Otero, the site manager (in white) and Frances McDade, far right, seem to expect mayoral approval.

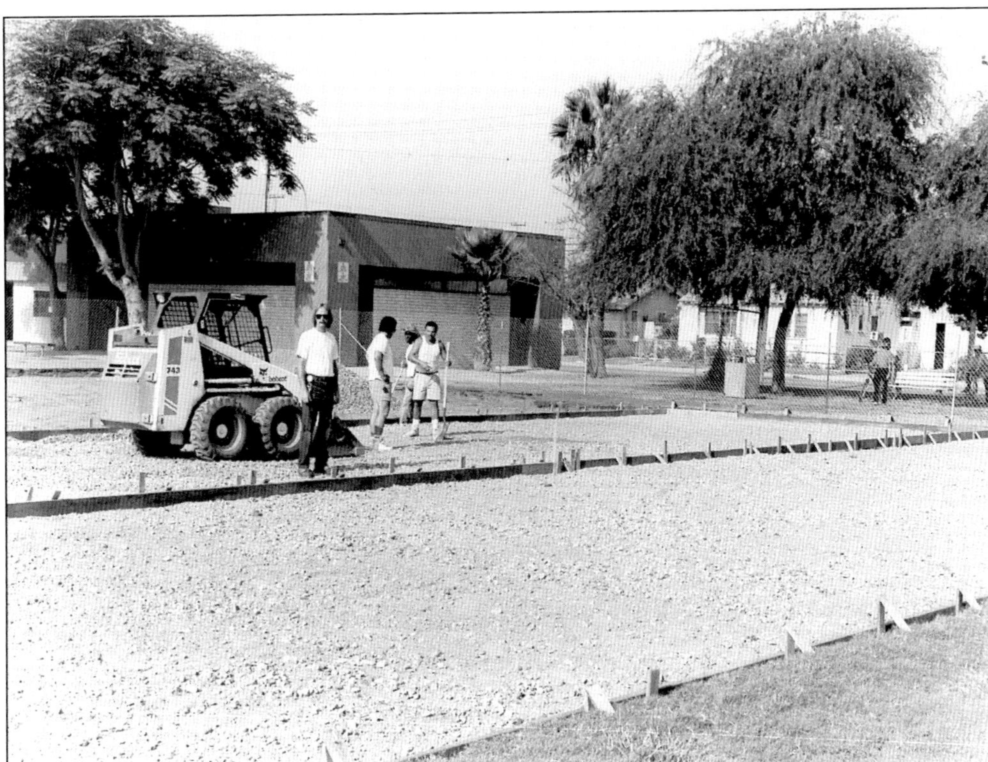

Construction is underway for the new basketball court at Maywood City Park in the mid-1980s. Current city employee Brad McDade is looking toward camera.

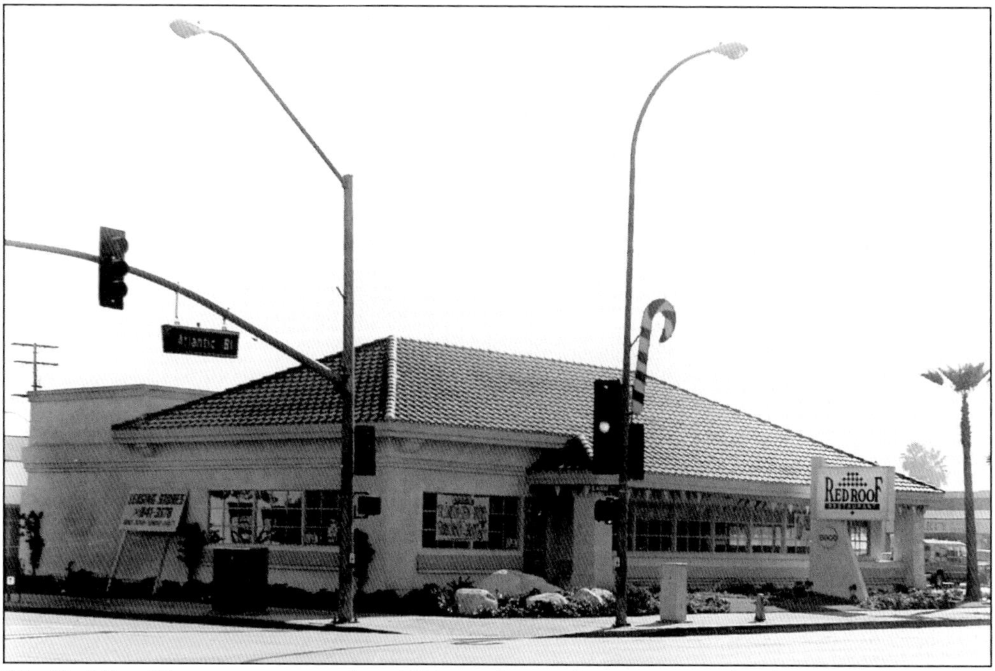

The Red Roof Restaurant opened in 1989 on the southeast corner of Atlantic Boulevard and Slauson Avenue.

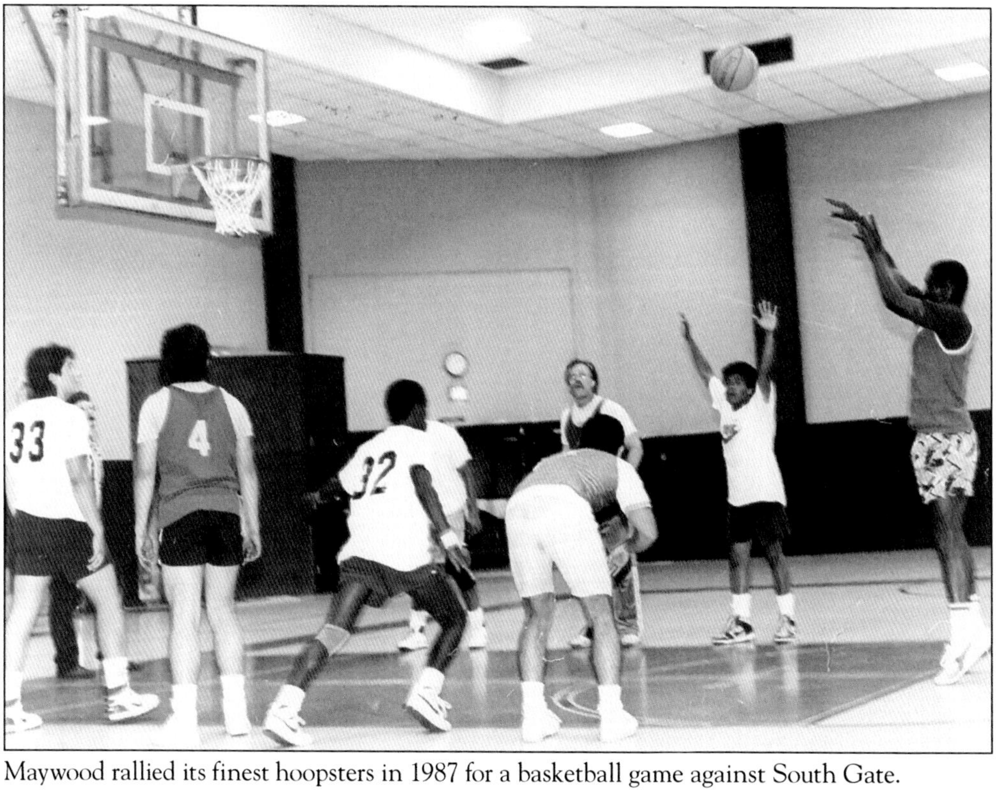

Maywood rallied its finest hoopsters in 1987 for a basketball game against South Gate.

Eight

The 1990s

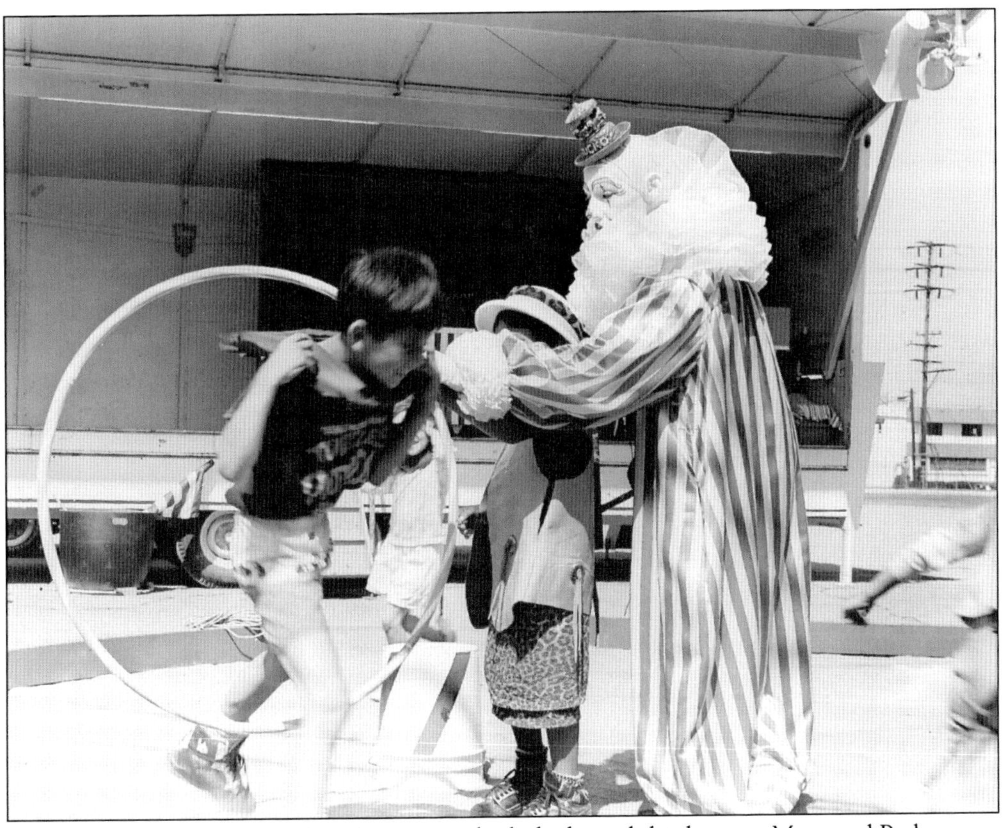

In the early 1990s, Chucko the Clown runs the kids through his hoop at Maywood Park.

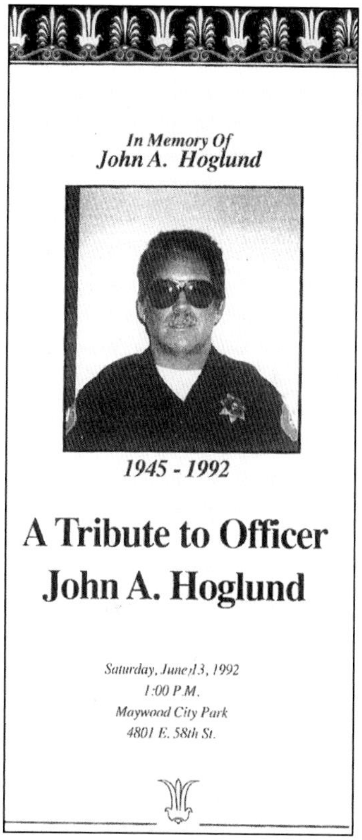

Maywood police officer John Hoglund was shot and killed in the line of duty on May 29, 1992, when he responded to a silent alarm and encountered five armed men fleeing a neighborhood market. His June 4 burial followed a funeral service in Downey's Calvary Chapel, attended by Los Angeles police chief Daryl Gates, Los Angeles County sheriff Sherman Block, and district attorney Ira Reiner. More than 2,500 mourners, including many police officers from across the state, attended. A tribute to Officer Hoglund was held on June 13.

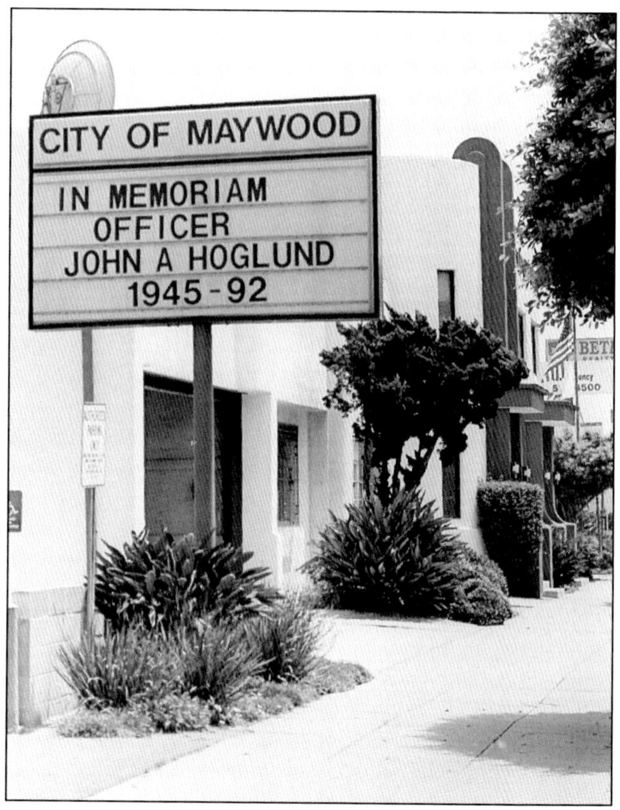

The message board at Maywood City Hall recognizes fallen officer John Hoglund.

Maywood City Council members in 1990 included, from left to right, (first row) Thomas Engle and Henry Santiago Jr.; (second row) William Hamilton; (third row) Rose Marie Busciglia and Betty Lou Rogers.

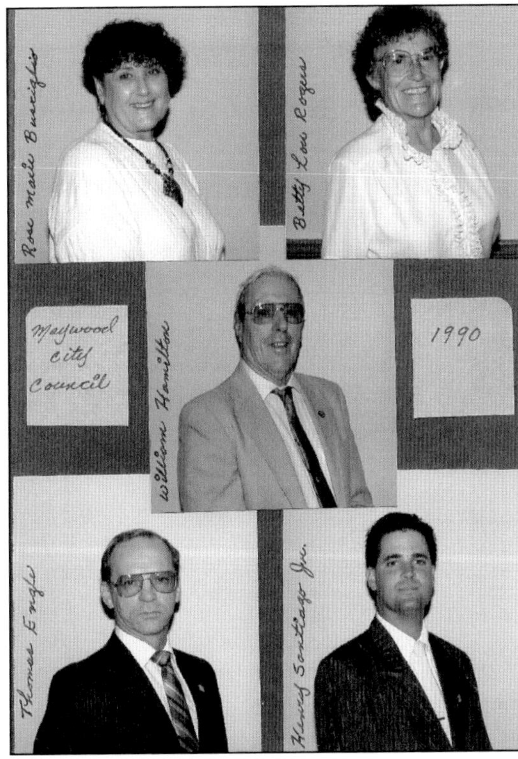

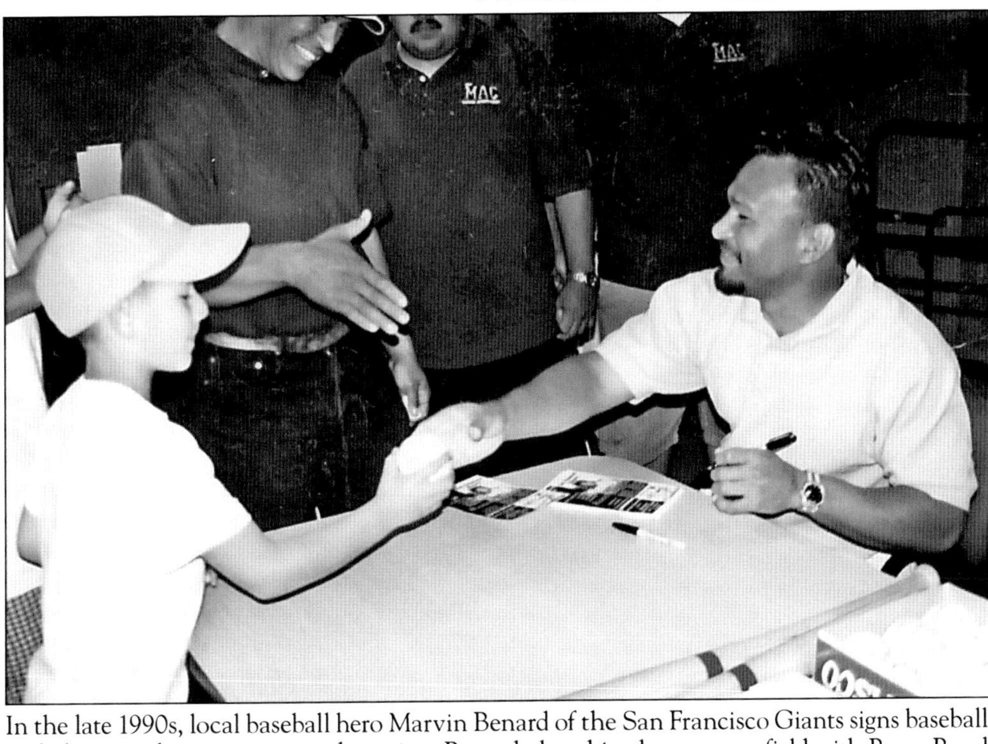

In the late 1990s, local baseball hero Marvin Benard of the San Francisco Giants signs baseballs and photographs at an autograph session. Benard played in the same outfield with Barry Bonds and had his finest season in 1999 when he hit .290, scored 100 runs, and clouted 36 doubles.

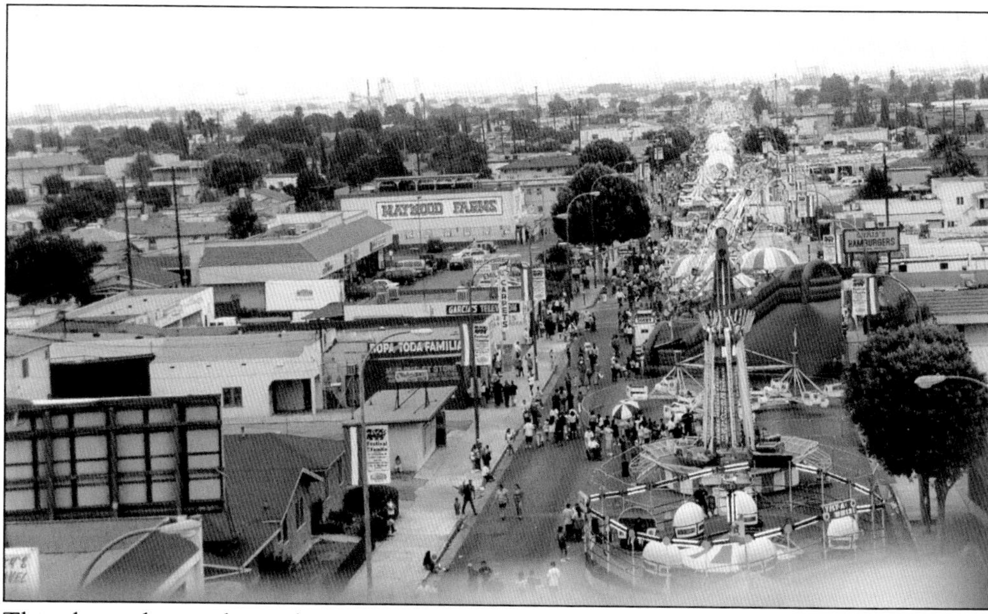

This elevated view shows the annual Maywood Street Fair. Note the Maywood Farms sign on the yellow building, center left, a throwback touchstone to the days when Maywood truly was farmland.

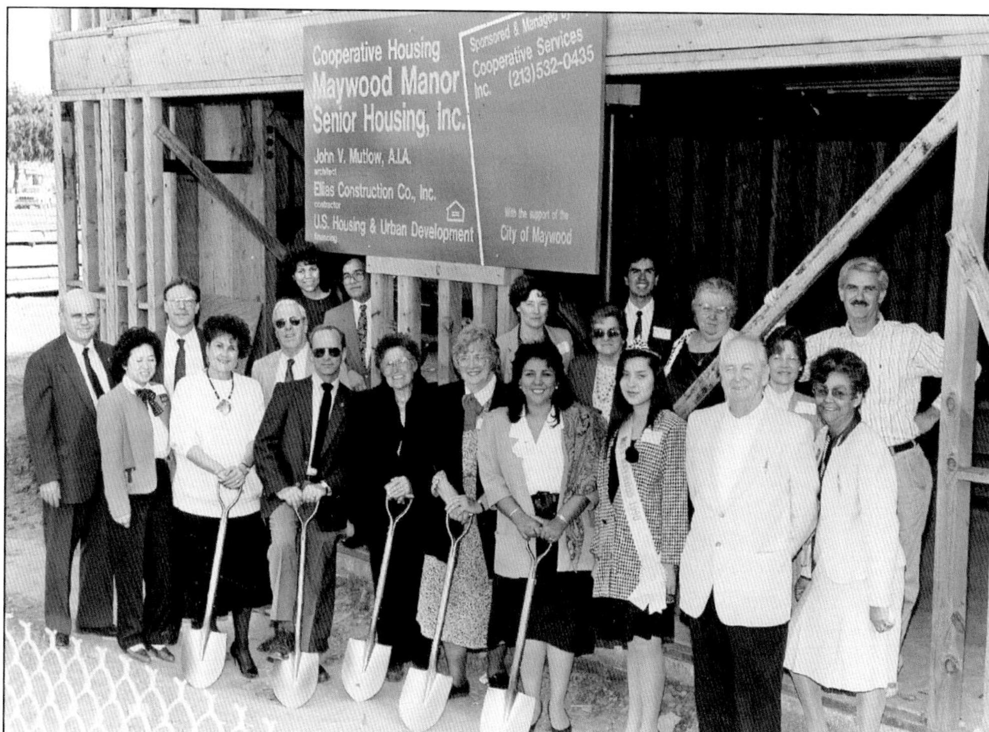

Maywood Manor Senior Housing building is under construction. This 1990s shot includes council members Rose Busciglio, Betty Lou Rogers, Thomas Engle, William Hamilton, chief administrative officer Leonard Locher, and Ron Lindsey, director of Building and Planning.

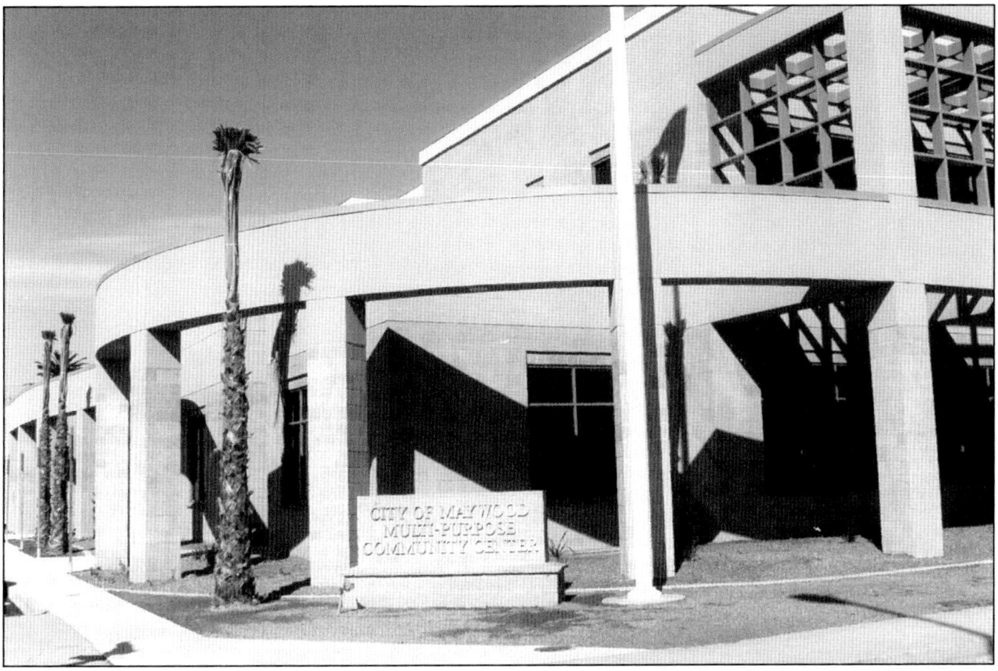

The Maywood Multi-Purpose Community Center was completed in 1999, adjacent to Maywood Park.

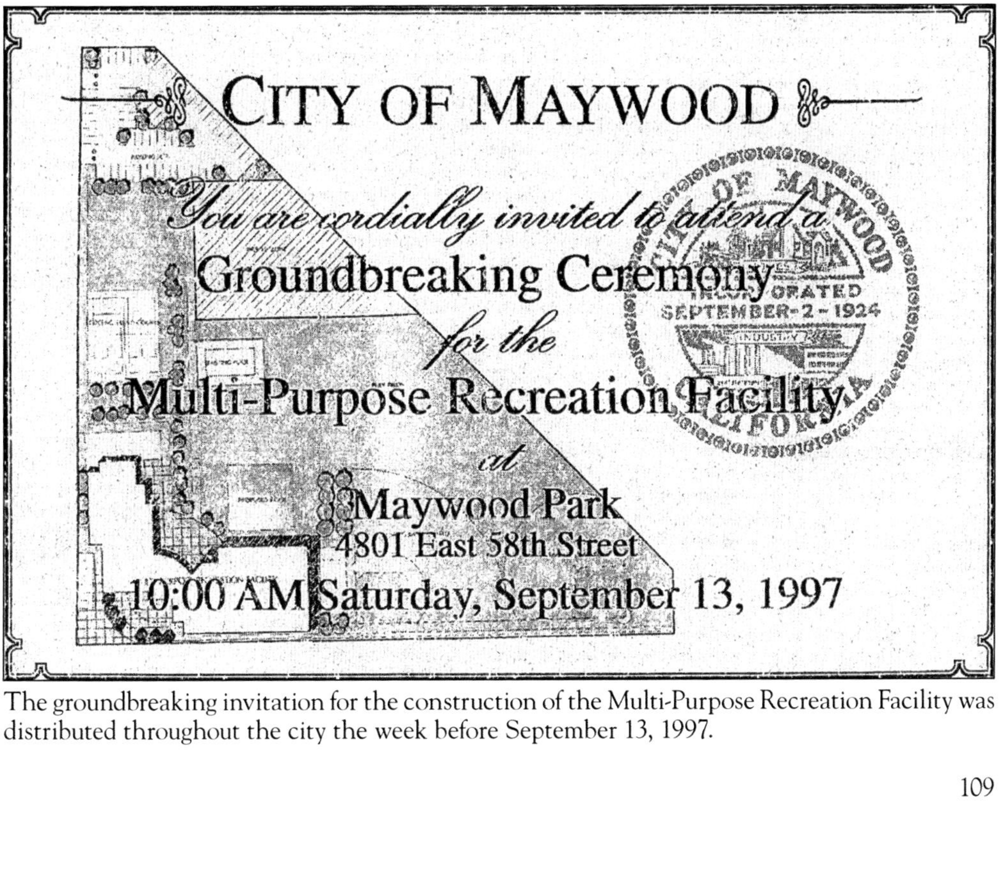

The groundbreaking invitation for the construction of the Multi-Purpose Recreation Facility was distributed throughout the city the week before September 13, 1997.

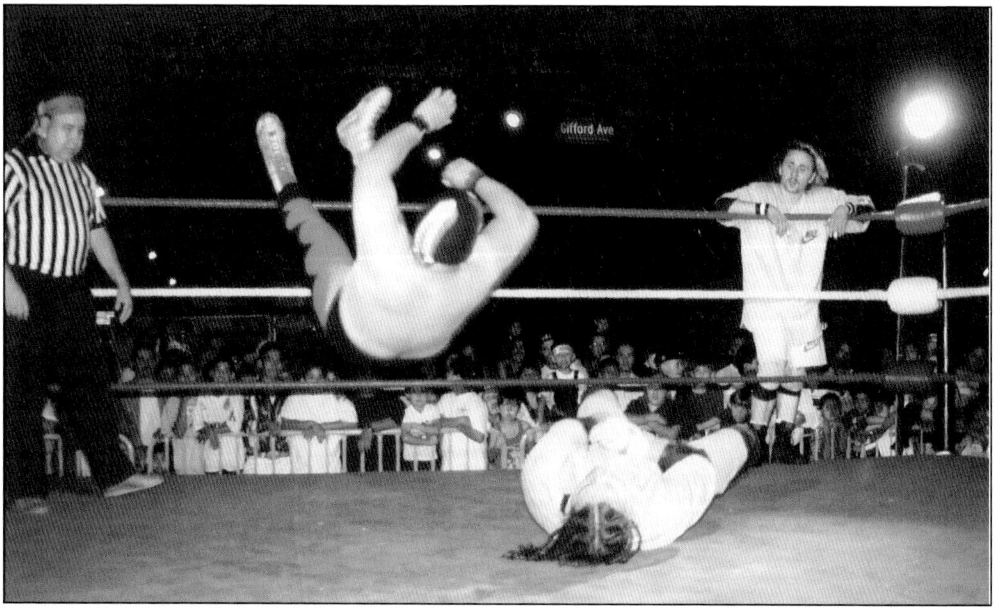

Pro wrestling is nothing if not filled with acts of gravity-defying mayhem by very large individuals. This 1997 match was held during the Maywood Street Fair.

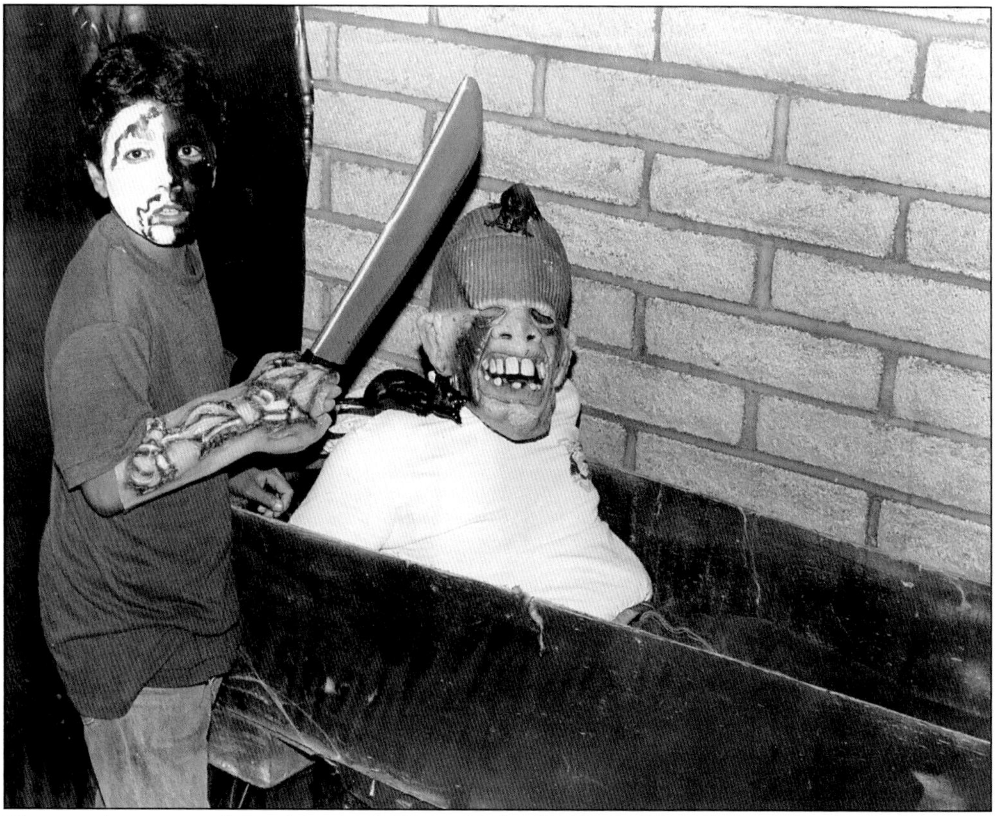

The gentleman on the right is in bad need of a dentist and a vermin exterminator during Halloween 1996.

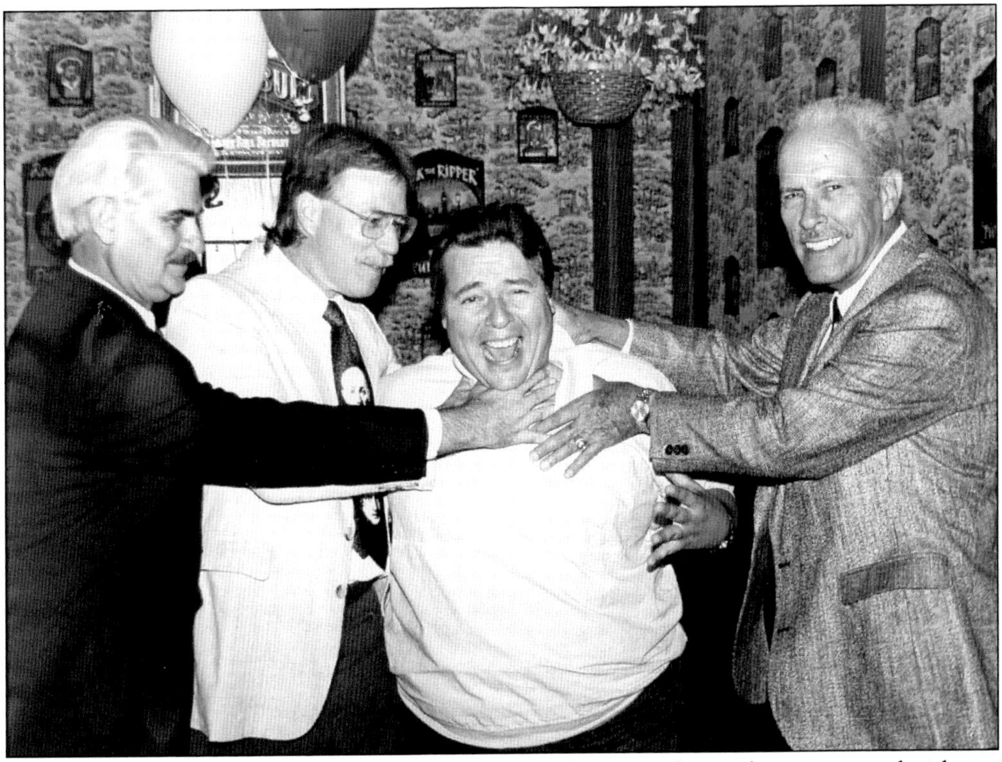

Pro wrestler Bubba Storm gets all choked up at a City of Maywood event horsing around with city officials, from left to right, Ron Lindsey, Ed Ahrens, and the late chief of police Ted Heidke.

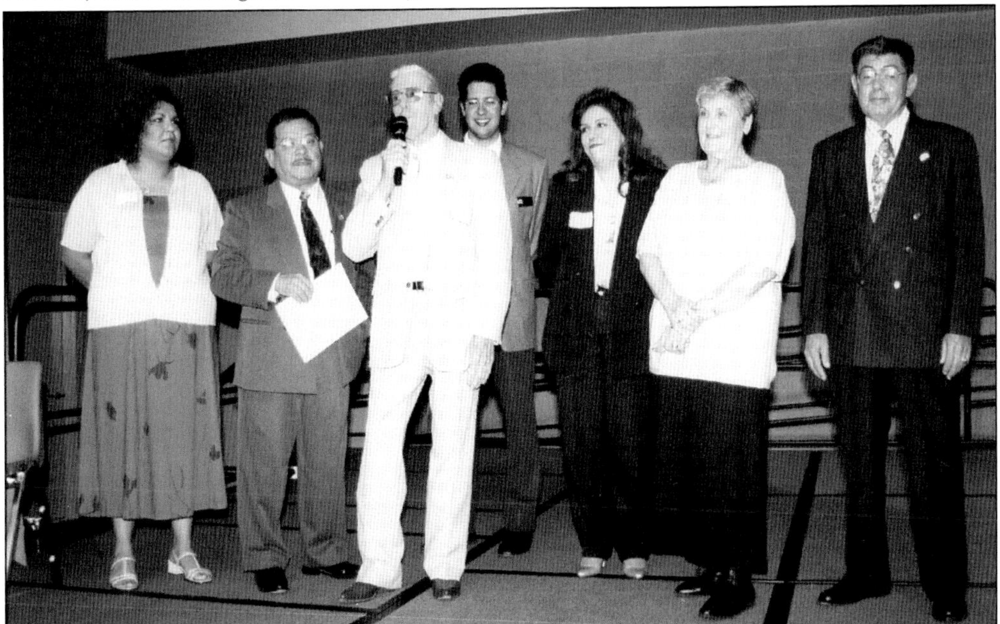

At the dedication of the multi-purpose building, councilman William Hamilton says a few words. Included here, from left to right, are Elvira Moreno-Guzman, Salvador Contreras, Hamilton, Thomas Martin, Dorothy Ramirez, Rose Busciglio, and Tomas Martin.

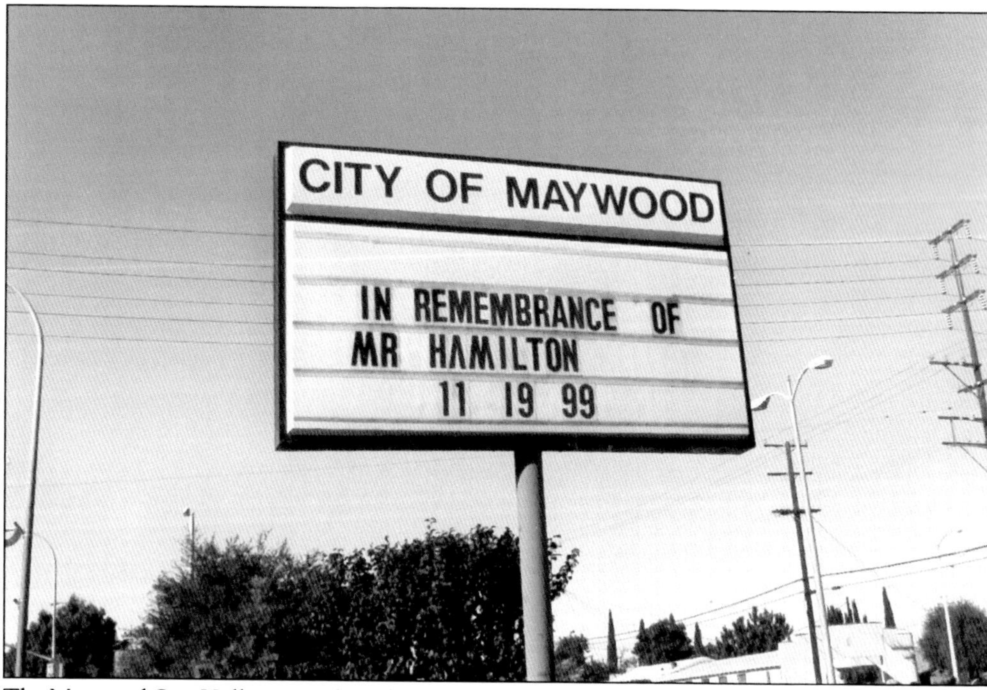

The Maywood City Hall message board recognizes the passing of former mayor and city councilman William Hamilton, who served the city for 21 years.

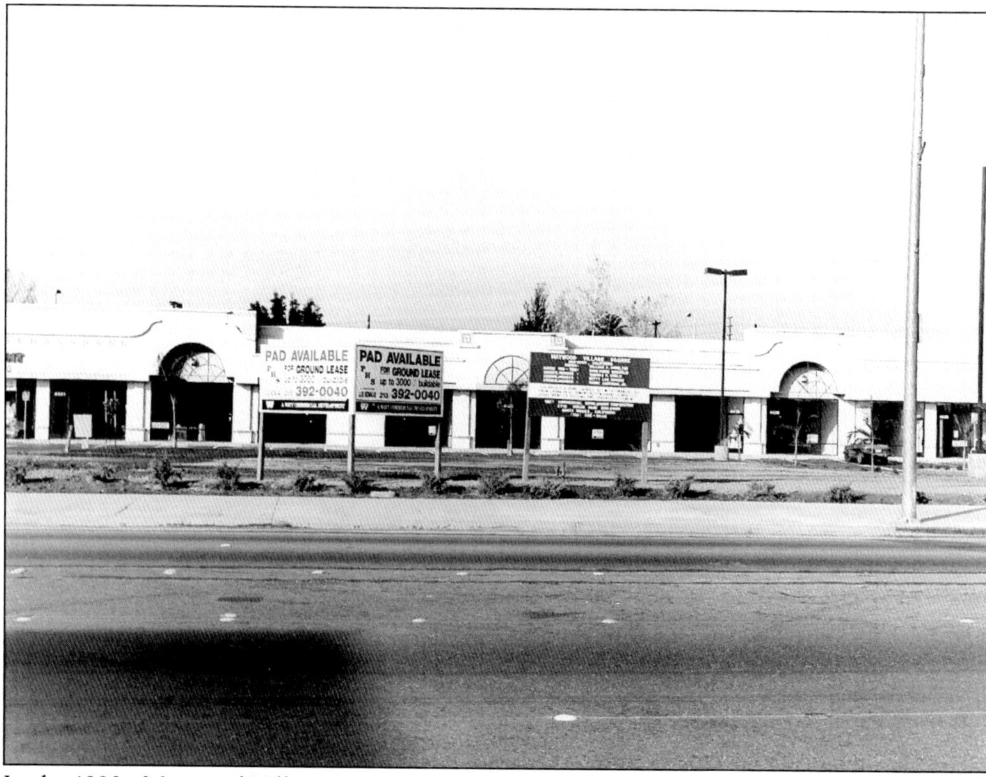

In the 1990s, Maywood Village Square opened for business.

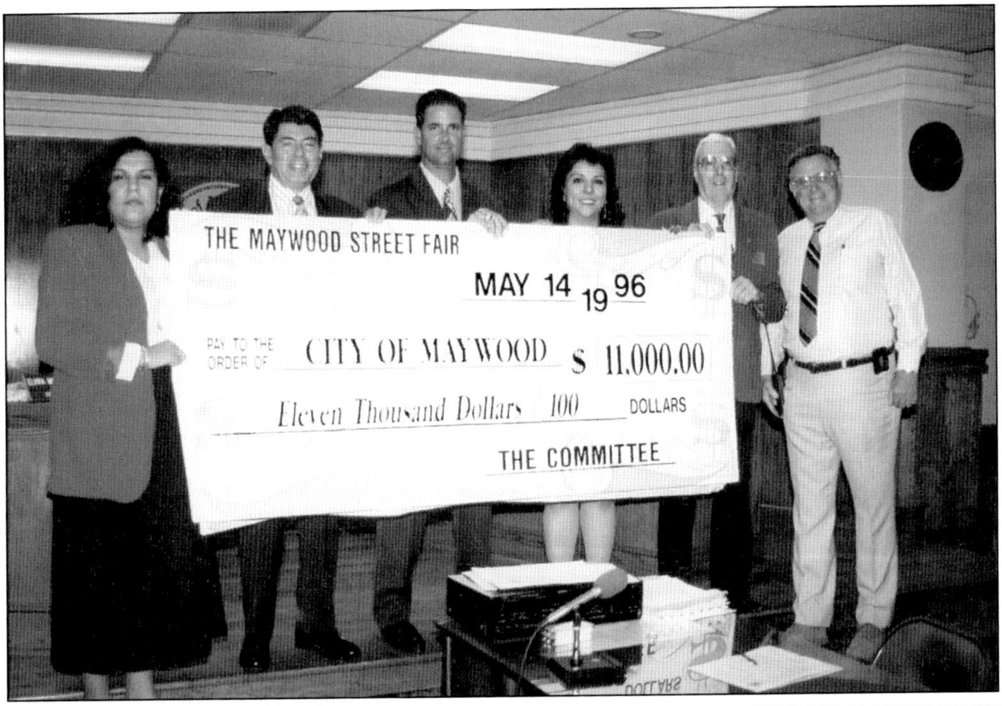

A big check was received by the City of Maywood from the 1996 Street Fair. At the presentation, from left to right, are Elvira Moreno-Guzman, Tomas Martin, Henry Santiago Jr., Dorothy Ramirez, William Hamilton, and Bill Lomas of Pageantry Productions.

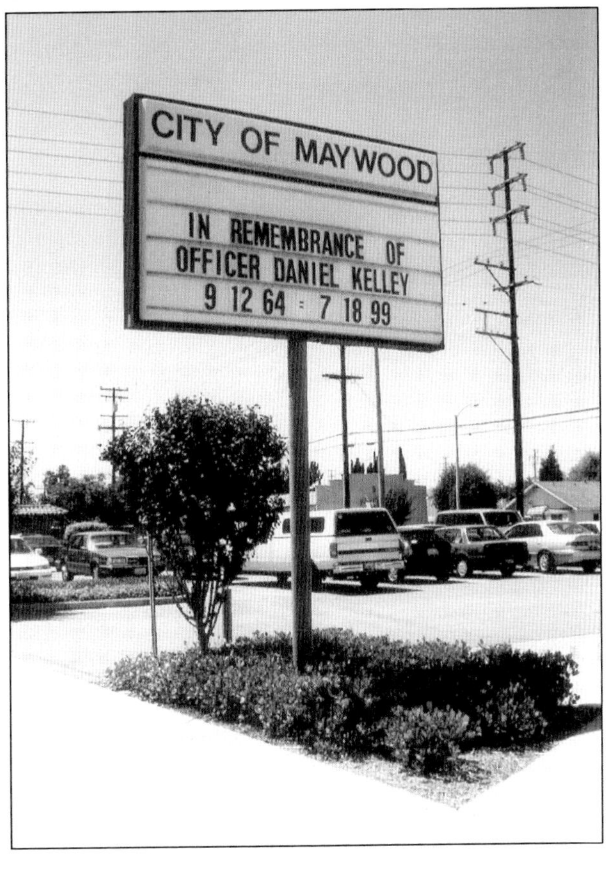

The Maywood City Hall message board commemorates the second Maywood police officer to die in the line of duty in the 1990s. Motorcycle officer Daniel Kelley succumbed on July 18, 1999, to injuries he sustained in an on-duty traffic accident.

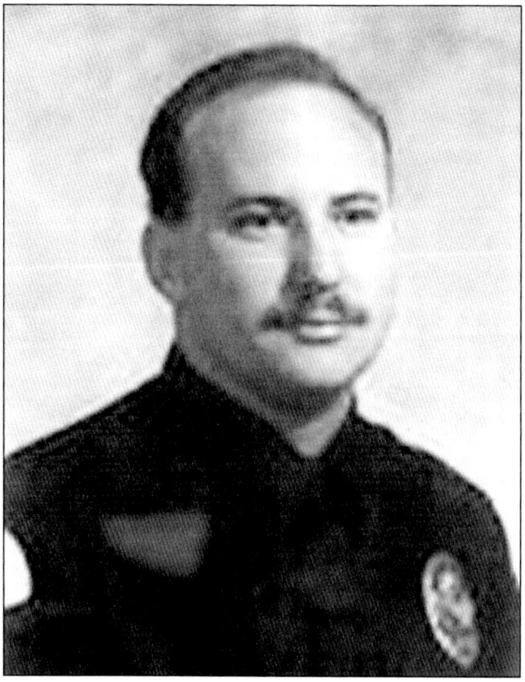

Maywood police officer Daniel Kelley died on July 18, 1999, of injuries sustained in an on-duty traffic accident 10 days earlier. He was the third officer to be killed in the line of duty in Maywood. Kelley had previously served with the Riverside and Orange County Sherriff's Departments and the Los Alamitos Police Department.

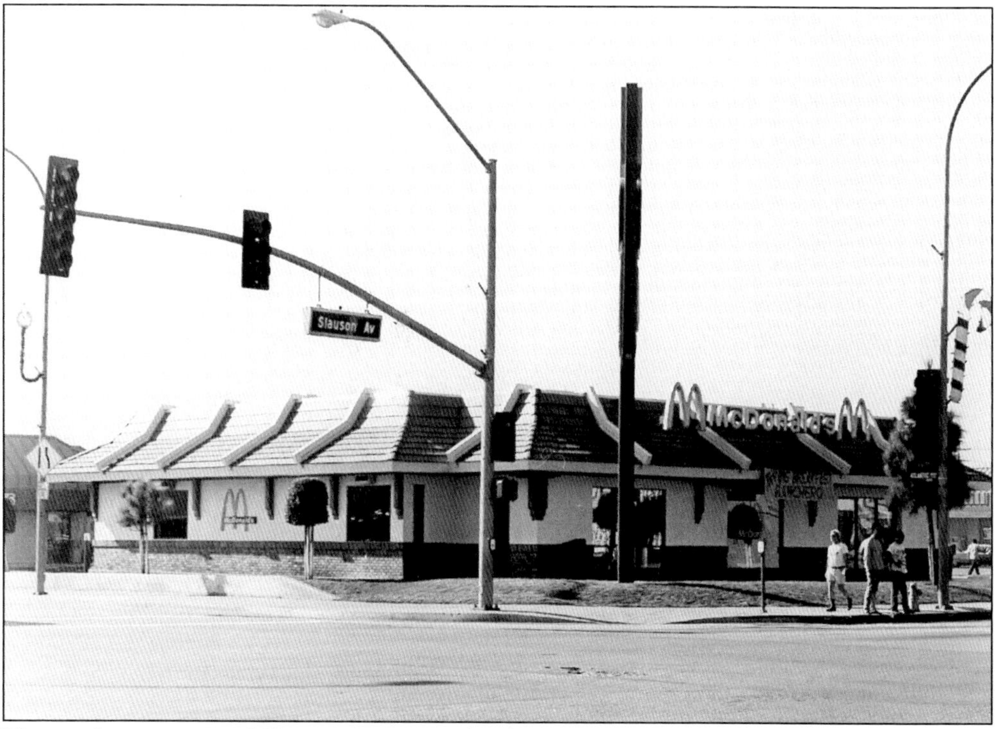

The southwest corner of Slauson Avenue and Atlantic contains one of the more popular places in Maywood—the local McDonald's.

Nine

THE 21ST CENTURY

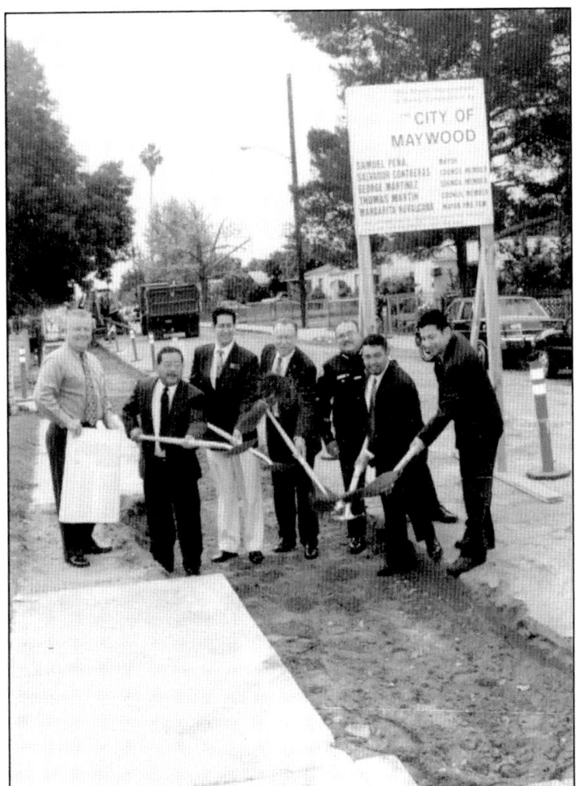

The groundbreaking for the start of a street improvement construction project includes, from left to right, city engineer William Pagett, council members Salvador Contreras and Thomas Martin, chief administrative officer Edward Ahrens, chief of police Rick Lopez, council member George Martinez, and Mayor Samuel Peña.

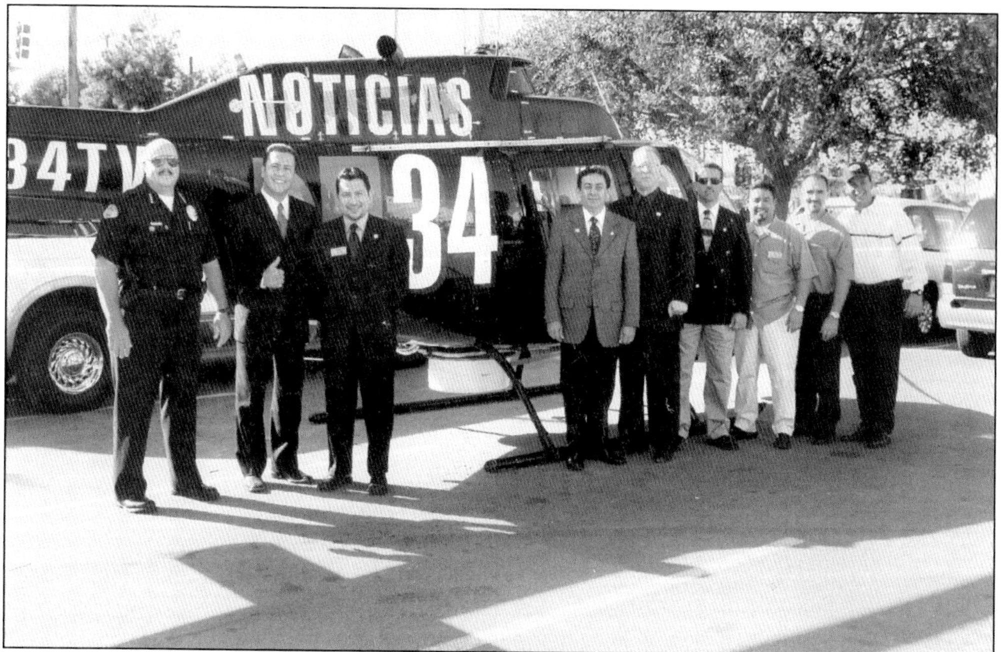

In 2002, the City of Maywood united with Los Angeles's premiere Spanish-language television station, Channel 34, for a Thanksgiving celebration.

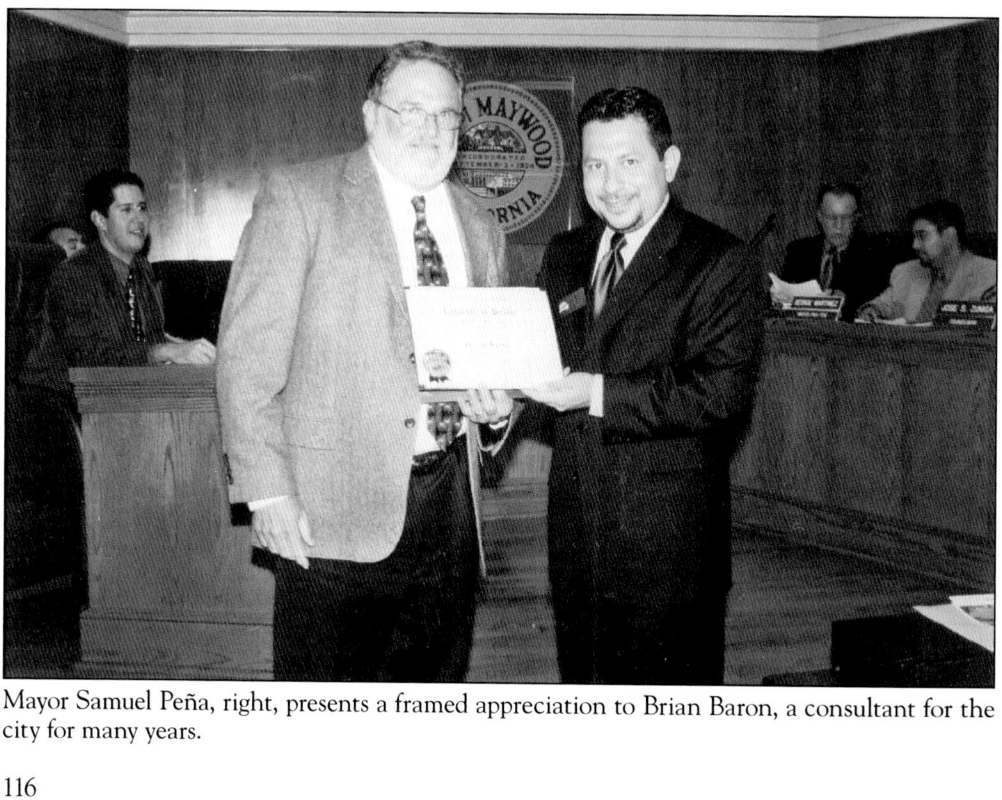

Mayor Samuel Peña, right, presents a framed appreciation to Brian Baron, a consultant for the city for many years.

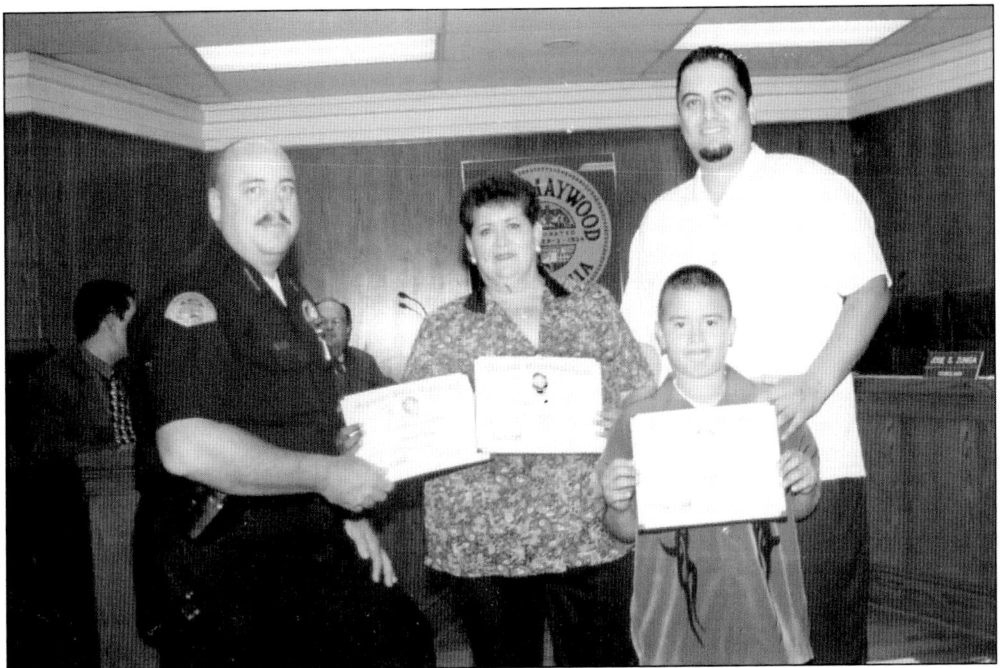

For assisting in the capture of an attempted murder suspect, awards for valor were presented by Bruce Leflar, chief of police, to Damien Zuniga and Maria Zuniga at a council meeting. Council member Jose Zuniga is on the far right.

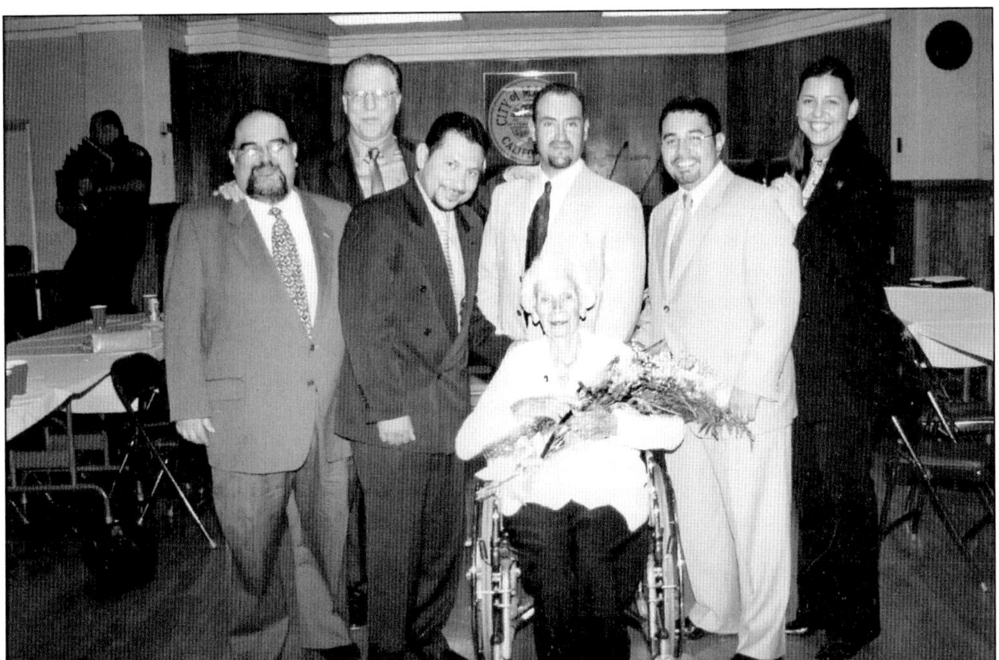

Joining former city clerk Isabel Dedmore, front, to celebrate her 100th birthday in Maywood, from left to right, are city attorney David Olivas, chief administrative officer Edward Ahrens, Mayor Samuel Peña, councilmen Luis Lara and George Martinez, and city clerk Veronica Barragan.

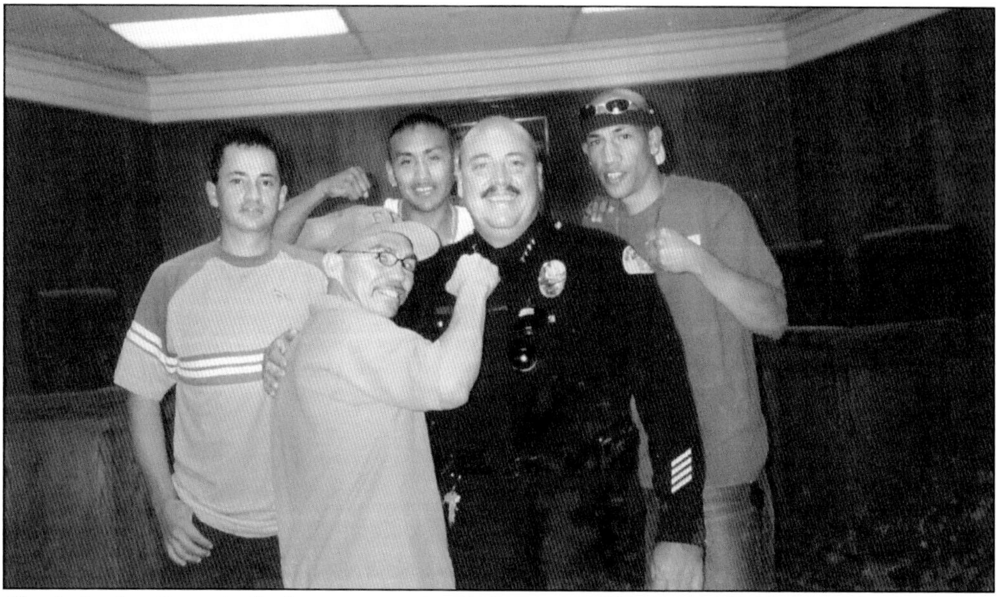

Chief of police Bruce Leflar horses around with former World Boxing Champion, Jorge Maromero Paez, before the 2003 Fourth of July parade.

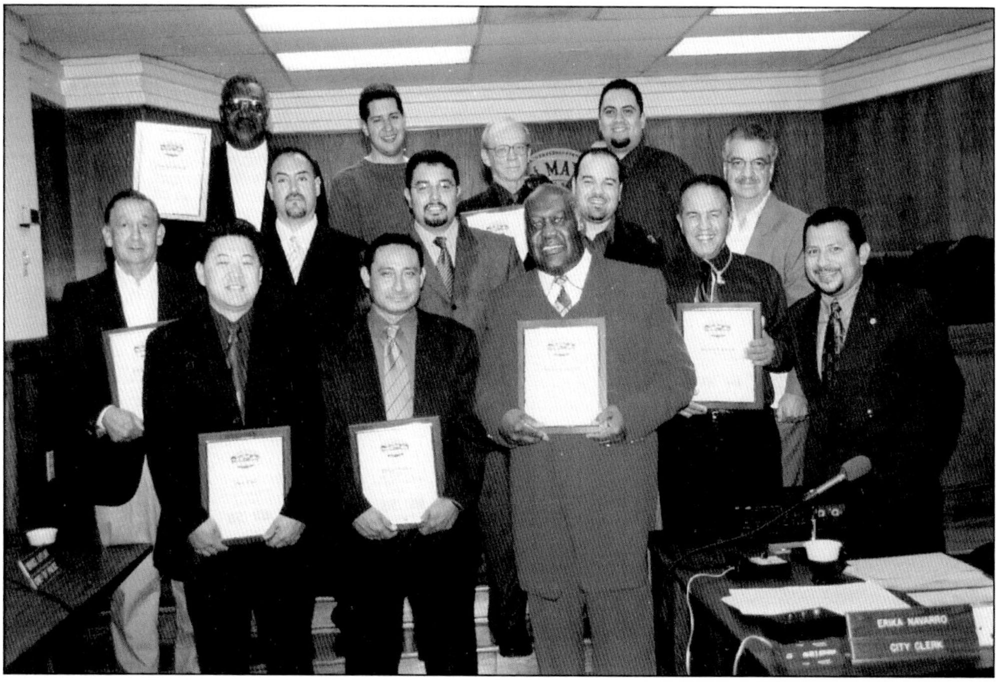

Presentations to community supporters and business members are a December tradition in Maywood.

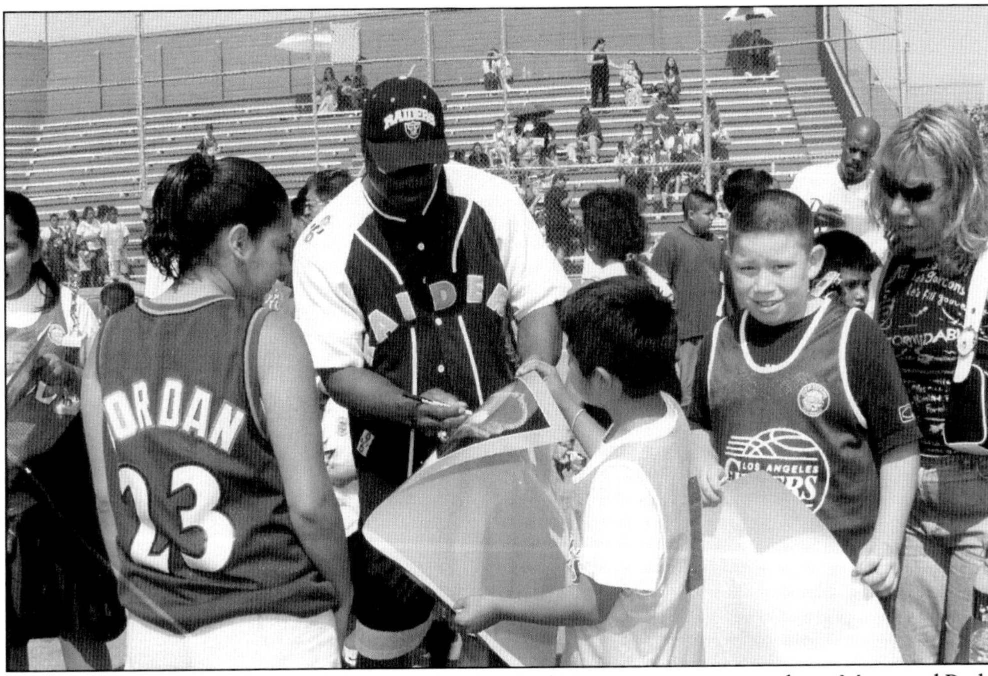

Former Oakland/Los Angeles Raiders linebacker Rod Martin signs autographs at Maywood Park. The two-time Pro Bowl participant intercepted three passes to lead Oakland to a victory in Super Bowl XV against the Philadelphia Eagles.

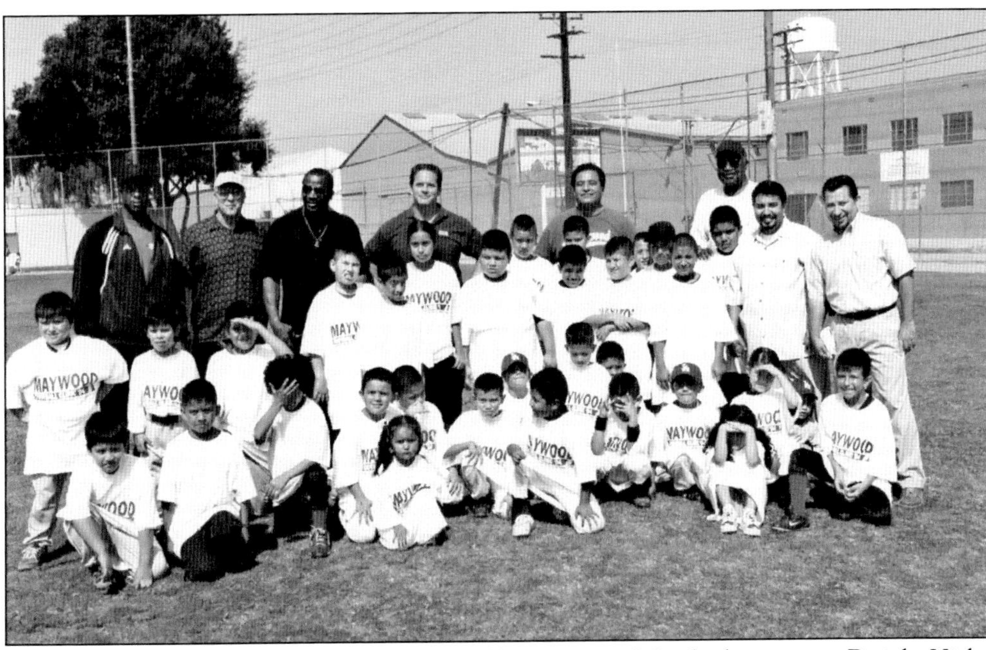
In 2004, the kids line up at a football clinic held in Maywood. In the last row are Dwight Hicks, who played for the San Francisco 49ers; former Pittsburgh Steeler Rick Moser; Charley Powell, who played for both the San Francisco 49ers and the Oakland Raiders; former world heavyweight boxing champ Mike Weaver; Maywood mayor George Martinez; and mayor pro tem Samuel Peña.

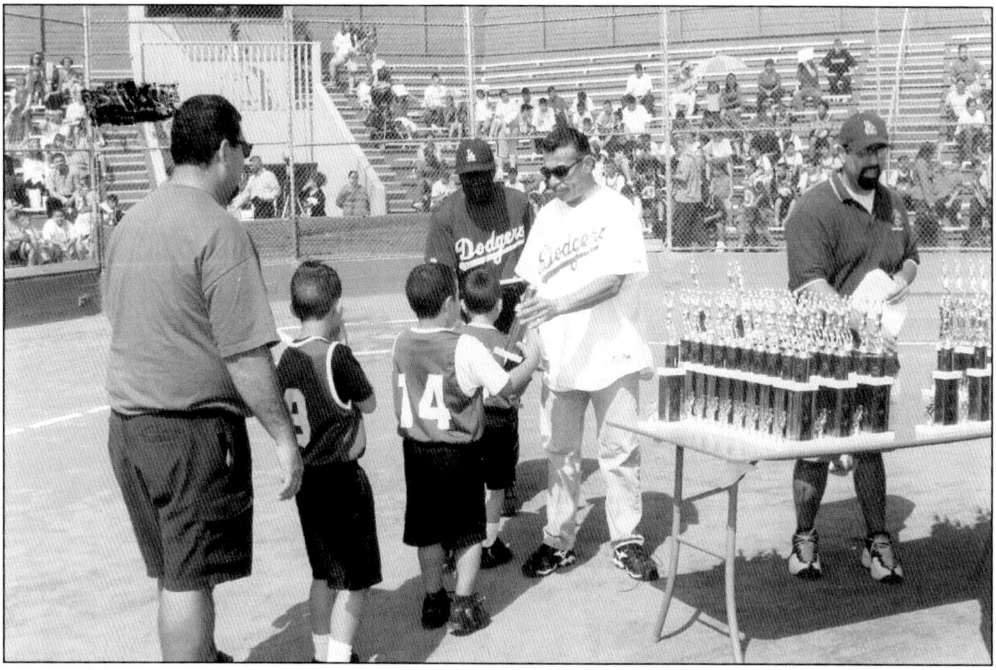

Pictured here are Bobby Castillo, former Los Angeles Dodgers outfielder Lou Johnson, and recreation supervisor Fernando Martinez, far right, during a trophy presentation.

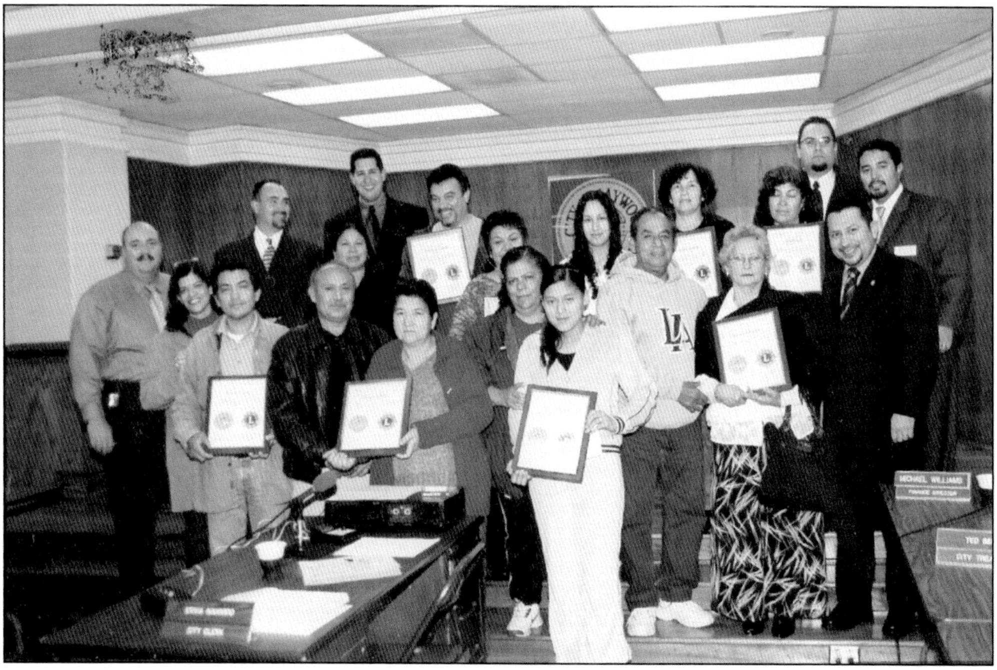

Maywood council members present the 2004 Christmas home decoration winners with their plaques.

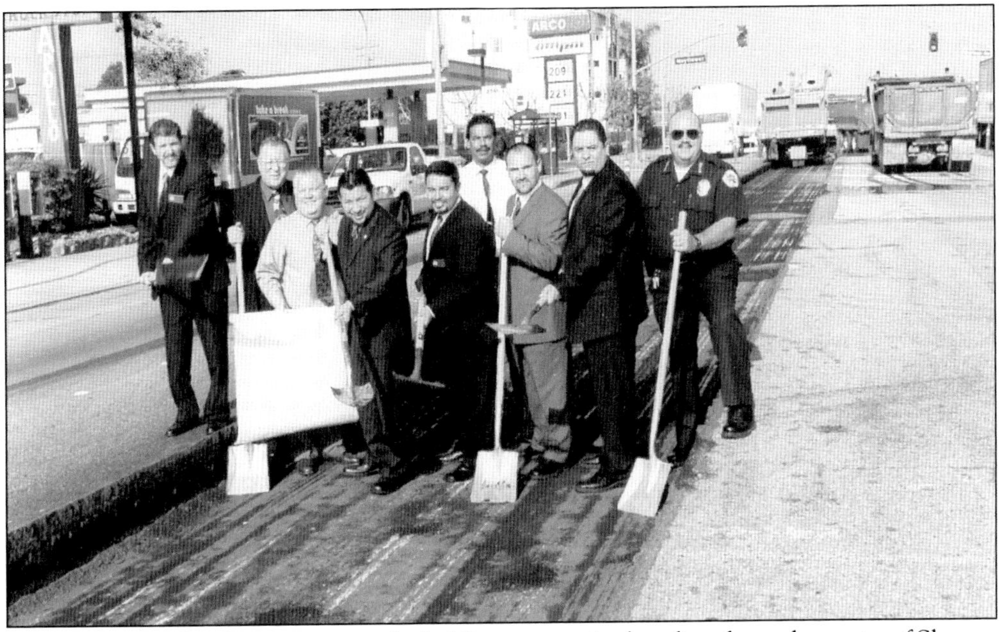

The Slauson Median Project consisted of adding a new raised median down the center of Slauson Avenue, and included signage, decorative banner poles, and the planting of trees. City officials on hand, from left to right, include treasurer Ted Serna, chief administration officer Edward Ahrens, city engineer William Pagett, mayor pro tem Samuel Peña, Mayor George Martinez, ACAO Michael Williams, councilmen Luis Lara and Jose Zuniga, and chief of police Bruce Leflar.

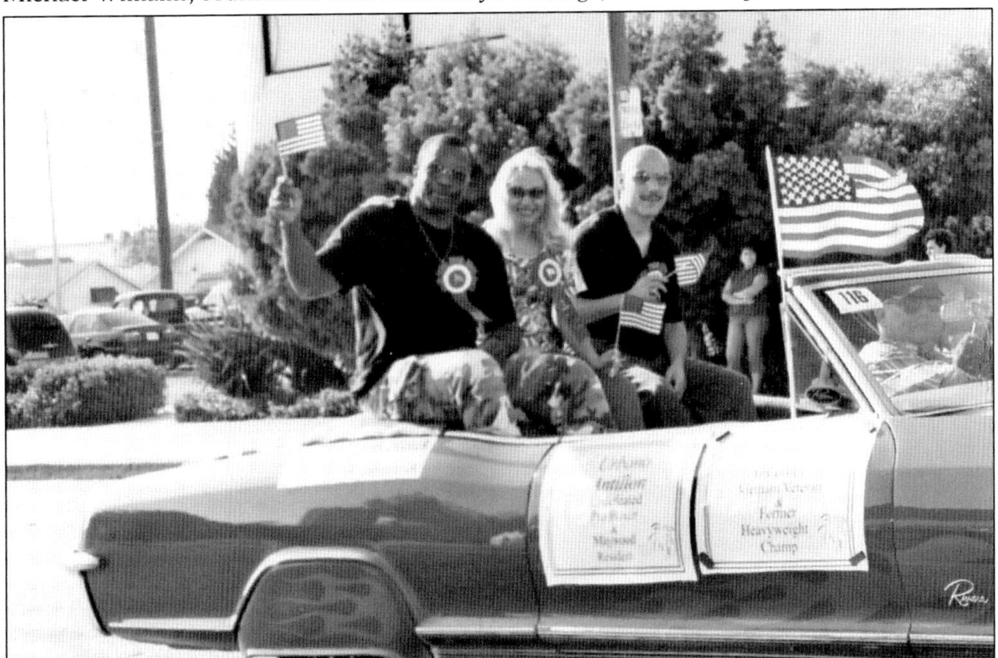

Former world heavyweight boxing champ Mike Weaver, Laura Ahrens, and Maywood resident and undefeated pro lightweight Urbano Antillon ride through the streets in the 2004 Fourth of July parade.

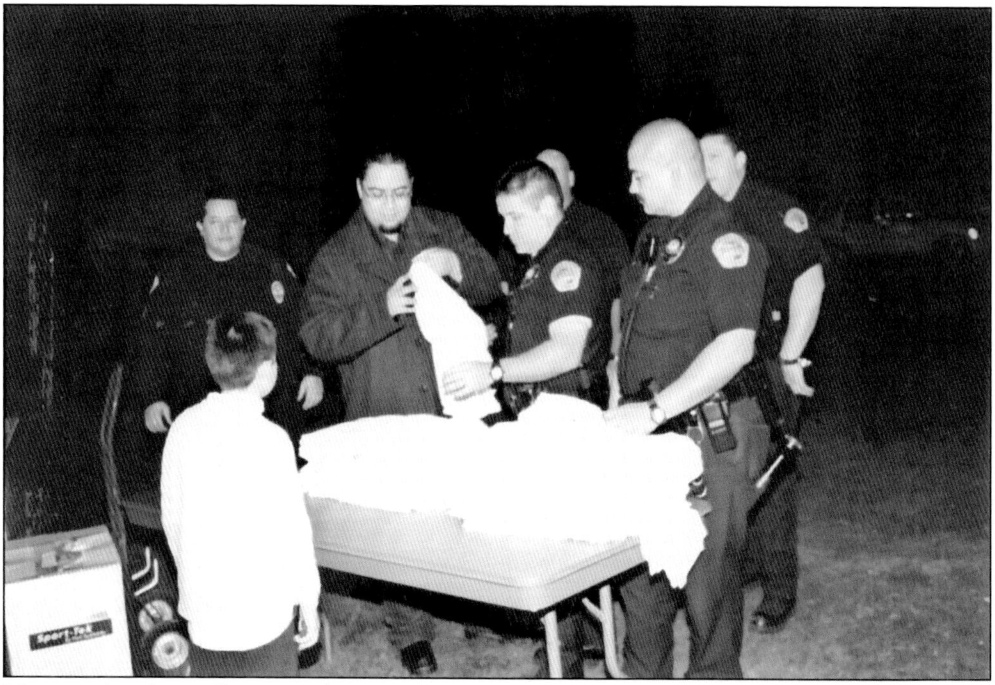

Maywood police officers and councilman Jose Zuniga present free antidrug T-shirts to area youngsters.

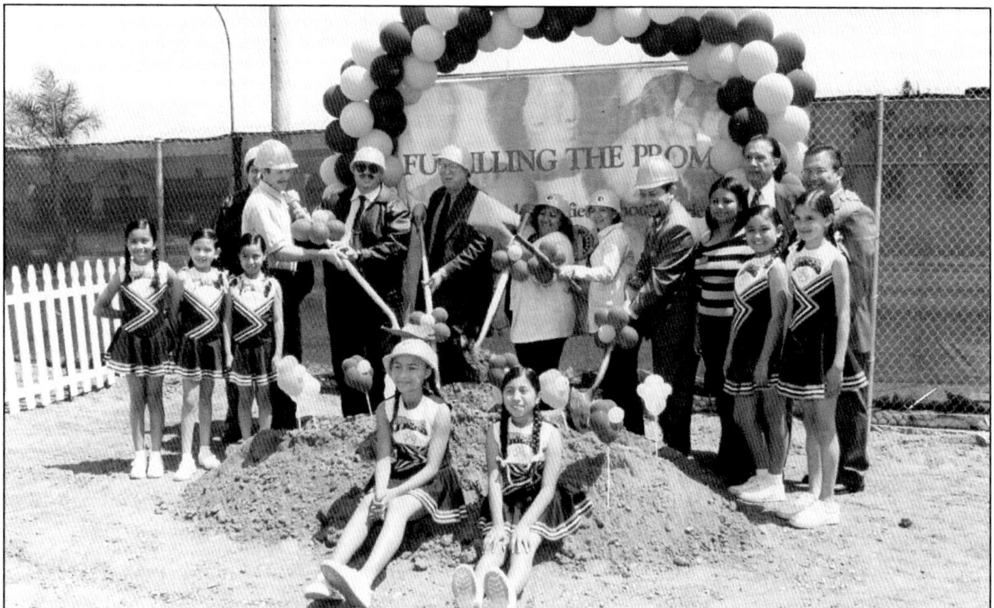

"Fulfilling the Promise" for the groundbreaking of the fifth elementary school in Maywood, Maywood No. 5 on Atlantic Boulevard, are mayor pro tem Samuel Peña, city treasurer Ted Serna, city clerk Erika Navarro, chief of police Bruce Leflar, and chief administrative officer Edward Ahrens.

Outstanding amateur boxer Charles Huerta has been garnering attention everywhere he competes, from Bucharest, Romania, to Alexandria, Louisiana. Huerta proudly represents the Maywood Boxing Club.

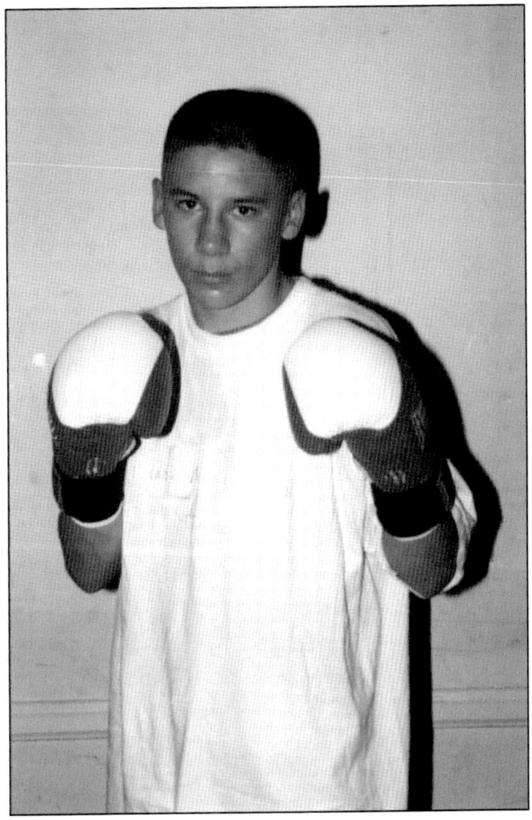

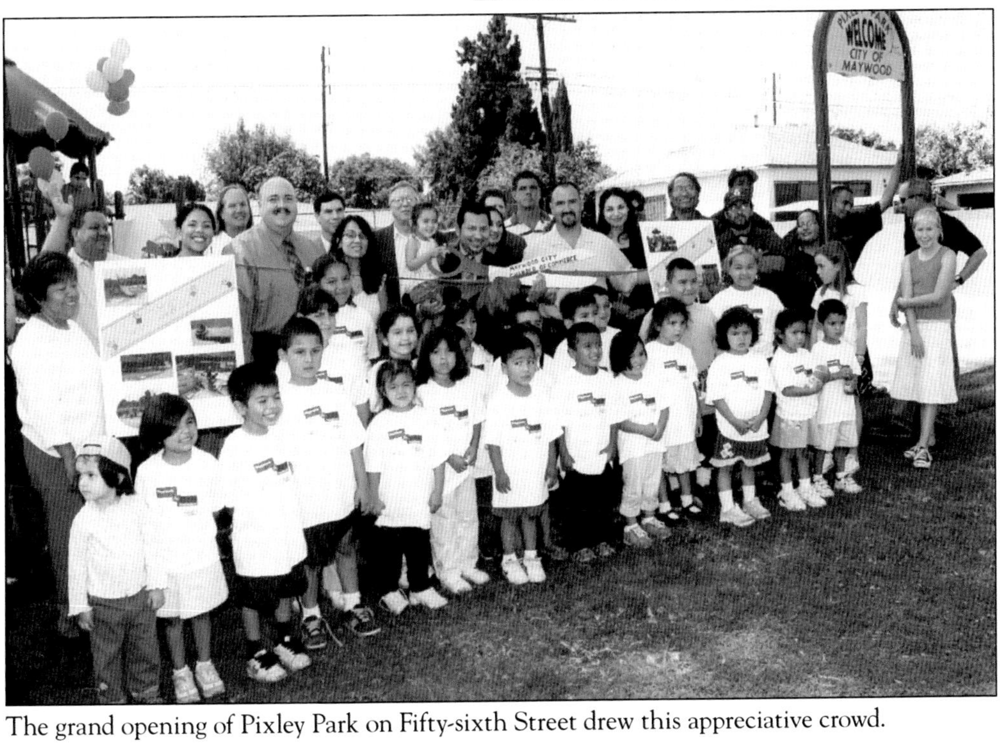

The grand opening of Pixley Park on Fifty-sixth Street drew this appreciative crowd.

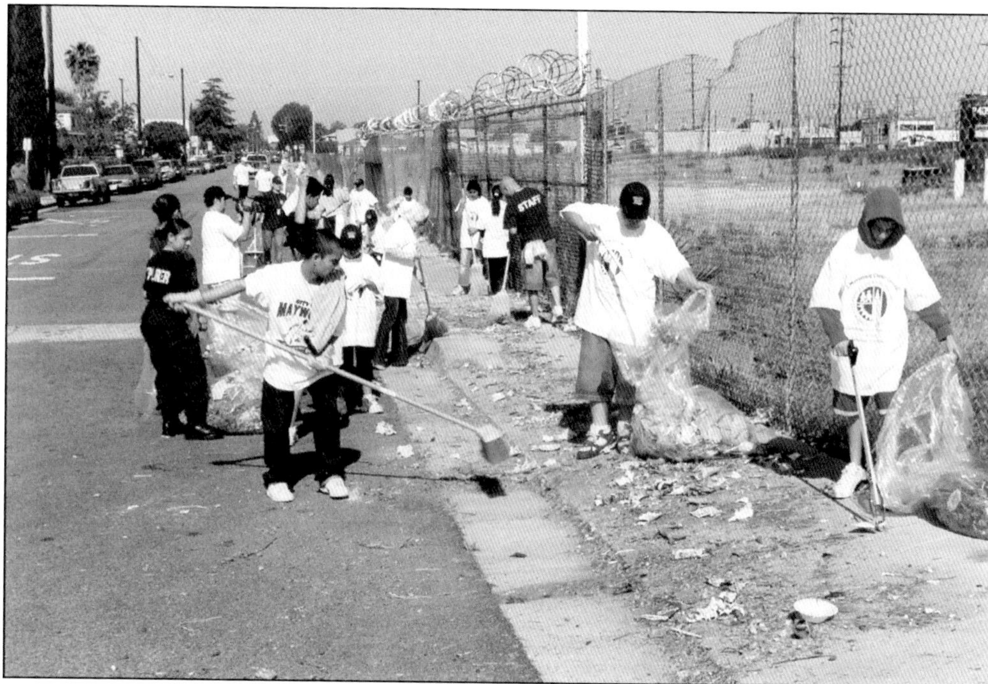

Absolutely no one can talk trash about Maywood's 2004 Clean Sweep.

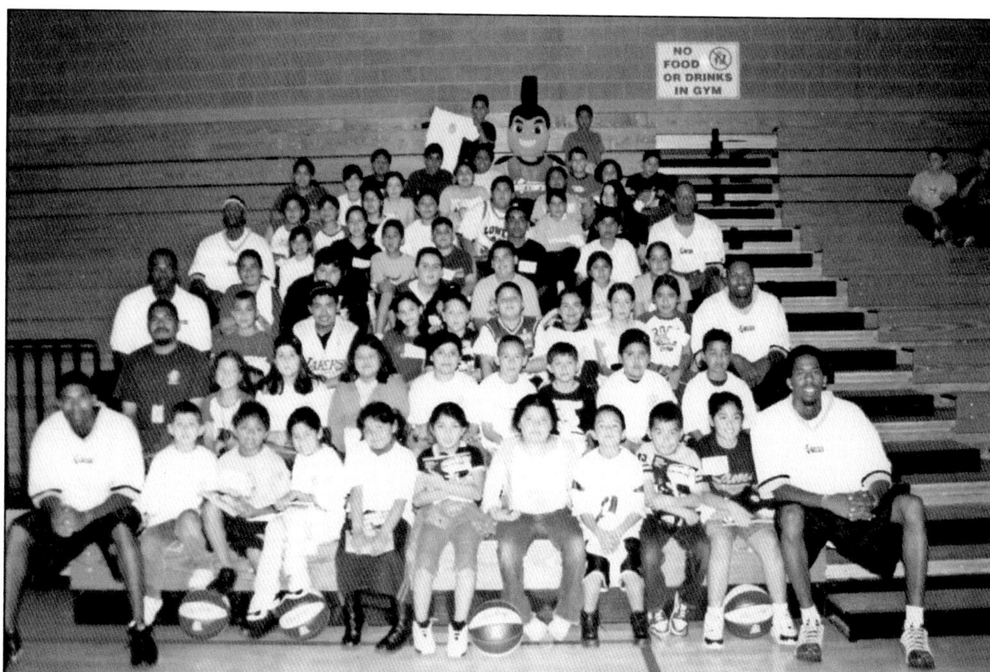

In 2004, the American Basketball Association Ontario Warriors presented a basketball clinic for youngsters.

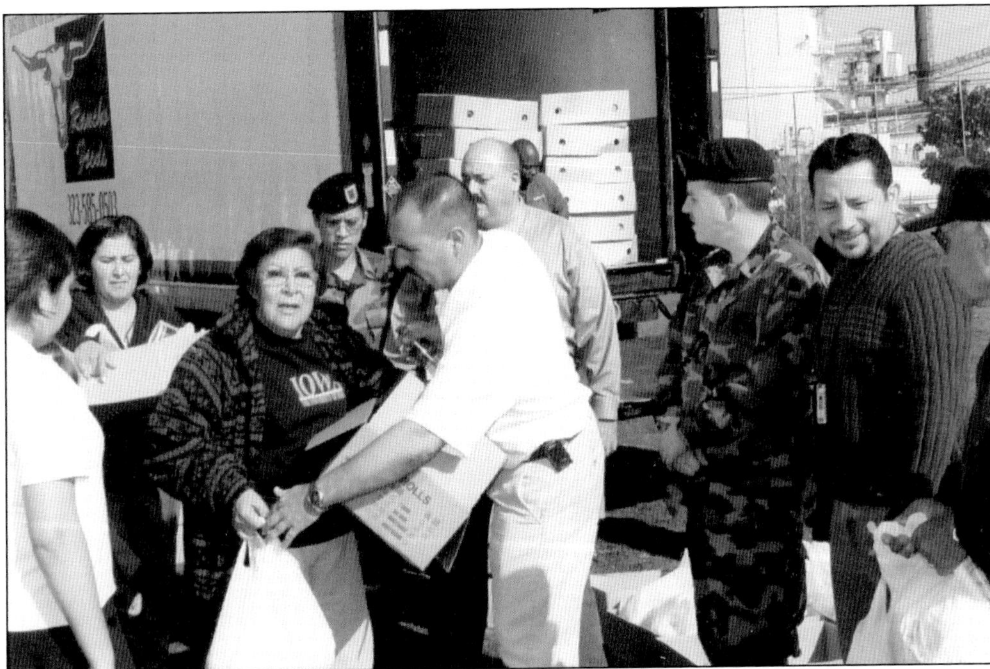

The annual November tradition of the Turkey Give-Away is shown in 2004 with a cast of characters including councilman Luis Lara, chief of police Bruce Leflar, and mayor pro tem Samuel Peña.

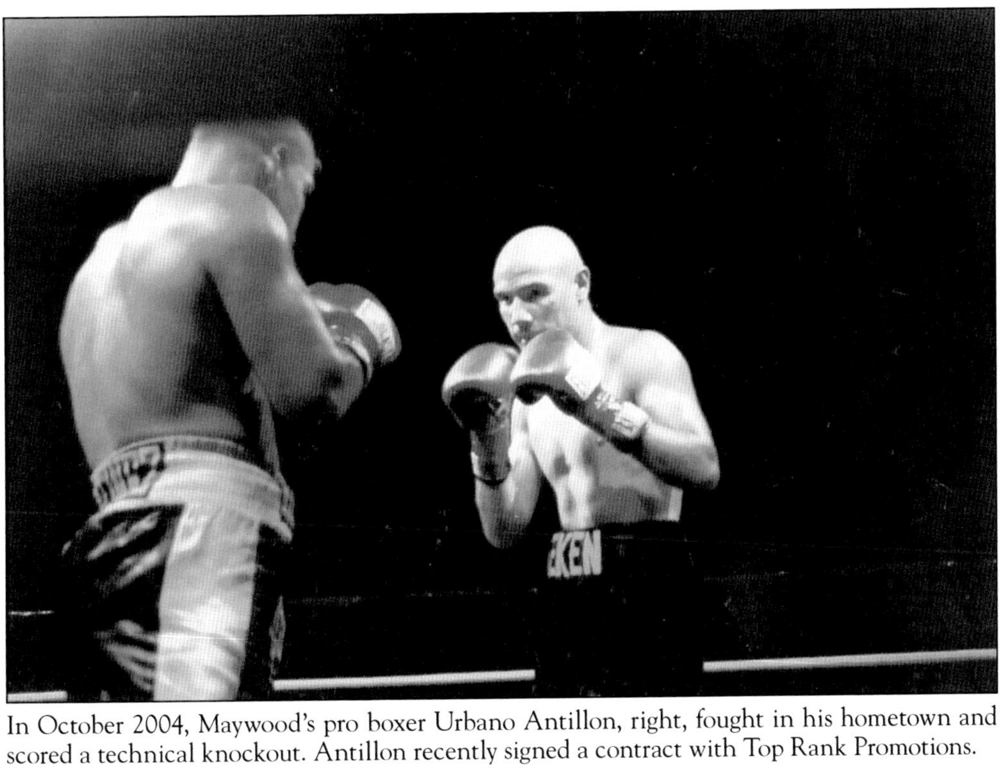

In October 2004, Maywood's pro boxer Urbano Antillon, right, fought in his hometown and scored a technical knockout. Antillon recently signed a contract with Top Rank Promotions.

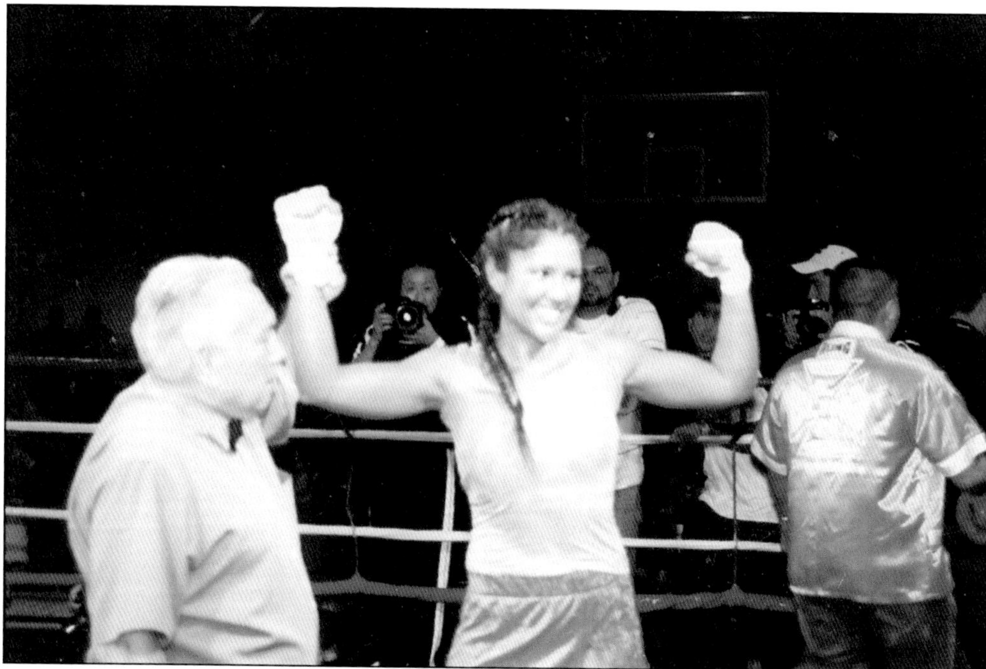

Mia St. John, the most well-known female boxer of her time, also scored a victory in Maywood in October 2004.

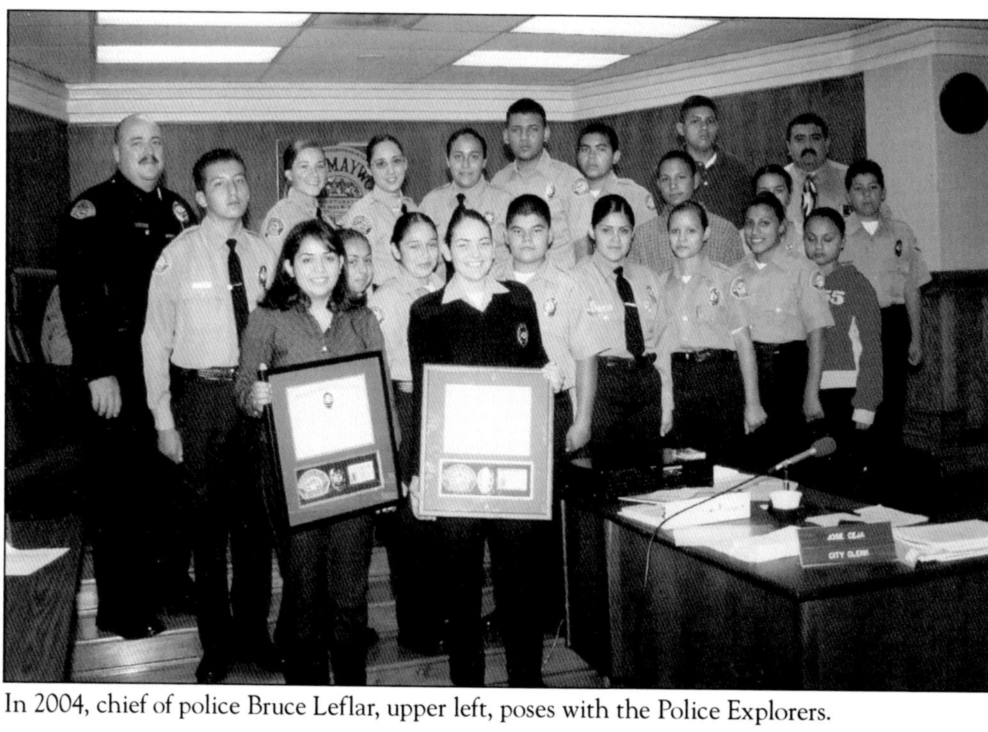

In 2004, chief of police Bruce Leflar, upper left, poses with the Police Explorers.

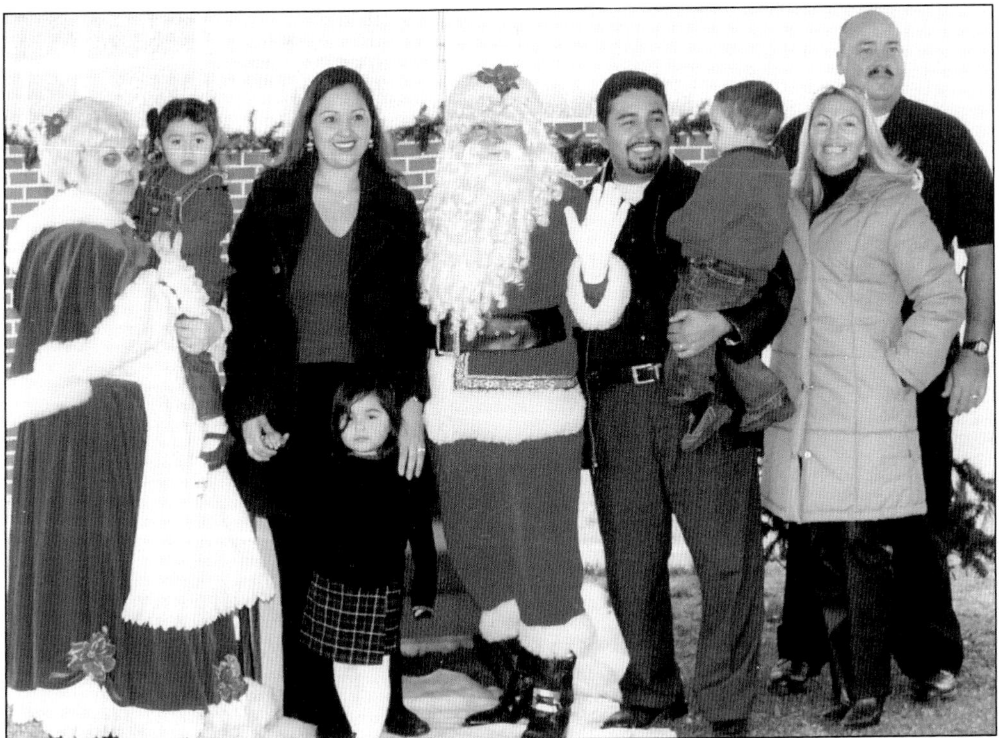

Mayor George Martinez and his wife, Angie, join chief of police Bruce Leflar, far right, Laura Ahrens, in front of the chief, and a couple in loud, red outfits from way up north in December 2003.

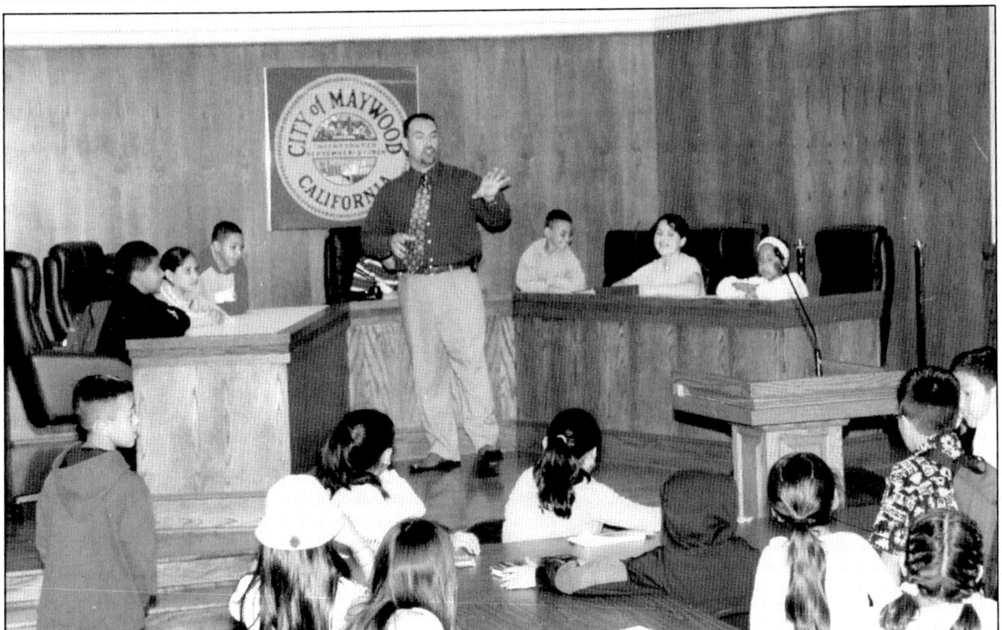

In April 2005, councilman Luis Lara addresses students from Heliotrope Elementary School in council chambers.

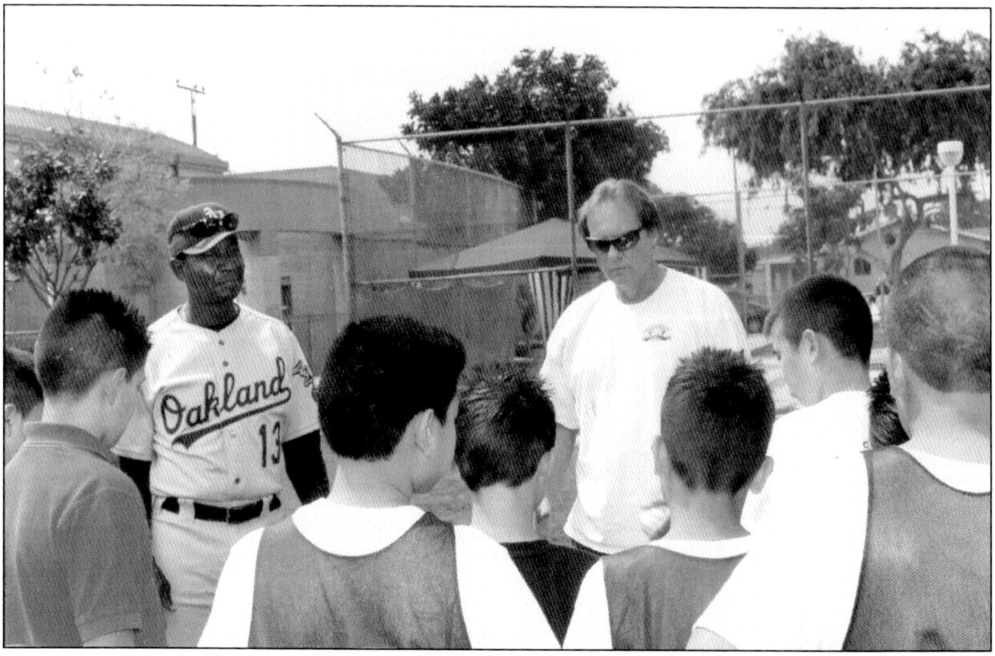

A Maywood baseball clinic featured former Oakland A's pitcher John "Blue Moon" Odom, left, and former broadcaster and outfielder Jay Johnstone. Odom posted two 15-6 seasons with A's and won 84 career regular season games. Johnstone played 20 years with eight different clubs, including the California Angeles and Los Angeles Dodgers.

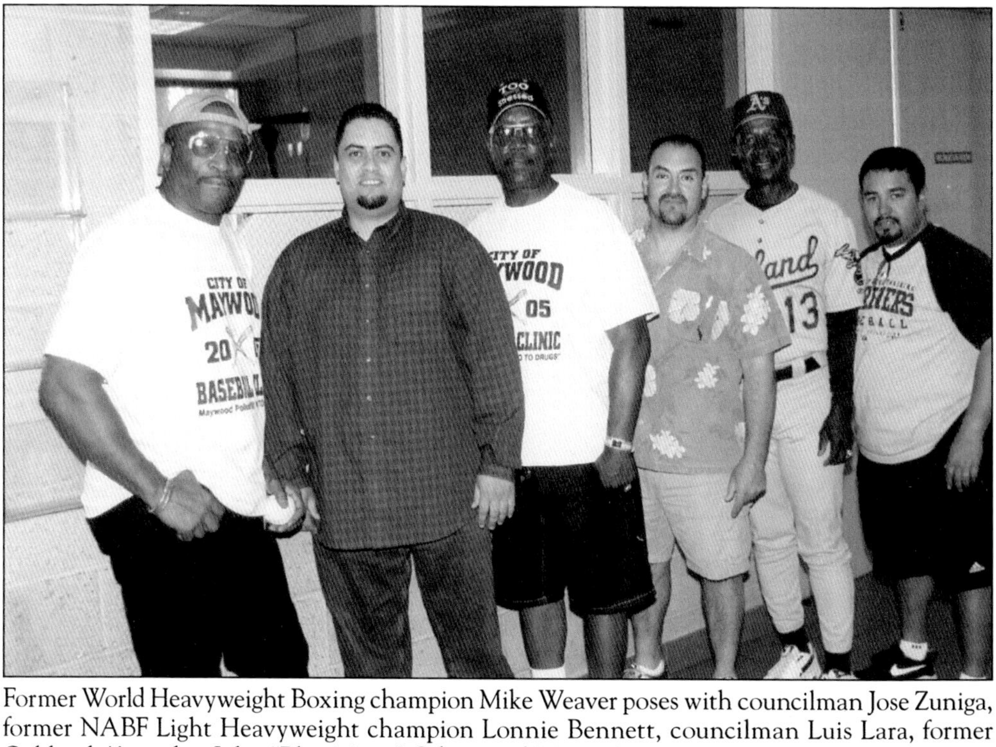

Former World Heavyweight Boxing champion Mike Weaver poses with councilman Jose Zuniga, former NABF Light Heavyweight champion Lonnie Bennett, councilman Luis Lara, former Oakland A's pitcher John "Blue Moon" Odom, and Mayor George Martinez.